Due Diligenc

M000266581

Due Diligence

The Critical Stage in Mergers and Acquisitions

PETER HOWSON

LONDON AND NEW YORK

First published 2003 by Gower Publishing

Published 2017 by Routledge
2 Park Square, Milton Park, Abingdon, Oxfordshire OX14 4RN
711 Third Avenue, New York, NY 10017, USA

First issued in paperback 2017

Routledge is an imprint of the Taylor & Francis Group, an informa business

Copyright © Peter Howson 2003

Peter Howson has asserted his right under the Copyright, Designs and Patents Act, 1988, to be identified as the author of this work.

All rights reserved. No part of this book may be reprinted or reproduced or utilised in any form or by any electronic, mechanical, or other means, now known or hereafter invented, including photocopying and recording, or in any information storage or retrieval system, without permission in writing from the publishers.

Notice:
Product or corporate names may be trademarks or registered trademarks, and are used only for identification and explanation without intent to infringe.

British Library Cataloguing in Publication Data
Howson, Peter, 1957–
    Due diligence: the critical stage in acquisitions and mergers
    1. Consolidation and merger of corporations – Law and
    legislation – Great Britain
    I. Title
    346.1'06626

Library of Congress Cataloging-in-Publication Data
Howson, Peter, 1957–
    Due diligence: the critical stage in mergers and acquisitions / Peter Howson.
        p. cm.
    ISBN 978-0-566-08524-6 (alk. paper)
    1. Consolidation and merger of corporations–Great Britain–Management. 2.
    Consolidation and merger of corporations–Law and legislation–Great Britain. I. Title.

HD2746.55.G7 H69 2003
658.1'6–dc21   2002028129

Typeset in 9 point Stone Serif by IML Typographers, Birkenhead, Merseyside.

ISBN 13: 978-1-138-24652-2 (pbk)
ISBN 13: 978-0-566-08524-6 (hbk)

Contents

List of tables

List of figures

Preface

This book is intended to be a practical, hands-on guide to the much misunderstood discipline of due diligence in M&A transactions. It is intended to be comprehensive, easy to read and, for a change, not slanted exclusively either towards the legal aspects or written from the adviser's perspective. However, buyers contemplating an acquisition would be well advised to take appropriate professional advice and not rely on this book to complete a transaction.

1 *Introduction*

Who is this book for?

Due diligence is variously described as boring, expensive or time consuming and, more often than not, all three. To many it is a way of spending a lot of money to tell you what you already know. It is also incredibly time pressured. Sellers have absolutely nothing to gain by giving a buyer time to probe and question. The buyer, on the other hand, has to gather and digest an awful lot of information on a whole range of quite specialist topics in a very short time and often with less than perfect access to the sources of information. Despite what many may believe, this in practice makes due diligence not some clever financial modelling exercise or a fascinating legal challenge, but essentially an exercise in project management.

The secret is to be very focused. This book is aimed at helping the practitioner to focus. The practitioner is the person who is going to drive the due diligence process. By knowing what information is needed, where and how to get it, and how the various due diligence professionals, lawyers and accountants as well as management consultants, go about their work, due diligence becomes more manageable, much more fun and much more cost-effective. It allows acquirers to focus on what is important and therefore to make better decisions.

The book should also be helpful to the professional adviser. Even experienced advisers may find something new in the sections which follow covering disciplines other than their own. Advisers tend, unfortunately, to work exclusively on their own area of investigation without reference to any of the other advisers. Although one of the aims of this book is to change that, it is nonetheless true that even lawyers with many deals to their credit may not know much about what accountants and management consultants do and how they go about their work.

The acquisition process

Due diligence is obviously only one part of an acquisition or investment exercise. In order to understand where it fits into the overall acquisition process, let us, for convenience, assume the process falls neatly into the four generic categories shown in Figure 1.1.

Stage one is about identifying an acquisition target and making an approach. This can only sensibly be done following a proper strategic review in which acquisition has been identified as a logical strategic tool. If an approach leads on to agreement to take things further, the deal enters the second stage. The two parties sketch out the broad terms of the deal and the buyer will begin due diligence. Successful due diligence leads to negotiation and, if all goes well, the deal completes. Then the buyer enters stage four, in many ways the

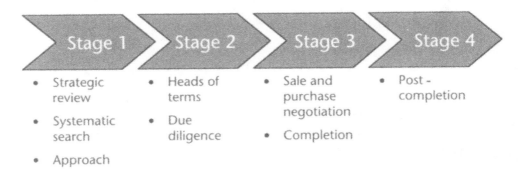

Figure 1.1   The acquisition process

most important stage of all, where the acquisition must be bedded in and made to pay its way. Each of the four stages is described in more detail below.

STAGE 1   STRATEGY, SEARCH AND APPROACH

Strategic review

It is a long time now since Barings advised Asda not to buy MFI. Asda did the deal anyway. Barings lost a client and a big fee. Standard corporate finance 'advice' has changed a lot since then. Now advice seems to be along the lines of 'Here is a good idea: we advise you to buy this business'. Acquisitions can and do happen as a result of banks hawking round ideas. They can also take place for a host of other not very good reasons. Often the chairman comes across a 'bargain', usually from one of his mates down at the golf club. Even today management may decide it would be a good idea to go on an acquisition spree to diversify shareholders' risk. Goodness knows why, when shareholders can do that better for themselves. At other times it is a case of the acquirer having a large cash pile to spend, management wanting a bigger empire, or, closely related, management persuading themselves that they can manage anything.

Acquisitions are very risky. All the academic research points to a failure rate well in excess of 50 per cent. Because of the risk, acquisitions should take place only after a thorough review of strategic objectives and then only after very careful consideration of the alternatives. They should be seen as a means of achieving strategic objectives – nothing more and nothing less. They will never be an antidote to poor performance in the core business or a means of management self-aggrandizement. Acquisitions are strategic tools, a means to a strategic end and given their very high failure rate, should be seen only as a last resort.

However, strategic reviews do often identify acquisition as the most logical way forward. If the strategic review has been carried out properly then the next step will be an organized, systematic search for acquisition targets.

Search

A systematic search for acquisitions often starts where the strategic review leaves off. The ideal targets have to be characterized. In turn this means creating a set of criteria for the types of company that should be looked at. A search will then seek to identify every company which meets those criteria, and to gather basic information about each one.

The potential targets will then be ranked according to their ability to meet strategic objectives and categorized according to whether they are strong contenders for purchase or merely fallback options. More detailed information will be put together on those companies which seem to be strong contenders, and a shortlist drawn up for approach.

Approach

Acquisition targets are like London buses. None come along for ages then all of a sudden there are three to choose from. Getting from first approach to a deal can take a long time. Approaching a company can produce extreme reactions. Some potential vendors will rejoice, thinking they are about to become rich, others may be deeply offended, others say 'no' when they mean 'yes' and yet others go away only to come back again. Reactions will vary according to the target's ownership, nationality, industry, and the personalities of those involved, but if a deal is to happen at some point both parties will perceive a mutual interest and decide to take preliminary discussions further.

STAGE 2   THE PRELIMINARIES TO NEGOTIATION

Heads of terms

If an approach does lead to mutual interest, both parties will want to begin serious negotiations. Heads of Agreement/Heads of Terms/Letter of Intent is the document which records an agreement to negotiate the purchase of a business. It is a non-binding agreement (see page 20) which sets out the main points on which the parties to a transaction have agreed and the basis on which they are prepared to proceed.

As far as due diligence is concerned, the critical thing about signing Heads of Agreement is that there is a deal underway. Drawing up the document usually focuses the minds of both parties. The buyer will now have assured the seller of its seriousness, both parties will have decided that there is sufficient agreement between them to continue and both can draw comfort that the deal will go ahead because they can point to a document setting out the fundamental issues. Due diligence can therefore begin.

Due diligence

As explained in greater detail below and indeed in the rest of this book, due diligence assesses the deal from a commercial, financial and legal point of view. It is concerned with understanding more about the business being bought, confirming that the buying company is getting what it thinks it is buying, unearthing any risks in the deal, finding negotiating issues and helping to plan post-deal integration.

Skeletons found in due diligence should not normally break a deal but they will be negotiating points on the way, with luck, to agreement.

STAGE 3   NEGOTIATION AND AGREEMENT

Sale and purchase negotiation

With due diligence over, next comes the stage of finalizing the details of the deal. This is where everyone falls out, but eventually, after much posturing and horse-trading, negotiations are concluded, agreement is reached and the deal is signed. As mentioned above, due diligence feeds into the negotiations by identifying risks against which the buyer should negotiate some sort of protection. This could be through a price reduction or through a guarantee by the seller to compensate for any loss.

Completion

The due diligence is over, the terms of the deal are agreed, and completion is the process of actually signing the sale documents. For some strange reason there is an unwritten law that completion always happens at 4 o'clock in the morning, and usually at the weekend, even though all the participants struggle to avoid this!

STAGE 4   POST-COMPLETION – THE BIT THAT EVERYONE FORGETS

Of course the negotiating process is highly charged and extremely challenging. Not surprisingly a satisfactory conclusion, with the new acquisition in the bag, is often seen as an end in itself. Management are left exhausted and, after the thrill of the chase, too apathetic to manage the integration process.[1] But, to paraphrase a well-known slogan, 'a deal is for life, not just for Christmas'. Once the deal is signed, the really hard work starts: that of making the return from the new acquisition justify the price paid. In the chase and excitement of the deal this phase is often overlooked. As is discussed in some detail below, due diligence should play a major role in shaping the post-completion plan. This leads on to the next topic, what should due diligence aim to achieve?

What is due diligence?

There is no dictionary definition of due diligence. There is no standard legal definition either. A lawyer would probably define it roughly as follows:

> a process of enquiry and investigation made by a prospective purchaser in order to confirm that it is buying what it thinks it is buying.

Caveat emptor (buyer beware) is central to the whole acquisition process in Anglo-Saxon countries. Due diligence is the way buyers make sure they understand exactly what they are buying.

A dealmaker might go further. A dealmaker would say that due diligence is about reducing risk. There is no shortage of surveys which show how risky acquisitions are. As already noted, according to these surveys, at least half of all acquisitions fail. The true failure figure is probably more like three-quarters. The better the due diligence, the more buyers know about a target and therefore the more they know about the immediate risks they are taking on. As far as the dealmaker is concerned, therefore, due diligence allows an acquirer to:

- identify issues which feed into price negotiations, and hence reduce the risk of paying too much;
- de-risk the deal by identifying points against which legal protection should be sought.

In other words, the dealmaker sees due diligence as an aid to working out what contractual protection is required from the vendor and what risks the purchaser should avoid completely.

The problem with this thinking is that it sees the short-term issues specific to negotiations as being the same as those which in the end will dictate whether or not the deal will be a success. This may very well not be the case.

Again, there is no shortage of surveys purporting to show where the risks in an acquisition lie. The trouble with a lot of them is that they are carried out by consultants with a post-acquisition integration consultancy service to sell. Nonetheless, it is probably true that more acquisitions fail because of shortcomings at the post-acquisition implementation stage than at the pre-acquisition investigation stage. For example, according to one piece of research[2] there is an 83 per cent correlation between implementation success and overall acquisition success. Of course, this may be because pre-deal due diligence is so well carried out that risky deals never complete, but the need to think beyond pre-deal 'tyre kicking' to the post-deal aftermath is confirmed by a 1999 study by KPMG.[3] As shown in Figure 1.2, this found three hard keys and three soft keys to acquisition success. The KPMG research tries to pinpoint the factors which give deals a better chance of success than average.

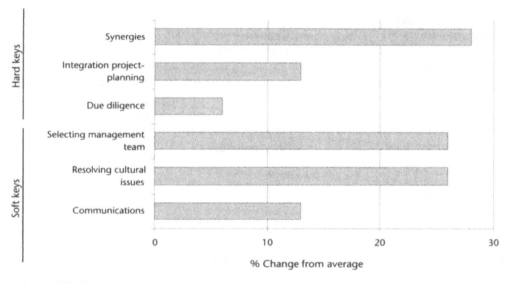

Source: KPMG

Figure 1.2   Pre-deal activities and the increased chances of deal success

Pre-deal synergy evaluation emerged as the main hard key to success. Acquirers who carried this out thoroughly had a 28 per cent better than average chance of overall deal success. KPMG describe this as the 'what and where' of obtaining value in a deal. Companies can only hope to avoid bad deals by working out how extra value is going to be achieved. This calls for a thorough exercise early on in the acquisition process, involving operational managers, to confirm both the robustness of synergy assumptions and their deliverability.

Integration project-planning is the next most important hard key. This is the mechanics of the 'how'. According to KPMG, the survey confirms, 'that the chances of merger success are increased if the process of working out 'how' is started well before the completion of the deal.'[4]

The third hard key highlights the power of 'proper' due diligence. 'Proper' due diligence, according to KPMG, as used by 'sophisticated and forward looking acquirers' uses a 'springboard approach to due diligence which often uses a range of investigative tools designed to systematically assess all the facts impacting on value.' 'Value' is only created once the deal is done.

In other words, the successful acquirer's definition of what due diligence is all about goes much further than any legal or deal-doing definition. According to the successful acquirer, the objective of due diligence is not just to 'audit' or verify past performance, it is not just to look for black holes or reasons to chisel the price. It aims to do all of these but, more important for success, it should aim to assess future prospects and show how they can be realized. Of course due diligence is going to look out for vulnerabilities but at least equal importance needs to be given to identifying opportunities. After all, there is really only one reason for buying a business. Not because it has done well in the past, nor because it is cheap. The only reason is because it has a great future with you as the new owner. As KPMG put it, 'with more money chasing fewer deals, a greater proportion of the valuation is made up of strategic and synergistic elements'.[5]

Sadly though, as the statistics show, there are few successful acquirers around. The long and the short of it is that 'acquirers keep making the same mistakes over and over again: not enough planning, too obsessed with the financials to the detriment of other areas'.[6] Again this can be seen from the KPMG study where getting the soft keys right is more important to increasing the chances of deal success than getting the hard keys right.

In summary, pre-acquisition due diligence should be constructed to give as good an insight as possible into post-deal implementation as to isolating pre-deal risks. This contrasts with the quaintly traditional way in which due diligence is still mostly performed, biased towards:

- getting the deal done
- the financial and legal aspects
- unearthing 'skeletons'.

A proper due diligence programme, therefore, should have five strands:

- the verification of assets and liabilities
- the identification and quantification of risks
- the protection needed against such risks which will in turn feed into the negotiations
- the identification of synergy benefits (which may also feed into price negotiations)
- post-acquisition planning.

This is easy to say, but the reality is that managers working on an acquisition are first going to have to satisfy the Chairman, the board, their boss or themselves that the deal itself is under control otherwise they may very quickly find themselves working on something less high profile.

So the number one priority from due diligence is to understand what is being bought, where the immediate risks are in doing the deal and what protection is needed. But, number two, do not underestimate the benefits a well thought-through programme of due diligence can bring to the long-term success of the deal. Due diligence should be seen as integral to post-acquisition planning. In the heat of a deal, there is always a tendency to delay or play down the importance of planning for the aftermath. The evidence above would suggest that there is no substitute for early post-deal planning. The KPMG and other studies[7] suggest that unless there is an integration plan which is properly communicated, and the mechanics of that plan implemented within a couple of months of completion, acquirers will lose value from their acquisition. Never mind 2 + 2 = 5; if due diligence is not used to help put together an integration plan, a buyer may well end up with 2 + 2 = 3.

The arguments for carrying out due diligence

The above is all very well, but what about the deals where the buyer knows the company very well, knows the market and quite frankly does not need to go to all the expense and trouble of due diligence? The answer is that it is possible to buy a company without doing any due diligence, but there are a few snags.

First of all, the information disclosed by the seller to qualify the warranties will be the only material formally available to the purchaser with which to confirm a decision to buy the company. Nothing at all wrong with that in certain circumstances. In addition, there will only be fairly standard warranties and indemnities available for legal protection. This is hardly surprising given that the buyer has not made the enquiries which give a basis on which to negotiate non-standard warranties and indemnities or other forms of protection. Again, this may be fine in certain circumstances. It is fairly common where the deal is quite small in relation to the size of the buyer or where the buyer's knowledge of the target is very good.

However, for reasons discussed below, just relying on warranties and indemnities is not a good idea. For a start, the protection they offer may be limited or impractical to enforce. Also if the seller is plain dishonest, which is not entirely unknown, just taking warranties and indemnities without further investigation is unlikely to uncover any fraud or other wrongdoing. Due diligence can sometimes identify suspicious activity.

Leaving aside the integration questions, the real value due diligence can add, even where buyers think they have a lot of knowledge, is in what can best be described as unearthing problems no one really knew existed. Sellers, usually quite genuinely, believe their companies to be problem-free. Often they will have lived with what outsiders would see as 'problems' without any harmful effects. This does not mean that the buyer would take the same view. However, without identifying and quantifying the 'problems', the buyer can take no view at all. For example, it is often the case that important pieces of software in early stage IT companies have been developed by programmers who are not employees of the company. The law is quite clear about copyright: it resides with the author. In this case buying the company will not buy the intellectual property central to its success. Clearly this would be an issue for the purchaser whereas for the current owners the software has been developed, it works and is selling so there is not a problem.

The second real value of due diligence is what can best be described as its comfort factor. Everything in this universe is relative. Accountants and lawyers may be expensive, but not when compared with going to law. Comparatively speaking, due diligence is cheap, litigation is not. This is why most buyers are much more comfortable knowing about problems beforehand rather than being left with the possibility, however remote, of making warranty or indemnity claims or having to sue the seller after completion. However good the warranties and indemnities, a buyer really does not want to litigate. Litigation is expensive, in both time and money, and its outcome is far from guaranteed. In fact, a buyer's aim should be never to have to open the sale and purchase agreement once it is signed.

Finally, knowledge is power. Due diligence gives the buyer knowledge. The more that is known about a seller's business, the better the buyer is armed, both physically and psychologically, for the negotiations which lie ahead.

Contrary to popular myth, due diligence can be a worthwhile investment.

ISN'T DUE DILIGENCE REQUIRED BY LAW?

Due diligence is not legally required. The nearest it comes to being a legal requirement is in the following circumstances:

- The Cadbury Report recommended that significant acquisitions should be reviewed by the full board of directors of the purchasing company. To ensure that the board considers all the issues, due diligence reports may be required.
- With listed companies, which are subject to the London Stock Exchange's regulations, if an acquisition is a major one and therefore needs shareholder approval, a financial report on the merged group will be required. This makes a detailed accountants' investigation necessary so that the necessary circular can be drawn up.
- In European public deals, synergy papers are increasingly becoming a critical element in pre-deal planning. In these cases the financial robustness of an acquirer's cost savings, and in some cases their revenue enhancement targets, are vetted and approved as being realistic.
- As a defence against charges of negligence in a transaction. The US courts have found that, 'due diligence is equivalent to non-negligence'[8] having earlier 'established that it is not reasonable to rely on exclusively management for key data. Data must be double-checked through an independent investigation.'[9]

The different due diligence disciplines

There are a number of different types of due diligence which can be carried out. Table 1.1 summarizes the three main areas, while Table 1.2 shows the other usual due diligence topics. It looks like a forbidding list. In any deal, some of these will be more important than others. Some will be carried out as topics in their own right and others subsumed under other headings.

Table 1.1   The main due diligence topics

Due diligence topic	Focus of enquiries	Results sought
Financial	Validation of historical information, review of management and systems	Confirm underlying profit. Provide basis for valuation
Legal	Contractual agreements, problem-spotting	Warranties and indemnities, validation of all existing contracts, sale and purchase agreement
Commercial	Market dynamics, target's competitive position, target's commercial prospects	Sustainability of future profits, formulation of strategy for the combined business, input to valuation

Table 1.2 The other due diligence disciplines

Due diligence topic	Focus of enquiries	Results sought
Human Resources and culture	Make-up of the workforce, terms and conditions of employment, level of commitment and motivation, organizational culture	Uncovering any employment liabilities, assessing the potential Human Resources costs and risks of doing the deal, prioritizing the HR issues that need to be dealt with during integration, assessing cultural fit, costing and planning the post-deal HR changes
Management	Management quality, organizational structure	Identification of key integration issues, outline of new structure for the combined businesses
Pension	Various pension plans and plan valuations	Minimize the risks of underfunding
Tax	Existing tax levels, liabilities and arrangements	Avoid any unforeseen tax liabilities, opportunities to optimize position of combined business
Environmental	Liabilities arising from sites and processes, compliance with regulations	Potential liabilities, nature and cost of actions to limit them
IT	Performance, ownership and adequacy of current systems	Feasibility of integrating systems; associated costs. IT plans for operational efficiency and competitive advantage
Technical	Performance, ownership and adequacy of technology	Value and sustainability of product technology
Operational	Production techniques, validity of current technology	Technical threats; sustainability of current methods; opportunities for improvement; investment requirements
Intellectual Property Rights (IPRs)	Validity, duration and protection of patents and other IPRs	Expiration; impact and cost
Property	Deeds, land registry records and lease agreements	Confirmation of title. Valuation and costs/ potential of property assets
Antitrust	The various national filing requirements (some of which can be expensive if not complied with); degree of market/ information sharing with competitors	Merger control filings and clearance; an assessment of any antitrust risks posed by the target's activities; an assessment of the enforceability of the target's contracts
Insurance/Risk	Present, future and, most importantly, past exposures of the business. The structure and cost of the existing programme	The costs and benefits of retaining risk versus transferring it

As mentioned above, often these are combined, so that, for example, Human Resources, IPR and property could be covered by legal due diligence; tax, insurance, IT, operational and pension matters by financial due diligence and management and technical by commercial due diligence. All the above, except property and operational, are covered in later chapters. Property is covered under legal while operational is so highly tailored to the target company it is difficult to generalize about it much beyond what is said in Table 1.2 and in the appropriate headings in the chapter on financial due diligence.

Different types of due diligence

As well as different due diligence disciplines, there are also different types. Most of this book is concerned with the traditional, buyer-commissioned due diligence prior to the purchase of a private company. There are other forms.

VENDOR DUE DILIGENCE

Vendor due diligence (VDD) is the name for any due diligence which is commissioned by the current owners of the business in preparation for its sale. It is a relatively new phenomenon which grew out of the sellers' market of the late 1990s and in particular with the rise of data rooms.

Vendor due diligence is commissioned for a number of reasons most, but not all, designed to control the information flow and so maintain negotiating advantage. As such, vendor due diligence:

- allows the seller to argue that it has provided all the information a buyer could want and therefore no further access to management and customers is necessary;
- gets all the bad news out up front so discovery of problems later is not used as an excuse to chisel the price;
- may be a device for hiding or 'spinning' problems.

And it:

- stops management, advisers, customers and suppliers being deluged by questions;
- is used in some cases by the seller to understand exactly what is being sold.

Buyers should be wary of due diligence reports presented by the seller. The tone of reports, if not the facts, can always be varied according to the brief. Even if the investigations have been conducted by an independent organization of the highest reputation, the buyer will not have been privy to the original briefing. I once witnessed a vendor due diligence briefing involving a UK public company which had a potential buyer interested in one of its very weak, and probably unsaleable, businesses, a corporate finance boutique determined to earn its fee and a similarly fee-hungry due diligence consultancy. The 'briefing' consisted of a discussion on what the vendor due diligence should, and should not, say. It amounted to nothing more than a shockingly blatant conspiracy to pull the wool over the eyes of the potential buyer who, sadly, would be blissfully unaware of what had gone on.

The message with vendor due diligence, then, is 'watch it'. Vendor due diligence makes it more difficult for a buyer to form its own opinions, and in some cases it is *designed* to do exactly that. If given vendor due diligence a buyer should:

1. read it.
2. assess the reputation of the firm which carried out the work – do some due diligence on the due diligence providers.

3. read between the lines. Note what is not there, but which should be. Sherlock Holmes once solved a mystery because he spotted that a dog did *not* bark in the night (proof that the crime had been committed by the dog's owner).
4. meet the firm(s) which produced the vendor due diligence (be very suspicious if the seller will not allow this). Ask:

- if the bill was paid in full – if it was not, probe for the reasons. There may have been an argument about the wording in the final report.
- how many drafts were produced. The more drafts the more the client interference.
- what was re-drafted?
- their overall impressions of the target. (Watch the body language as they answer and listen out for direct questions indirectly answered or not answered at all.)

Given most advisers' paranoia about legal action, these conversations will have to be off the record. Be very sceptical and if the slightest doubt remains, either insist on commissioning further due diligence or pull out. Due diligence which does not rely on the target for information, can, if necessary, be carried out without the seller's knowledge.

DUE DILIGENCE IN PUBLIC BIDS

Due diligence in public bids can be very different to private or semi-private transactions. With hostile bids, expect, at best, the minimum of cooperation and be prepared to rely on external intelligence gathering and publicly available information about the target company. Commercial due diligence is a good example of intelligence gathering that can be done without the target's cooperation. It is often commissioned prior to an approach that may turn into a hostile bid in order to reassure the buyer that the bid is sensible before it embarks on what is a painful and costly exercise.

If a public bid is friendly, that is recommended by the target's board, some due diligence is possible although given the price sensitivity full unfettered access is going to be a problem until the deal is announced. Even then, due diligence can be a big headache for the seller in public bids in the UK. If a competitive offer comes along, there is a right to information under Rule 20 of the City Code. Rule 20 says that where there are competitive bids the target company has to supply the same information to the new bidder as it did to the original bidder. The slight get-out is that the second bidder cannot just ask for all the information supplied to the first bidder but has to ask specific questions. Nevertheless, this can act as a constraint on due diligence in public bids. It is not unknown for competitors to enter the fray on fishing expeditions rather than as serious bidders. A target company may therefore not want to disclose sensitive information, even to a recommended bidder, just in case a competitor announces a bid and the information has to be handed over.

Warranties and indemnities are unlikely to be given in public bids. Once the deal is done there is usually nobody left willing to give them, although management might give warranties in public to private transactions as a means of helping bankers get comfortable enough to back the deal.

DUE DILIGENCE IN PUBLIC OFFERINGS

Due diligence for an offering of securities is different from that for an acquisition. The focus is on complete and reliable information on the target company so that underwriters do not misrepresent to potential buyers.

DUE DILIGENCE WHEN BUYING FROM THE RECEIVER

Receivers often allow buyers only a few days to complete a deal. This can severely limit what can be achieved by due diligence. If anything, due diligence is more important with receiverships than with normal acquisitions. If you cannot get proper access for a reasonable time for due diligence you should seriously consider whether or not to go through with the deal, however cheap the target might seem.

For many, the quid pro quo of compressed timescales is that the price is so low a few transaction risks are worth taking. However, compared with even distressed prices, risks can be huge and warranty protection will be almost non-existent. In addition, there may be issues around title to stock or the costs of maintaining the goodwill of key suppliers who might have incurred relatively large bad debts as a result of the receivership.

Others will maintain that risk can be reduced by buying the business rather than the company. The issue with picking and choosing which assets and liabilities to take on is that the buyer still needs due diligence information to make a proper, informed judgement.

But the most compelling reason for proper due diligence may be the post-integration issues. The truth is that businesses get into trouble for a reason. Understanding why a company is in receivership could be crucial not only to making an offer but also to turning it round. Turning companies round always takes longer and costs more than was ever envisaged.

Different types of deal

Due Diligence is a term traditionally used for the review process applied to an acquisition. Exactly the same process is, can, and should be applied to a whole range of other transactions, for example:

- the investment by private equity investors to provide development capital to a private company or to finance a management buy-in (MBI) or management buy-out (MBO)
- the provision of bank facilities either prior to lending or when there is concern about an existing loan
- joint ventures
- strategic alliance
- divestment
- public to private.

Finally, other types of business arrangement might benefit from some, possibly scaled-down, due diligence. For example, a company embarking on a new distribution relationship might wish to make enquiries about the abilities and track record of its new partner.

Different contexts

The book tends to concentrate on Anglo-Saxon legal practice and on UK law. This is not because European acquisitions are not important, or that it is meant for an Anglo-Saxon audience; quite the opposite. It is simply because:

- The acquisition process, and therefore due diligence, is much more developed in Anglo-Saxon jurisdictions, so much so that even purely continental European transactions sometimes adopt Anglo-Saxon practices.
- The acquirer should *always* take local advice in international transactions. This, therefore, is not the place to deal with the differences between law and practice in different jurisdictions. Appropriate advisers will take care of that.
- Despite what many believe, due diligence is not just about the law. The law comes into it in quite a big way but it is not the most important element of the process. It is far more important to grasp the principles of due diligence than to get bogged down in the legal differences between a myriad of different jurisdictions. Again, the important thing as far as the practitioner is concerned is to stay focused on the big picture, using advisers where advice is needed.

Conclusion

Due Diligence is not simply a tool to unearth black holes. Nor is it just to provide ammunition for the negotiations. It does both of these but should also be used as a tool for the longer term.

The academic research in this area shows quite clearly that half of all mergers and acquisitions do not achieve their intended purpose. Other research shows that in the majority of cases this is because the acquisition is not effectively integrated. However good the strategy, however good the choice of target and however good the negotiation of the sale and purchase agreement, poor post-deal integration will seriously increase the probability of a poor deal. Integration must be carried out so that it generates the value the acquisition is expected to bring. It must be conducted quickly, with minimum uncertainty for the acquired workforce and minimum disruption to operations. The key to integration is advance planning. Pre-deal due diligence is the ideal vehicle for the investigative work needed for advance planning. The aim of due diligence should be to give the buyer an assessment of the risks and benefits of the deal both as an aid to negotiation and as an aid to delivering value post-completion.

2 How to structure a due diligence programme

One of the most common mistakes in starting a piece of due diligence is to instruct accountants, lawyers and other experts and let them get on with it. Every deal is different and so, therefore, is every due diligence exercise. Time spent planning and thinking carefully about what is needed will pay enormous dividends when the programme gets going. Time will be short; it always is. Anticipating, and dealing with obstacles is another useful task to make sure is completed very early on. However, even the perfect due diligence exercise will have its shortcomings. This needs to be recognized from the beginning and to be factored into the negotiations.

The preliminaries

The sensible starting point for due diligence is some due diligence on yourself, the buyer, because if you do not know what you want from the exercise you can be pretty sure that no one else will. However stupid that may sound at first, simple answers to many of the acquisition 'process' questions can help prevent wasting a lot of time, money and effort on due diligence and, more important, prevent long-term disappointment with the acquisition in question.

Before diving into due diligence, have the buying team ask itself the following questions:

- What is the business strategy?
- How do acquisitions fit into the business strategy?
- Does the target fit the strategy?
- Have we carried out sufficient pre-acquisition planning? (Buyers can be amazingly slapdash in this area.)
- Are we sufficiently prepared for the due diligence exercise?
- Which areas are we going to investigate? Why?
- Do we know what we really need to know in each area of investigation?
- Do we have enough time to complete the process? If not, what are we going to do about it?
- Do we know, do we really really know, where the synergies are going to come from? Have we tried to quantify them in detail? What further information is needed?
- Have we set a walk-away price or are we so emotionally involved that we will pay any price?
- Have we worked out an adequate implementation plan?
- Have we explored all the consequences of the deal, for example the effects on current operations, existing personnel, the industry and competitors?
- Have we set materiality limits for the due diligence investigation?

- Have we explained the process to the seller?
- Have we agreed access to people and documents with the seller?

The programme

Doing no due diligence at all is not really a good idea except in the most exceptional circumstances. At the other end of the spectrum, if a buyer carried out every investigation possible to the nth degree, due diligence could end up costing more than the target itself. Structuring a due diligence programme is a balancing act between cost and perceived risk. There are two elements:

- which areas to cover
- how much investigation to do.

AREAS TO COVER

Which areas should be covered by due diligence? There are a number of answers to this.

Answer one

The first is that there is no right answer. Due diligence does not have to cover everything and often there will be special areas of concern depending on the deal. Every deal is different and a buyer must decide early on what areas are likely to be the most important. Like very many topics in due diligence, what to cover is a matter of judgement that depends on the business involved. Rather self-evidently, for example,

> inquiries regarding the frequency of returned goods are more relevant to a consumer goods retail business than to a management consulting business. Similarly, questions regarding environmental violations are obviously more critical in acquiring a manufacturing operation than in buying a department store chain.[1]

It is also true that different industries tend to have different risks. In the pharmaceutical industry, for example, the first concern is likely to be intellectual property and the second the state of the distribution. Poor distribution = poor sales. In the defence industry or in construction, the possibility of corrupt practices will be a concern. In other industries, chemical for example, there will be great sensitivity to environmental risks.

In the end, deciding what to cover in due diligence is a function of how much the buying company thinks it knows about a business and how much risk it attaches to areas where its knowledge is limited. If an acquirer is in the same business and territory as the target company its management will feel more relaxed about the level and scope of due diligence required than, say, when buying a business with a new product or which operates in different geographical markets.

Answer two

The second answer is custom and practice. It would be surprising if a deal were done without some form of legal and financial due diligence. These are the two areas most likely to satisfy the Chairman and the board that the deal is under control. But as pointed out above, 'not enough planning' and being 'too obsessed with the financials to the detriment of other areas' is not necessarily going to result in a successful deal.

Answer three

A third answer, therefore, would look at the integration phase as well as the pre-deal phase. The extent and form of post-deal integration will owe a lot to the reasons for making the acquisition in the first place. Assuming an acquisition is being made for logical, well-thought through, strategic reasons, (possibly an optimistic assumption given the evidence!), as Joseph L Bowyer points out[2], there will be a link between the strategic intent behind a deal and the implications for integration that result. The same link can be made to due diligence. Bowyer lists five good reasons for mergers and acquisitions (M&As), each of which, as shown in Table 2.1, is going to mean a different due diligence focus.

Table 2.1   The different types of M&A

M&A type	Strategic objectives	Due diligence focus
The overcapacity M&A	Eliminate overcapacity, gain market share, achieve scale economies	Retaining market share, rationalization costs – especially Human Resources and IT
The geographic roll-up M&A	A successful company expands geographically; operating units remain local	Retaining customers; strength of product relative to competition
Product or market extension M&A	Acquisitions to extend a company's product line or its international coverage	Cultural and systems integration; strength of product relative to competition
The M&A as research and development (R&D)	Acquisitions used instead of in-house R&D to build a market position quickly	Technical and intellectual due diligence; retention of key people
The industry convergence M&A	A company bets that a new industry is emerging and tries to establish a position by culling resources from existing industries whose boundaries are eroding	Commercial due diligence; technical due diligence; retention of key staff

Following Bowyer's logic, the due diligence process is likely to be most effective if it concentrates on those areas for which the deal is occurring. If market share is the aim then commercial due diligence is called for and it should be structured to give a thorough customer interview programme and a realistic assessment of post-deal competitive position. For example, despite a host of acquisitions, American companies have failed to capture as large a share of the UK greetings card market as perhaps they should. The reason for this is that apparently retailers prefer to multiple source their greetings cards so as one company is swallowed up by another, customers simply take their business elsewhere. Buying for market share just does not work.

Answer four

A fourth answer is to do with the likely degree of integration and the speed of its planned implementation. The faster a buyer wants to do things, the more it is going to want to know about the target up front.

Answer five

A fifth answer is to investigate at least those areas where key exposures are likely to lie. To an extent these will be deal specific and they are often in non-financial areas:

- IT systems – non-compatibility with existing systems
- Contract commitments
- Employment terms
- Financial instruments and hedging activities
- Environmental matters
- Compliance with existing laws
- Outstanding litigation.

Answer six

A sixth and final answer is to cover those areas which pose the greatest risk in transactions, unless the buyer's existing knowledge is good enough for it not to have to bother with some of them. Surveys based on acquirers' past experience show these to be (in order of importance):

- Market/Customers
- Management
- Financial records and projections
- Competition
- Product/technology
- Legal issues
- Environmental investigations.

HOW MUCH INVESTIGATION TO DO

There is absolutely no right answer to the question, 'how do you know when you have done enough due diligence?' There is a theory that the more extensive the contractual protection, the less the need for due diligence. This is dealt with later, but is only partially true. In the end it comes down to comfort. When you feel comfortable making a firm recommendation which, if it is for the deal to go ahead, is supported by synergy papers and a fully costed list of post-acquisition actions, you can stand down the due diligence team.

In structuring a programme buyers should always remember that due diligence is not about ticking boxes on a checklist. It is not just about collecting lots of information. It is undertaken so that the correct decisions can be made. These could be:

- Buy/Don't buy
- Negotiate a lower price
- Prioritize warranties and indemnities
- Draw up a proper post acquisition implementation plan

And so on.

Instead of ticking issues off a list, focus on issues as they arise. 'View the effort as a series of independent mini-investigations with respect to key issues'.[3]

An acquirer cannot discover every possible risk. The effort required would mean running out of time, resources and testing the patience of the seller to the limit, not to mention cost. Regardless of what would be ideal, in practice time, money and the seller are going to dictate how much investigation a buyer can do. The key is to be thorough but reasonable.

Doing too much could, in fact, be counter-productive. The reason for this can lie in the terms of the acquisition agreement. With the normal purchaser-drafted acquisition agreements, what due diligence has found is not really an issue. These usually say exactly that by including a clause to the effect that the purchaser's prior knowledge of a particular matter is no defence by the seller to warranty claims unless the matter is actually disclosed in the disclosure letter (warranties and disclosures against them are covered on page 27 below). This is a common approach and means that only matters disclosed in the formal disclosure letter are treated as qualifying the warranties. The commercial objective is obvious: the parties are clear as to the warranties given in the sale agreement, and to the disclosures which qualify them. However, the courts have not always been entirely comfortable with this approach, as in the case of *Eurocopy PLC v Teesdale*.

In *Eurocopy PLC v Teesdale* the court held that the purchaser's knowledge outside the matters disclosed in the disclosure letter might be pertinent in assessing (that is, reducing) the purchaser's claim for breach of warranty. In this case, the vendors had warranted that all material facts had been disclosed. The acquisition agreement also contained the standard clause mentioned above that, apart from information set out in the disclosure letter, the purchaser's knowledge of the target was irrelevant. The Court of Appeal's logic was, among other things, that when the purchaser decided to pay over the odds for the shares it must have taken into account the matters that it was now complaining about so it was no good coming along and claiming a loss now.

There are all sorts of problems with this judgement but it will be a long time before it is tested again. In the meantime, purchasers should be wary of making warranty claims for matters on which there is evidence that they had knowledge. This could mean limiting due diligence and it certainly means not disclosing due diligence findings to sellers even if they request them in the nicest possible way. Their request could just be a ruse to limit liability under warranties based on the precedent set up in *Eurocopy v Teesdale*.

Getting the information

The specific sources of information for each of the specialist due diligence areas are covered under the relevant chapter headings, but there are a number of general points to be made.

It almost goes without saying that throughout the process, the buyer should be sensitive to the stress on its own personnel and on its relationship with the seller:

- Due diligence is a major disruption.
- In non-Anglo-Saxon countries, it is often seen as a sign of mistrust by the seller.
- Sellers will always be afraid of the consequences for the future of the business and/or its sale to someone else if the deal does not go ahead.

Even with a perfect relationship between buyer and seller there are a number of obstacles to contend with.

Dealing with obstacles

It would be nice if buyer and seller could draft Heads of Terms, shake hands and then spend a couple of months helping the buyer's advisers find, comb through and make sense of the mass of information they will inevitably want. It never quite works like that. For a number of reasons, buyers must overcome a number of obstacles which may be placed in their way.

CONFIDENTIALITY AGREEMENTS

Due diligence relies heavily on information from the seller and on access to the target's management, facilities and advisers. Nothing very much is likely to happen until prospective buyer and seller have agreed on confidentiality undertakings.

The fact that negotiations are taking place probably gives rise to an implied obligation on the part of the buyer to keep everything confidential which the seller and its advisers disclose. Nevertheless, sellers usually require the comfort of a signed confidentiality agreement before they release any information.

As a minimum, the seller will want such an agreement to require the purchaser and its advisers to:

- keep all disclosed information confidential
- take all reasonable steps to keep it safe and secure
- disclose the information only to those employees and advisers who need it for the transaction
- use the information only for assessing the prospective transaction
- return all documents (including copies) at the seller's request or at the conclusion or termination of negotiations.

Where buyer and seller are direct competitors there may be further clauses through which the buyer promises not to solicit any of the targets customers or employees during negotiations and for some time after if the deal does not complete.

Although notoriously difficult to enforce, sellers, or more likely their legal advisers, take confidentiality agreements extremely seriously. As a result they are tending to become excessive in their demands. This means that these agreements have to be negotiated which in turn adds delay to what is usually already a fairly tight timetable. The thing to remember is that rarely do parties go to law over breaches of confidentiality agreements so it is better to sign them and get on with the due diligence than waste a disproportionate time quibbling. Restricting the due diligence programme is definitely something which is in the seller's interest and a protracted fight over the terms of the confidentiality agreement could be exactly what the seller had in mind.

On the subject of confidentiality, it is worth asking the target before due diligence gets underway whether it itself is bound by any confidentiality obligations. For example, joint venture agreements may prevent the target disclosing certain information to a purchaser without the partner's consent.

CROSS-BORDER CONSIDERATIONS

Many of the obstacles listed below, and throughout the rest of the book, arise because of an inherent conflict between buyer and seller. The buyer wants to see and understand everything before being bound to a deal. The seller wants to give nothing away until the buyer is bound. These natural differences are often exaggerated in cross-border deals:

- for cultural reasons
- to gain a tactical advantage.

The technical issues in cross-border deals are usually quite straightforward, especially with good local advice. For example, even where civil codes, in theory at least, mean there is no need for warranties, warranties are usually acceptable because there is an acceptance that where a deal is being done with an Anglo-Saxon, an Anglo-Saxon format can be used. Cross-border deals do require more management, and language can be a problem, but what is really difficult are the cultural issues. Very often these cultural difficulties can be avoided by simply trying to understand where the other party is coming from. Differences brought about by different legal philosophies are a good example of how simple ignorance can lead to major difficulties.

For example, the French civil law system is radically different to the English common law system. An important difference as far as the law of contract is concerned is that whereas English company law favours complete freedom in contract negotiations, French law seeks to protect the weakest party to the transaction, the buyer. As a result, French law imposes a duty of good faith on the seller. This is the complete opposite to the English doctrine of *caveat emptor*. In France, the seller owes a duty to the buyer to disclose any fact which might have a bearing on the value of the target. As a result, there is no need for most forms of due diligence, at least not to find deal breakers or negotiating issues, and much less emphasis on contractual protection.

Hardly surprisingly, therefore, the comprehensive Anglo-Saxon approach to due diligence, followed by an exhaustive set of warranties and indemnities, is sometimes viewed by French vendors as over the top. On the other side, failure by the French vendor to discuss such issues seriously is often viewed by a potential UK acquirer as an indication that the French vendor has something to hide. Knowledge of, and sensitivity towards, such differences will go a long way towards diffusing them as obstacles. Flexibility, patience, persistence and the use of local specialists all help too. An aggressive approach normally succeeds only in exacerbating cultural obstacles.

In short, standard approaches will not work with cross-border transactions.

HEADS OF TERMS

The whole point of due diligence, as far as the buyer is concerned, is to find out more about the target company. Not surprisingly, therefore, the buyer will want to retain its freedom to re-negotiate some of the fundamental issues that might have been included in the Heads, such as the price. Also, a buyer will not want to be fully committed until the investigation has been completed and there is adequate contractual protection in place against pre-sale liabilities through clauses in the main agreement.

Unfortunately, the legal consequences of 'Heads' differs markedly by country. In civil law jurisdictions, Heads of Agreement can virtually commit the acquirer to doing the deal on the terms specified, unless they are carefully worded. In general, courts examine the intent of the parties and the completeness of the agreement to determine its enforceability. In common law countries, such as England, the document is little more than a non-binding agreement to negotiate.

At this point a sensible purchaser will also insist on a period of exclusivity. Exclusivity is a period during which the seller agrees not to discuss the sale with other interested parties or encourage such interest. Due diligence is expensive and time consuming and a would-be purchaser does not want to go to the trouble and expense if there is a risk of another bidder walking away with the target before it has had a fair chance to bid. The sanction for breaking the undertaking is often that the seller will pay the potential purchaser's due diligence costs.

Therefore, if there are Heads of Agreement, before starting due diligence it is vital for the buyer to make sure that the document:

- is legally non-binding on the buyer
- contains 'lock out' or 'standstill' clauses giving the buyer exclusivity (although in many countries the existence of Heads of Agreement – or even negotiations – creates obligations to negotiate in good faith).

The seller will probably also want to see confidentiality provisions and both may want clauses which deal with liability for costs in the event of an abortive transaction.

All the above, especially in civil law jurisdictions where the risk of inadvertently creating a binding agreement is greatest, means a short document which:

1. has an introductory paragraph clearly stating that the purpose of the letter is to create either wholly non-binding, or a combination of binding and non-binding, obligations on the parties
2. refers throughout to 'prospective buyer' and 'prospective seller'
3. uses the conditional, words like 'would' and 'might', in non-binding clauses
4. includes a list of all conditions that must be satisfied before the agreement is binding
5. has a summary at the end which:

   - says the agreement is generally non-binding
   - lists the paragraphs that are binding
   - states that the existence of the document is not proof of intent on the part of either party

6. is possibly left unsigned.

It is perfectly possible to start due diligence without Heads of Agreement. Heads of Terms are by no means universally employed and in many transactions are actually quite difficult to draft in any detail prior to due diligence, which rather defeats the object.

SENSITIVE INFORMATION

For understandable reasons, the seller will often not reveal sensitive commercial information until the last possible minute. Sellers do not want to hand potential (or in many deals, existing) competitors information which could damage the business if the deal does not go ahead. The profit made on each product and from each customer, gross margin by product by customer, is not something a seller wants outsiders to know. Unfortunately late disclosure may lead to last-minute negotiations, especially if the information turns out to be different from what the buyer had expected.

In other types of deal, such as public bids, the limits on the amount of information available to the acquirer are often severe, forcing the acquirer to rely more on alternative sources of information than those provided by the target.

RESTRICTED ACCESS TO THE SELLER'S EMPLOYEES

Site visits are important means of collecting due diligence information. From the seller's perspective it is natural to want to keep the proposed sale from employees. However, a seller should provide reasonable access to key personnel, and it is worth pushing very hard for proper access for the following reasons:

1. If the seller is intending to prevent top management from responding to the due diligence request, any meaningful due diligence investigation will be virtually impossible.
2. Top management often proves more willing than the seller to disclose matters that the purchaser should know, such as:

   * who else is bidding
   * what sort of prices have been offered
   * where the real problems are and which of the 'problems' are not problems.

Target management will often have been incentivized to get the deal done but, unless the deal is known for certain to involve their wholesale removal, they know which side their bread is buttered – which is why smart sellers will try to deny access to management in the first place. If access is given, make sure you and your team treat management with respect. Do not let your advisers mess them about or make life difficult for them, do not let them make unreasonable or silly requests and remember they also have a business to run. Make sure their life is as pleasant as possible and you will get a lot more out of them.

If the buyer is denied proper access but still wants to go ahead with the deal, it is a question of using whatever mechanism possible to gather information. In one transaction the selling company insisted that its (female) group financial controller sat in on all discussions between the financial staff of the target and the buyer's financial due diligence investigators. Needless to say the most controversial topics were covered in discussions in the gents' toilet.

Of course in trying to restrict information, access or time, a seller may be playing to one of the few negotiating strengths it has. As a buyer, it is a good idea to test this early on by making it clear that you want to do due diligence before buying the business, that you are going to do it right, and on your terms, and if this cannot be agreed then you will abandon the purchase.

NO ACCESS TO CUSTOMERS

It is absolutely reasonable for a vendor to wish to protect the confidentiality of the discussions; indeed it is in the acquirer's own interest to avoid any rumours in the market which may harm the target's relationships with its customers. Nor does a seller want customers' suspicions aroused by a sudden volley of phone calls from consultants purporting to be studying the market or carrying out a customer care programme on behalf of the target. The seller will have to live with these customers afterwards if the deal does not complete.

What is not reasonable is for the vendor to seek to prevent a would-be acquirer in exclusive negotiations from talking on a confidential or undisclosed basis (more about this later) to the people who know the real strengths and weaknesses of the company and/or the company's technology or products. Again the seller may only be playing a negotiating game. Test this. If you still get no joy, remember that not even the most bloody-minded of sellers can prevent consultants finding and talking to customers on an undisclosed basis. Just allow extra time.

RESTRICTED TIMETABLES

Every seller will do everything possible to convince a would-be buyer to accept the shortest possible due diligence period. Corporate finance firms in particular are very good at creating time pressure. It is in both their interests to do so. The more time a buyer has, the greater the chance of it finding something it does not like. If the timetable imposed on a buyer is unfeasibly tight, alarm bells should ring. Most timetable issues are moveable and indeed by the time discussions get round to due diligence timetables, the seller is so close to a deal it would be foolish to alienate a prospective purchaser for the sake of a couple of weeks' extra investigation – especially if the business is as good as it appears to be from the seller's sales pitch.

Most advisers will need three weeks to carry out their work and more if they come across unexpected issues or problems which need further investigation. Add to this, time to digest their findings and you can see that due diligence needs a month at the absolute minimum. If the seller or the seller's advisers will not budge, you should seriously consider walking away. If not, try to negotiate a break fee, at least then due diligence costs will not be wasted if the work is not completed in time.

It is not always the seller's fault that the timetable is too tight. Often the buyer is to blame. Many buyers hold off from briefing advisers until the very last minute, just in case the deal does not happen, only to find that they have ended up not leaving anywhere near enough time for proper investigations.

If the timetable is genuinely not moveable, and only a limited due diligence exercise is possible, the purchaser should at least seek to investigate key issues and take other precautionary steps, for example, ensuring that the warranties and indemnities are appropriately wide or by negotiating a retention of the purchase price to cover potential warranty claims. A selling company which has restricted the would-be acquirer's due diligence programme will be in a weak negotiating position if it then tries to restrict warranties and indemnities as well.

SEEING THE WOOD FOR THE TREES

A common due diligence problem is the sheer volume of material available during the process, leading to useful information becoming concealed in irrelevant or unfocused data. As mentioned above and in the next chapter, focus is paramount.

DATA ROOMS

There is an art to dealing with the straightjacket that data rooms attempt to impose but this is probably beyond the scope of this book. The objective of a data room is to give potential purchasers enough information for them to submit indicative bids. It is in the seller's interests to put in as much non-sensitive information as possible, and especially all the problems. If a seller gets all the problems out at the beginning of the sale process while there are a number of interested parties, it leaves itself much less vulnerable to purchasers chipping away at the price. If there is only one bidder left, the seller is much more vulnerable to a 'take it or leave it' type of negotiating stance if the buyer comes across unexpected problems.

Following indicative bids, a shortlist of bidders will be drawn up. These will usually have access to the more confidential or sensitive information and be allowed to conduct normal due diligence.

MISREPRESENTATION

Not all sellers, or their advisers, tell the whole truth all of the time. In certain cases in the UK this is a criminal offence.

According to The Financial Services and Markets Act 2000, Section 397,

(1) This subsection applies to a person who –

    a) makes a statement, promise or forecast which he knows to be misleading, false or deceptive in a material particular;

    b) dishonestly conceals any material facts whether in connection with a statement, promise or forecast made by him or otherwise; or

    c) recklessly makes (dishonestly or otherwise) a statement, promise or forecast which is misleading, false or deceptive in a material particular.

(2) A person to whom subsection (1) applies is guilty of an offence if he makes the statement, promise or forecast or conceals the facts for the purpose of inducing, or is reckless as to whether it may induce, another person (whether or not the person to whom the statement, promise or forecast is made) –

    a) to enter or offer to enter into, or to refrain from entering or offering to enter into, a relevant agreement; or

    b) to exercise, or refrain from exercising, any rights conferred by a relevant investment.

(3) Any person who does any act or engages in any course of conduct which creates a false or misleading impression as to the market in or the price or value of any relevant investments is guilty of an offence if he does so for the purpose of creating that impression and of thereby inducing another person to acquire, dispose of, subscribe for or underwrite those investments or to refrain from doing so or to exercise, or refrain from exercising, any rights conferred by those investments.

The wording is very wide. As already mentioned, the offence is criminal. Sellers, and their advisers, involved in UK transactions should therefore think very carefully before they say or conceal anything they think might be material to a buyer trying to decide about a transaction. The provision would apply even to the old estate agent's negotiating trick of telling a potential purchaser that there is another buyer who has offered to pay more.

Another side of Section 397 is that vendors will be particularly concerned to avoid liability for statements made by employees during due diligence that are negligent or innocently made but just plain wrong. They will seek to do this with a clause which says something along the lines of,

> The purchaser has not relied on any representation or undertaking whether oral or in writing save as expressly incorporated in the agreement.

Note, however, that where fraudulent misrepresentations can be proved, this clause in an agreement is not sufficient to exclude liability under the Misrepresentation Act 1967.

RELIABILITY OF DUE DILIGENCE ANSWERS

As is discussed later under commercial due diligence, respondents can be misleading without deliberately lying. This can happen for perfectly innocent reasons: for example they can get facts confused or try to hide the fact that they are not as knowledgeable as they should be. The due diligence practitioner, whatever the discipline, should always:

1. bear in mind that the nature of information impacts on its reliability:

   - Internal information is usually more reliable than external.
   - How and from whom it is obtained can be important.
   - More reliance can be placed on information that is independently verifiable.

2. Be on the lookout for inconsistencies that are material.
3. Ask open-ended questions in interviews.
4. Remember that past behaviour can be a good predictor of future behaviour.

Much of the really useful information will come from interviews. Where these are face-to-face, say with target management, it is always useful to have two interviewers. One is there to listen to the answers, the other is there to watch the answers. It is amazing how much body language can tell you.

There is no substitute for walking around. Even the relatively inexperienced eye can spot a poorly run factory so imagine what the experienced eye can see. The world of due diligence is full of stories of what has been unearthed simply by going to look. 'If the new automated welding system really is bedded in and working, why is there a crew of welders at the end of the line? Are they there, by any chance, to correct errors?' 'If the new computer system has truly created the paperless office, the workforce have not been told because there are piles of paper everywhere.'

How much information is verified is going to be largely based on the buyer's or due diligence investigator's opinion of the source of the information. As a rough guide, the following will always require verification:

- Information that is not publicly available

- Any details of future contracted business
- The existence of physical assets
- Product warranties
- Anything which does not seem believable
- The background of directors and senior staff

Dealing with the shortcomings of due diligence

The fairest and probably most sensible way of apportioning liabilities is to make the seller liable for everything pre-completion and the buyer for everything post-completion. Trying to achieve this happy balance cannot be achieved through due diligence alone. However thorough the due diligence, it is not a substitute for legal protection in the contract. Due diligence and warranties and indemnities should be seen as separate weapons:

- Due diligence cannot uncover or quantify the size and likelihood of every acquisition risk. Legal protection therefore serves as a second line of defence.
- If the seller does not tell the purchaser the truth or does not tell the purchaser the whole story in response to questions, the buyer might find that there are very few remedies. The Financial Services and Markets Act 2000 mentioned above does not provide a civil remedy and so does not give the purchaser the right to seek monetary compensation. Although a purchaser induced to enter into the sale agreement by misrepresentation may be able to rescind the sale and/or claim damages, oral misrepresentations are notoriously difficult to prove and so purchasers usually seek express representations.

The case for express written representations (or warranties) in the sale agreement is further reinforced, at least in Anglo-Saxon jurisdictions, for the following reasons:

- Under English law, the principle of *caveat emptor* or 'buyer beware' means that virtually no terms are implied in favour of a purchaser of shares in a target company. Consequently, protection must be dealt with by express contractual provision.
- Purchasers cannot even rely on audited accounts (see Chapter 4, Financial Due Diligence, for more details).

The theory that the more extensive the contractual protection, the less the need for due diligence is only true to a certain extent. The normal form of contractual protection, warranties and indemnities, is only as good as the covenant of the giver. If, for example, the giver does not have the financial wherewithal to meet warranty claims, or simply disappears, the purchaser will be left out of pocket. A purchaser must, therefore, use all the means of protection available: due diligence, warranties, indemnities, reductions in the purchase price, retentions from the purchase price, earn outs, guarantees, insurance, the exclusion of certain assets and remedial work at the seller's cost.

Furthermore, there is no substitute for knowledge of the target and its affairs in trying to negotiate comprehensive warranties and indemnities, and no better means of getting it than through due diligence. The better the due diligence, the more specific the 'express contractual provision' can be.

Legal protection is therefore used alongside due diligence and usually takes the form of warranties and indemnities. It is the function of both to limit the workings of *caveat emptor*. They do this in different ways.

WARRANTIES

A warranty is in effect a 'guarantee' by the seller that a certain state of affairs exists. Warranties are statements of fact which the seller confirms to the purchaser as being true. An example might be that the target company is not involved in any litigation. If the seller knows that this is not actually true, the seller discloses the real facts (for example, the details of the actual litigation) in a separate letter. With a touch of creativity rare in the legal profession, this is called the disclosure letter. If the seller disclosures exceptions to the warranties, it will not incur any liability under the warranties for the matters disclosed. If the buyer tries to claim for one of these items, the seller can say, 'but I told you about that, you went into this with your eyes open, it is no good trying to claim now.'

As the purchaser is to a large extent relying on what the seller has disclosed, it would be wise to seek extra protection in the form of warranties guaranteeing the accuracy of information. If the information then proves to have been wrong, the purchaser can claim damages.

As no warranties will be given for items disclosed, buyers must be careful of incomplete disclosures. Partial disclosure can make the contractual protection of any associated warranty ineffective.

Warranties have two functions as far as a purchaser is concerned. The first is that the disclosure letter usually contains a lot of useful information about the target company. Clearly if it flags up liabilities which were previously unknown, the purchaser may try to negotiate a price adjustment before the deal is done. The second is contractual. Any breach of the guarantee given by the warranties which has a bearing on the value of the target entitles the purchaser to a retrospective price adjustment. That is to say, where there is a breach of warranty, a seller company who can prove loss is entitled to damages to put itself back in the position it would have been had the warranty been true.

The problem with warranties is that there may be difficulties in relying on them in the event of a breach. These are normally one of two types:

- Difficulties of proof – either that there has been a breach or that there has been a loss resulting from it.
- Disclosures – the warranty will not normally apply if breaches of the topic in question have been disclosed.

INDEMNITIES

An indemnity is a guaranteed remedy against a specific liability. The buyer is entitled to it regardless of whether:

- or not the value of the target is affected
- the liability in question is disclosed to the purchaser in the disclosure letter.

Indemnities enable the purchaser to adopt a 'wait and see' policy, especially where the liability in question is contingent and it is uncertain to what extent, if at all, it will crystallize.

The sale and purchase agreement can identify the particular problem and provide that if that liability crystallizes the purchaser will be compensated for the loss suffered. One of the most common indemnities is an indemnity against tax liabilities. Here the vendor promises to meet a liability should it arise.

Whether or not a warranty or indemnity is adequate depends on the financial worth of the seller. If the sellers are not particularly creditworthy or, for example, have moved their assets to an offshore jurisdiction, some security may be called for. This could take the form of a deposit of funds in an escrow account, a third party guarantee or even retention from the purchase price for a stipulated period after completion.

The width of an indemnity will depend upon its wording and it should not necessarily be assumed that all losses will be recoverable. Indemnities have the following limitations:

- They will not cover wilful and culpable acts.
- Difficulties of proof may make indemnities difficult to rely on, as can difficulties in establishing quantum.
- Indemnities may not always cover economic loss.
- Indemnities may be limited in time and be financially capped.

There are all sorts of twists and turns on these basic themes which get the lawyers terribly excited but these are beyond the scope of a book on due diligence. For example it is possible for a tax liability to give rise to both a breach of warranty and an indemnity claim. The most important issues as far as due diligence is concerned are:

- First, as mentioned above, to what extent will what you have found out in due diligence be treated as actual knowledge as if it had been in the disclosure letter?
- Second, and related to the first point, should a buyer reveal its due diligence findings to the seller?
- Third, what are the issues to be taken into account in establishing a loss or a breach of warranty (because this might have a bearing on how much due diligence to do and how to make sure claims are properly made once the deal is done)?

It is usual for the buyer's solicitor to produce a standard set of warranties and indemnities. These should be tailored to meet the buyer's specific concerns before being sent to the seller. In cross-border transactions the flow of information may not be quick enough to allow this so warranties may need to be revised later once the information does come in.

CLAIMING UNDER WARRANTIES AND INDEMNITIES

As warranties tend to be the bigger issue here, the comments which follow are addressed specifically to warranties although many of the principles also apply to indemnities.

As already mentioned, for warranty claims there has to be breach of a specific warranty and there must be loss. The issues around claiming include:

- Time limits: the seller will usually try to restrict the time in which a claim can be made.
- Procedure: the agreement will set out formal requirements for making a claim.
- Loss: the general principle is that the purchaser is entitled to the difference between the value of the company as warranted and its actual market value. It goes without saying that

in assessing market value each party will argue for a valuation method that produces the most favourable valuation for them.

- Amount: the seller will normally seek to impose both a minimum and a maximum level of claim with the ceiling often fixed at the consideration paid.

Because of the difficulties with warranty claims it may be better in some circumstances for the purchaser to pursue a claim for damages instead.

There is one final and very important point under this heading. Whoever is responsible for integrating and/or running the target business once the deal is done must be made fully aware of what warranties and indemnities have been agreed and what the procedures are for claiming under them. When a deal is done, the acquisition team tends to move on and hand over to line managers. Line managers do not have a natural inclination to go to law when a problem appears and unless the notion that there is contractual protection is thoroughly ingrained there is a strong chance that they will not make use of it.

Other forms of protection

As mentioned above, apart from legal protection in the form of warranties and indemnities, other forms of protection can always be negotiated following adverse due diligence findings. These include:

- Price adjustment
- Retention from the purchase price
- Earn outs
- Third-party guarantees
- Insurance
- Asset sale rather than a share sale
- Exclusion of certain assets and liabilities from the acquisition
- Rectification of any problems at the seller's cost.

Conclusion

One of the secrets of due diligence is knowing what is required, from whom, and when – in other words, project management, pure and simple. Good planning and active management are paramount. Start right at the very beginning. Why you are doing the deal and what you hope it will achieve will be vital pointers as to what due diligence needs to achieve and therefore which areas need to be covered to what degree. However, there is no escaping the fact that in due diligence judgement plays a big part. There are few right answers. What and how much to cover in any deal is a matter of judgement.

Managing the project means managing not just advisers (the subject of the next chapter) but managing the seller and its advisers also. Obstacles to honest investigation cannot be helped, but they can be managed.

One of the great benefits of a properly executed due diligence programme is that it highlights areas of uncertainty which can be ring-fenced by warranties, indemnities or other forms of protection. The buyer should not regard either due diligence or legal protection as substitutes for each other. They are separate, complementary weapons to be used in tandem.

3 *Working with advisers*

The one thing all principals need to remember about due diligence is that to get the best out of it, it has to be managed. The pace of the deal and the diverse range of expertise which must be deployed means that advisers are usually a feature. It is very important to select the right ones and as they are expensive, getting the best out of them is as much of an issue as anything else in due diligence. Like all project management, the keys are to plan what needs to be done by when and by whom, coordinate the efforts of all involved and communicate, communicate, communicate.

Why bother with advisers?

Whatever they tell you, and whatever some of them may actually believe, there is no particular magic to what due diligence advisers do. There is also no rule which says a buyer cannot do due diligence with its own internal resources. In fact every buyer usually does take an active part in some part of the due diligence process. Doing it yourself has the advantage of saving money and it also develops an in-house acquisition expertise. Some even claim that using in-house due diligence teams improves confidentiality. The fact is, though, that most due diligence exercises use outside professionals to a greater or lesser extent. The question, then, is why? Why do buyers usually instruct professionals to carry out the investigations?

The reason is that they can bring a lot to the event:

- Experience. Advisers have done it all before. Advisers should, therefore, be pretty efficient at getting through the task in the ridiculously short time available.
- Expertise. Advisers will be experts in their own specialist field. As such they will not only be good at spotting problems, they are usually pretty good at solving them too.
- Judgement. Due diligence often calls for judgement. Good judgement is helped greatly by experience and expertise. Not just anyone can provide reliable judgements, for example legal due diligence findings will need legal judgement.
- Resources. An acquisition is a time-consuming exercise. A buyer simply may not have the manpower to conduct due diligence. Using outside professionals will leave the buyer to concentrate on the bigger commercial picture.
- Access. Accounting firms are normally given access to the target's auditors' working papers and tax files. This would usually be denied to others. Often sellers will tell third parties a lot more than buyers who are often also competitors.
- Speed. More often than not the possibility of buying a business presents itself as a fleeting opportunity. Deadlines are always tight. It is very difficult to ensure that adequate due diligence and planning have taken place without bringing in external resources to aid in the process.

- Comfort. Knowing that a professional has investigated the target company is much more comforting than doing it all yourself and wondering what you might have missed. It is also a lot more comforting to third parties in a transaction such as banks, stockbrokers and merchant banks.
- Internal politics. Acquisitions can very often mean empire building. Advisers are usually not part of the politics. Not only can they just get on with the job but they can also deliver any bad news much more easily than an employee whose first thought might be the career-limiting implications of delivering the 'wrong' message.
- Objectivity. As an acquisition proposal is tabled, discussed and analysed within the acquiring company, it builds up a momentum all of its own. Once the proposal has been put to the target company, agreed in principle, and all the negotiating and investigating machinery has swung into action, that momentum becomes a powerful force. By this time a number of people within the acquiring company – some of them quite senior – have invested significant amounts of time, energy and credibility. Other things being equal (which often they are not) it is much easier for someone who is not from the acquiring company to bring an objective viewpoint.
- Corporate Governance. As mentioned in Chapter 1, The Cadbury Report recommended that significant acquisitions should be considered by the full board of directors of the purchasing company. Cadbury recommended that non-executive directors should play a 'devil's advocate' role. This role is virtually impossible without independent reports from professional advisers. Without them the non-executives could only rely on the executive management.
- Anonymity. Unless an in-house team goes to some length to disguise its identity, it will be unable to use certain sources of information (for example, competitors). Its activities may well also advertise what is going on and spark interest from other parties.
- Confidentiality. Confidentiality is probably easier to maintain in firms of professional advisers.

Taking control

Managing advisers means controlling the process right from the start. Sadly for most buyers, this means spending time planning the due diligence campaign. Time is always constrained, so to make the most of it, prepare properly. The rules of control are:

- First, the buyer controls the process, not the advisers.
- Second, advisers are there to give advice and not to make decisions. It is for the principals to make decisions.
- Third, do not be unrealistic about your demands.
- Fourth, advisers must be properly briefed. However much they are under your control, advisers will not do what is expected of them if they are not properly briefed.

BRIEFING ADVISERS

Advisers cannot be expected to turn in a half-decent job unless they know what is going on. Before they start they need to know:

- Which other professionals will be working on the deal, what they are doing and where the focus of their investigations will be. Naturally this should include a briefing on any due diligence which the purchaser will be undertaking himself.
- The reasons for doing the deal and the areas of greatest worry.
- Acceptable risks/materiality limits. The last thing you want is a report that covers every little detail. Setting materiality levels helps avoid this by specifying acceptable risk thresholds. If only risks above £100 000 are a worry, say so then the adviser does not have to report on anything beneath the threshold, unless there is a chance of it turning into something much bigger.
- The specific industry risks. For example the risks in the food industry are quite different to those in the pharmaceutical industry.
- The structure of the deal. A share purchase has very different implications to an asset purchase.
- What the key issues are and what is irrelevant. A colleague, for example, tells a story of due diligence which identified a downward sales trend in one product line. Before setting off to investigate why, he thought what had been found out should be mentioned to the client. The client in fact already knew and was not in the least concerned as it was the client's own product range which was picking up the lost share.
- Precisely what is wanted from the exercise. One of the reasons why due diligence reports run to several hundred pages of often unrelated, but very detailed, facts is that the client has not specified (or not got across) what is wanted both in terms of the information needed and how it should be presented. Raw data is no good; it needs to be evaluated by seasoned professionals. Say so. In the absence of a proper briefing, advisers will go out and collect everything.
- The deal timetable.

At the end of the briefing it is a good idea to test advisers to make sure they know what they think they are looking for and that they definitely know what the buyer wants them to look for. Professional advisers are very good at pretending that they know everything about everything. It pays to disabuse them of this nonsense. Encourage them to sit with you, probe, ask questions and listen to the answers. Review their information request or question set before they send it to the target. Above all, do not let them set off to solve a problem before it has been properly explained to them. Many do.

All of the above just serves to reinforce the second last of the above bullet points. Before you commission due diligence, you must think pretty carefully about what information and analysis is needed. This will not only keep the due diligence team focused, but will also keep costs down. Saying to advisers, 'tell me everything you can possibly find out' is a little like writing an open cheque. If the potential acquisition has been properly researched and the rationale for its purchase evaluated, a fairly logical set of due diligence issues should fall into place.

Beware: left to their own devices advisers will work quite independently of each other. This you do not want. Encourage them to work together. For example, accountancy firms are notoriously reluctant to put their names to a forecast. A commercial due diligence provider will gladly come up with forecasts, but will usually not provide numbers. Getting the two to work together has got to make sense. Similarly, lawyers will examine legal structure and may find that liabilities will be triggered if the target leaves its present group. These could, for example, be capital gains tax liabilities because of inter-group transfers of assets or additional costs because the target company can no longer benefit from group discounts. The accountants need to build these into their model.

Selecting advisers

There are two aspects to selecting advisers

- Which services do you want?
- Who do you choose to provide them?

The answer to the 'which services' question is going to be different for every deal. The question was covered under 'The programme' in the previous chapter. It will be a function of deal size, knowledge, and perceived risk.

The most reliable way to select the right advisers is to find key advisers and, over time, build personal relationships with them. You are not going to be able to build working relationships while under the stress of a deal so take the time and trouble to do that before you get stuck into a transaction. To find individual advisers who have expertise and integrity, ask people's opinions. Take time to meet advisers and get references from previous clients to understand exactly what their role was and how they performed. By taking time to build working relationships, advisers will get to understand your business and your long-term strategy; for your part, you will feel comfortable with the prospect of working with them. The people element is at least as important as the technical element. Appendix A1 gives a checklist for selecting (and working with) advisers.

INTERPERSONAL FACTORS

Technical ability and experience are important in choosing which advisers should carry out what work, but so are personal chemistry and seeing what lies behind the typical adviser's sales veneer. The following is an extract from a letter to the *Financial Times* describing Enron, but the sentiments could easily be applied to a great many due diligence advisers.

> It promoted itself beyond the limits of truth; it offered for sale things it had not quite finished buying; it spoke of funds it had almost, but not quite, garnered.[1]

Honesty and integrity should be important selection criteria. What every acquirer wants is an adviser who is looking out for the acquirer's best interests and who is not just interested in getting a deal done in order to earn a fee. The DTI report into Robert Maxwell's business affairs[2] recognized advisers' pursuit of the fee as one of the problems which allowed Maxwell to carry on as he did. 'Maxwell was an attractive client. He was a prolific deal doer . . . and he paid well.'[3] A 3i executive sums up the problem as follows,

> I am fed up of reading due diligence reports which conclude, 'from our initial inquiries we conclude that this would not be an attractive MBO candidate' and then go on to say, 'we look forward to continuing with the investigation.' Who do they think they are kidding?

Besides the obvious questions like 'Can they get the job done?' and 'Are their fees reasonable?' the buyer should also be asking 'Can I really trust these people', 'Can I work with these people?', 'Are they really as good/as experienced as they claim?' and ' Will they give me strong opinions based on their experience or are they only interested in covering their back?'

EXPERIENCE AND SKILLS

After interpersonal factors comes the right mix of experience and skills. Experience required in order of importance is as follows:

1. Experience of carrying out due diligence
2. Experience of the purchaser
3. Experience of the target company's sector.

In other words, the most important skill is preparing due diligence reports for different companies; knowing the purchaser and the sector are additional benefits.

Sector knowledge

Sector experience is not, as some seem to believe, the answer to everything. For example when the Internet boom was nearing its peak one consultant published a brochure on doing business on the Internet. This consultant's knowledge of the theory of Internet trading, compiled over several years and from many sources, was good. However, when questioned about the more mundane practical issues of interest to prospective backers of these nascent businesses, like how much and how long it takes to construct a website that works, he was next to useless. Even cursory investigation of his output would have shown that its quality hinged not on Internet experience as such but on normal business investigation. In other words, what was important to the due diligence process in this particular industry was no different to that in any other industry. What counted much more than industry knowledge was having the right people asking the right questions of the right sources.

So, if you are one of those who is convinced that industry knowledge is important, it pays to think very carefully about just what experience you are being provided. You should also bear four other things in mind:

1. Consultants can usually 'buy in' industry expertise if it is needed that much.
2. The reality is that there is often no such thing as an 'industry'. Consider the engineering industry. The term 'engineering' covers a tremendous variety of activities from basic industries, such as steel making or forging, through industries with some special features, such as automotive components or aerospace sub-contracting, right up to some fairly high-tech areas like automatic test equipment. It would be naïve to believe anyone can be an expert in all aspects of the 'engineering' industry, and the same is true of every other industry.
3. Just because a firm has carried out due diligence before in certain industries does not necessarily make the whole firm an expert on those industries. If the people involved previously do not happen to be involved this time round, where is the industry experience?
4. Industry knowledge can be out of date. A lot of the commercial due diligence one-man bands are what are called 'industry gurus'. Normally these are retired or semi-retired professionals. Some are excellent, but some are not and the trouble with the ones that are

not is that their knowledge is out of date – even a couple of years away from an industry can be critical – and prone to prejudices and received wisdoms built up over many years.

THE TEAM

Although the reputation of the firm is important, the individual qualities of the team are most important. A buyer is going to look to these individuals for good advice in a period of great stress. Above all, advisers should have appropriate experience for the work required. Do not allow due diligence to be pushed down to junior levels unless this is appropriate. Be particularly aware of this if using large firms of accountants for due diligence work. Most of these firms recruit graduates for their audit departments and to give them more challenge and variety often give them the opportunity to work on due diligence projects. Although it might help with their development and retention, it might not always be the best way of servicing clients' needs.

But it is not just accountants that can be guilty of using junior staff. The DTI report into Robert Maxwell's business affairs stated that 'MGN's unsuitability for listing was the result of failures for which Samuel Montagu were responsible to the extent we have identified.'[4] According to the *Financial Times*,[5] some bankers believe that Samuel Montagu's use of inexperienced staff on the *Mirror* float was at the root of the problem.

Clearly, then, it is important to find out how much involvement the senior adviser will have. All too often he or she will 'sell' the work, then disappear and leave more junior members of staff to complete it. If time permits it is a good idea to meet the adviser's teams and satisfy yourself as to the level of their experience and how they would handle the assignment. You do not want to be lumbered with the B team. In gauging this, remember that carrying out due diligence requires the right people asking the right questions of the right sources. The right people need more than just analytical skills and a good grasp of accounting standards or whatever. Analysis is important, but due diligence also requires a healthy slug of streetwise detective work and a lot of judgement. It is therefore much more suited to advisers who have been round the block, and preferably several different blocks, a few times than it is to intellectuals or newly qualified professionals who have never had to get their hands dirty.

TEAM SIZE

Teams should be kept small. The main objective is an overview of the entire company. The more people working on an assignment, the more the information is dispersed between them. One of the problems with trying to compress timescales means more people are needed to cover the ground in time, but more people can also means less collective understanding.

THE ONE-STOP SHOP

Many advisers are now making a big play of being able to offer an integrated due diligence service providing financial, legal and commercial expertise plus many of the other disciplines. Their argument is that the end result is better because there is one team working on the transaction. This is stretching the truth ever so very slightly. But that is not the most important point. To be sure, buying 'best in class' usually means engaging a number of teams, but it also gives a number of different perspectives on the target. Due diligence is not a precise science. Buyers can benefit from having assessments from as many different perspectives as is practical. Besides, if the person in charge of due diligence is doing his or her job properly, communication and coordination between the various due diligence providers will not be an issue.

DANGER SIGNS

Due diligence is a fraught and time-compressed exercise, requiring the maximum expertise pumping out the maximum in usefulness. This is not the time to have to carry any passengers. It is important, therefore, to watch advisers for any danger signs.

Part of the routine is for advisers to ask lots of questions. To an extent this is to be welcomed although a good many will owe more to show than a genuine desire to understand. A failure to ask searching questions is a cause for concern. Either:

- The advisers are not thinking through their approach. Or
- They are going to rely on an 'off the shelf' approach which does not take into account the particular circumstances of your acquisition. Or
- They are that breed of professional adviser conditioned not to admit that they do not know everything.

Advisers may justify their relative lack of imaginative questioning by their emphasis on previous sector experience. Probe just how real it is, especially amongst the individuals who will be working on the project.

Having satisfied yourself that you have not been fobbed off with the B team, watch for team changes. Lack of continuity during the process may mean other assignments are more important to them and junior staff are being assigned to your project. Difficulty contacting senior team members may confirm this, as they may be busy on other projects.

Of course they may just not get to grips with the industry or the issues, in which case they will not be able to talk sensibly about their work as the project unfolds, or they may just not be suitable, in which case they will annoy management and/or customers by applying a process regardless. Advisers need to be aware that every acquisition is different and show sensitivity to the particular situation in which they are working.

Timetables: involve advisers early

A typical due diligence assignment is going to take at least a month. The exact time frame will depend on the scope of work and complexity of the company being investigated. It can be shortened but, if it is, there is a danger that quality will suffer. Putting more people on to a project may allow the ground to be covered and the boxes to be ticked, but it does not guarantee that the analysis of findings will be carried out with enough thought or thoroughness. Analysis takes time and familiarity with all of the findings. If you do not leave the adviser sufficient time, the analysis will not be done properly. In any case, due diligence reports frequently take longer than expected.

The message, therefore, is to give advisers as much time as possible and involve them as early as possible. Even if the deal has not been finalized it is still worth calling them in. They can begin to plan the work, think about putting a team together and even start some of the background desk research. Many acquirers seem to have the misguided belief that firms of professional advisers have teams of often highly paid employees sitting around on the off chance that a deal may come along. As a result they spend months talking to target management and playing with their spreadsheets, only calling in advisers at the last possible minute.

Involving advisers early also allows you to pick their brains. Very often advisers will have much more due diligence experience so, for example, time spent with advisers thinking through terms of reference in the early stages will be time well spent. It will help you decide what you need, when and from whom. However, do not:

- let the process start until you are sure of what you do need
- let the adviser dictate the scope of the work.

The other side of the coin is that if you involve advisers late, they will charge more – because they know they can.

A colleague tells a wonderful story which sums up how not to do it. The written briefing on the work to be done included something like the following,

Timing is tight. There are only two weeks in which to complete the investigation. We require a final presentation by Friday 27 April.

The initial phone call warning him of the deal was not made until Tuesday 17th, and the written briefing did not arrive until the following day, Wednesday 18th. The client wanted a written proposal before giving the go-ahead. That was sent on the Wednesday and approved late morning the following day. Assuming he could drop everything else he was working on, the adviser in question now had, not a 'tight' two-week timetable, but one week plus a day and a half – and he had not even begun to assemble a team. The work was completed on time but the client still had a moan about the relative lack of analysis, that, not surprisingly, the report did not answer all the questions that were included in the original briefing and that the cost was higher this time than it was last time. In this case the client only had himself to blame for not getting exactly what he wanted.

Under the heading of timetable, it pays also to consider the sequence in which due diligence advisers are deployed. The legal and financial teams are probably going to be quite expensive. It is pointless letting them get started if there are still some lingering doubts about the deal. If for example the deal involves a site with potential environmental liabilities you may want to get an interim report from a firm of environmental specialists which gives the site a reasonable bill of health before giving the go-ahead to the other advisers. Many US acquirers will not even brief their advisers until they are satisfied on environmental liabilities. Similarly, some investigations take much longer than others. This may have a bearing on sequencing advisers' work. Intellectual property, for example, can involve a lot of elapsed time, whereas most commercial due diligence investigations are more or less guaranteed to take three weeks.

Written terms of reference

Establishing written terms of reference is one of the most important aspects of working with advisers. What you expect each specialist to do, by when and for how much, should be properly reflected in writing. There are a number of obvious reasons for this. Two others are:

1. You will not wish to pay two or three advisers for investigating the same areas. All too often advisers will duplicate each other's efforts or try to improve on the efforts of another adviser if their respective roles are not properly defined. Tax is a good example. Who do you want to investigate tax? It is an area that could fall into legal or financial due diligence.
2. If due diligence is not properly coordinated, it is quite likely that something will fall between the cracks. The case of Atlantic Computers, below, is a good example of what can go wrong.

The written engagement letter for each adviser will set out:

- The scope of the due diligence work to be carried out. Incomplete scope is often a major obstacle to getting the best out of advisers.
- A clear demarcation of responsibilities, possibly showing how one adviser's brief fits with other advisers' work.
- To whom the adviser owes a duty of care.
- Their timetable.
- Whether an interim report or presentation is needed.
- Fees.
- Headings to be covered in the report. (Appendix A includes some suggested terms of reference for various due diligence advisers.)
- Who will manage the assignment.
- Confidentiality.
- The rights to the results.
- Assignability of the results.
- Liability insurance (if appropriate).
- What happens if the deal is abandoned and the work is terminated early.

ATLANTIC COMPUTERS

Atlantic leased computers with a unique proposal called the 'flex lease'. The flex lease had two elements:

1. A lease agreement (normally for 6 years)
2. A management agreement, between Atlantic and the company taking out the lease, which contained two options:

   - A flex option which allowed the leaseholder to take out a new lease for different equipment after three years
   - A walk option which allowed the lessee to terminate the lease after five years.

It was the management agreement which proved the killer. It meant that when the flex or walk options were exercised, Atlantic became responsible for the lessee's obligations under the lease. This in practice meant Atlantic paying the lease founders to discharge the obligations.

Atlantic could also acquire the equipment for a nominal sum at the end of the lease, but this was the 1980s when machines were quickly becoming out of date (which of course explains why the Flexlease was so popular). Not surprisingly, the liabilities Atlantic assumed were greater than the value of the equipment.

At the time B&C (British and Commonwealth) acquired Atlantic it failed to understand the full extent of Atlantic's potential liabilities. They were enough to bring down the group. The situation arose because of confusion over the role of B&C's professional advisers. No formal written instructions were given to merchant bankers to define their role in the acquisition, nor was it clear whether the specialist consultants, who had been instructed to conduct an independent investigation into Atlantic and the computer leasing industry, were the clients of B&C or the merchant bank. The merchant bank had not considered it within its mandate to investigate and subsequently advise upon the flex lease arrangements (they saw themselves as facilitators and coordinators) whereas B&C claimed their role was to assist and advise in the evaluation of Atlantic's business and its suitability for acquisition.

All this meant that although the consultants pointed out the high risks involved in computer leasing in general, and Atlantic's particularly high risks under Flexlease, the message somehow never got through. The DTI inspectors concluded that the resulting confusion over roles and reporting lines was a factor contributing towards B&C's failure to gain an adequate understanding of Atlantic's business prior to the takeover.

The Atlantic case is a clear example of why it is crucial that each area of due diligence is outlined in detail and clear, written instructions given to the relevant advisers. It also reinforces the message that advisers should be encouraged to work together and to share information properly.

Fees

Generally speaking, you get what you pay for in due diligence. You can have a cheap report or you can have a good report, but not both. Advisers will tell you that fees tend to be competitive and, in any case, the choice of consultant should not be overly cost-driven. They will maintain that the reputation and experience standing behind opinions are more important than simple fee considerations. To an extent they are right, but a firm of advisers is always going to charge what it thinks it can get away with. If it sees the prospective buyer as someone with deep pockets or too inexperienced to know any better, the proposed fee will be higher than if it thinks it is dealing with a mean and experienced acquirer. It is worth haggling and talking with people in other companies who have recently done deals to find out what sort of fees they paid (and whether they thought them reasonable). Do not be frightened of picking up the phone and talking to other companies who have been on the acquisition trail. There is almost a spirit of 'us' and 'them' as far as advisers are concerned and this brings with it a certain camaraderie and a willingness to help.

It is normal for due diligence to be carried out on the basis of a fixed fee. Of course it is extremely difficult to estimate how many hours a due diligence exercise will consume. It is really up to advisers to get their estimates right and a buyer should be reluctant to vary fee levels unless there is a change in the scope of work or delays outside the adviser's control. In the event of either of these, it is up to the adviser to convince the buyer of the need for additional fees.

Contingent fees are becoming increasingly common. Here the exact fee charged depends on whether or not the deal completes. The usual arrangement is for there to be a discount on the fee if the deal does not go ahead and an uplift if it does. How much the fee varies around the 'normal' is really up to the adviser and the buyer to negotiate. Contingent fee arrangements can vary from a small up/down right through to 100 per cent success fees (that is nothing if the deal does not complete but a considerable uplift if it does).

Although contingent fees are a good way to minimize costs if a deal does not go ahead, they do give the adviser a vested interested in producing a positive report and this provides a clear conflict of interest. In the words of a very experienced deal doer,

> I wonder how clearly people work in situations where they make half a million if the deal happens and get nothing if they tell me about a minor defect.[6]

On balance it is probably better to avoid fee arrangements which give advisers too much of a material interest in the transaction taking place, particularly in the light of tales such as the following,

> I was called by the lawyers on the other side. 'We have £400,000 on the clock,' they told me, 'and we're on a success fee. So if you really insist on these warranties, we'll make sure you're satisfied.'[7]

The fairest mechanism is one which at least allows the advisers to eat if the deal does not go ahead but gives them a reward if it does. As a rough rule of thumb, one-third of the price of a due diligence exercise will be profit. On a contingent fee basis this would mean knocking off a third of the fee if the deal aborts and adding up to the same again on to the 'normal' price if it completes. On this basis, for a £60 000 exercise, the high/low fee would be £40 000 abort and up to £80 000 success.

Sometimes advisers are paid on a success fee only basis where the fee is a percentage of the transaction. Not only does this give advisers a huge vested interest in the deal going ahead, but there is something not quite right about advisers getting more if they get the acquirer to pay *more* for the target. There are ways round this, though, like advisers being paid a bonus based on savings below a ceiling target price.

LIABILITY CAPS

Some advisers seek to cap their liability. Liability caps seek to limit the extent of an adviser's liability should the client succeed in establishing that it has been negligent. The basis of these liability caps varies between firms and indeed not all firms try to impose them. Typically they are linked to a monetary value. For example, the standard accountants' cap is the lower of £25 million or 1 per cent of the deal.

Liability caps are hard to justify. If the job is done properly, the adviser has nothing to worry about. At the very least the prospective client is owed a full explanation of why advisers deem it necessary to cap their liabilities. If buyers are not satisfied, they should say so and perhaps go elsewhere.

Advisers will try to justify liability caps because from their perspective there is always a risk of allegations of professional negligence if things go wrong. The test at law is what a reasonable professional would have done in the circumstances. This does not support the argument for liability caps. What it does support is the importance of advisers agreeing the extent of the due diligence work at the outset, setting out in formal letters of engagement what is expected and then doing a good job.

If the target's auditors are being used, they will attempt to slip a clause into their terms of reference which gives them an indemnity in respect of their audit work. This definitely needs taking out.

Plan the work

If establishing sensible terms of reference is the most important contribution to successful due diligence, probably the next most important is to plan how the work is going to be carried out.

Much due diligence involves analysing information supplied by the target company and interviewing members of its management team. In order to ensure that time is not wasted and that the information and people are available, it is vital to plan the work in conjunction with the management of the target company. There is little point in teams of expensive advisers arriving at a company only to find that the key people are not available or that it will take time to provide the information that they require.

It is therefore vital in planning the work that the target is supplied early on with detailed lists of information requirements and the people to be interviewed. Whilst more information and more interviews will normally be required during the course of the work, this initial planning should greatly help ensure that the work is carried out efficiently.

Coordination

Exactly who does the coordination depends on company style and the deal in question. In small and medium-sized companies, masterminding an acquisition may fall to the chief executive. In larger companies it may be the manager of the division which will be responsible for running the company after it is bought, or it may be an individual or a department which has responsibility for carrying out acquisitions.

There are advantages and disadvantages to each approach. If the business unit which will run the acquisition handles the deal more sector understanding may be brought to bear in the research and negotiation processes. If, on the other hand, acquisition specialists do the work, they can build on the experience of previous deals. There is a lot to remember during an acquisition and there is no doubt that practice makes, if not perfect, then improvements.

The preferred route is certainly to involve the operators fully at an early stage. Chapter 1 stresses the importance of thinking about the integration plan right from the very start. The only other rule is to have someone who is responsible for running the entire due diligence and who therefore sees the whole picture.

If coordination is not done by one of the buyer's personnel (which ideally it should), one adviser should be appointed to coordinate the due diligence (ideally the adviser who is closest to the commercial negotiations).

Coordination is also necessary with various in-house experts.

- What are the objectives and concerns of the line managers who either know the business or are going to have to run it afterwards? Are there any particular areas of concern or sensitivity both in terms of confidentiality and in terms of known problems?
- Internally who are the main points of contact? Who has authority for what? What are the main areas of responsibility?
- Internal advisers (tax, property and so on) may have excellent knowledge which can be applied to the target business. How are they to be used?
- Will the project manager act as the main interface between the internal experts, the commercial team and outside advisers, or will the outside advisers have direct access?

Communicate regularly

Whoever is coordinating due diligence should make sure there is regular communication with the advisers. Communication should not be a one-off event which takes place when the finished report is presented (or, more likely, when the executive summaries are circulated to management). This is not to say that there should be formal progress meetings on a weekly basis, the deal timetable is usually too short for that, but there should be reasonably regular updates from external advisers as the enquiries proceed. If nothing else, this allows the buyer to:

- communicate changes in its concerns
- identify significant issues early on
- make sure all advisers' efforts are coordinated

Also hold regular meetings internally so that:

- The commercial impact of what is being found out can be properly assessed, questions can be raised and fed back to the investigating advisers and areas where further investigation is needed can be identified. There may be issues which kill the deal and the sooner these are brought up, the better.
- The due diligence process itself can be evaluated. Are you getting what you want out of the process?

Code names

It is a very useful discipline to insist that all parties to the proposed sale use agreed code names. Very often code names can help protect the identity of the parties and the target company should any sensitive correspondence or other written material fall into the wrong hands.

Report

The form of report is also an important key to managing the process effectively. A buyer will want a written report. This is not just a record but fulfils several functions such as keeping all parties informed of matters arising. There is also much to be said for insisting on a presentation. This is the opportunity to pin advisers down as to what they really think and to watch them wince when asked for their assessment of the risks involved. Whether written, verbal or both, above all advisers must give opinions. Buyers must insist on getting opinions. The advisers are the experts, they have trawled through the detail, and they should be capable of giving an opinion.

Due diligence reports should be user-friendly and contain an executive summary. The executive summary is the most important chapter as this is the only part many recipients will actually read. Reports should be written in easy to understand, non-technical language. Lawyers, for example, tend to write in a form only other lawyers can understand. You should guard against reports becoming huge tomes without too much form or meaty content. It is not unknown for external advisers to get lost in detail and lose sight of the deal as a whole. Be clear from the outset about what you want and how much you want. It could be three bullets or 300 pages. You might even consider using a standard format. You will almost certainly want to 'audit' the reports before they are circulated. If you cannot understand what is being said there is a good chance no one else will either. It is also an opportunity to pull out parts that may be relevant for other advisers to review.

Finally, there is no point shooting the messenger. If a due diligence report comes back full of negative sentiments about the business, the deal may not be worth doing in spite of the amount of shoe leather that has gone into getting it this far. Unless they have totally misunderstood the target company and/or its market, it is not the advisers' fault. One investigation into a mature, but relatively fragmented industry revealed that stalemate in Europe meant that the buyer would not be able to put up prices post-acquisition if it did the deal. The reasons were quite clear:

- The combination of the buyer and the target would make it only marginally bigger than the other four competitors in Europe. The acquisition would not give the buyer sufficient clout in Europe to influence prices.
- Even if the acquisition gave the target sufficient clout in theory, in practice the target and the buyer competed in different segments of the market.
- Most big customers were now sourcing globally, based on price. Price rises would therefore be difficult to achieve, even with scale.

Although based on a very extensive European due diligence programme, these were not popular findings with local management who proceeded to whine and nit-pick, rather than revisit their original deal price assumptions.

Post-acquisition due diligence

As mentioned in Chapter 1, what normally happens post-deal is that the acquisition team moves on to the next project and another group of people come in to manage the newly acquired target. However, when a lot of experience, expense and late nights have gone into negotiating the deal and the legal protection around it, it is wasteful not to have a mechanism for identifying possible warranty and indemnity claims which may come to light after completion. It is best to make someone responsible for this and ensure that operating management understands that it is possible to claim certain things from the seller.

They will need to be fully briefed on time limits for claims and to understand the claims procedure. The statutory limitation period for notifying warranty and indemnity claims is six years or 12 years from the sale. Negotiated limitation periods can be as low as two years. Sale and purchase agreements often contain formal notification procedures for dealing with warranty and indemnity claims. It goes without saying that these need to be complied with.

Conclusion

A due diligence programme is likely to involve a number of different advisers. Even when the target is a business the acquirer knows well, perhaps competing in the same industry and sharing the same distributors, external advice can add a lot of value to a transaction. How much value they add will be heavily influenced by how well due diligence is managed. Planning, coordination and communication are as important as any other input and project management should be given top priority.

It may be an obvious point but advisers cannot be expected to perform to their full potential if they are not properly briefed, do not understand the brief, or are not kept informed of relevant findings of other advisers. If in doubt, over-communicate.

Getting the best out of advisers also means using the right ones. A mix of technical ability, chemistry, due diligence experience, possibly sector experience, fee levels and the degree of involvement by senior professionals will all be factors in the final choice. One thing is certain, you will not have time to get to know advisers in the heat of a deal so get to know them and select them before the pressure is on. Then you can involve them at the earliest possible stage.

Finally, you will need a user-friendly written report with an executive summary and opinions and a presentation which gives you the chance to probe the advisers and their findings.

4 *Financial due diligence*

Very few deals are carried out without financial due diligence. Scandals such as Enron make it unlikely that its importance will diminish. There is, however, a lot more to financial due diligence than examining accounting policies or information systems. Good financial due diligence aims to give a view of underlying profit which can be used, if not to predict the future, then to provide a canvas on which the picture of the future can be painted. It also pays to remember that reporting accountants are well-trained business professionals who are going to spend a lot of time in the target company. They can be an extremely good source of other, non-financial, business information about the target.

As most companies produce audited accounts it might seem a little surprising that so much time, effort, angst and expense is devoted to financial due diligence (FDD). There are two reasons.

First, contrary to popular belief, accounting is not a science. This means that even audited accounts contain many uncertainties as far as the purchaser is concerned:

- All accounts are subject to a number of judgements. Some, such as the valuation of stock and depreciation policies, can make a big difference to reported profitability. Also the time when income is recognized can vary depending on accounting policies or judgements. As a result trends in profits can be distorted.
- Accounts will probably contain a number of 'one-off' profits or expenses which distort the profitability of the business and which need to be found and removed from the numbers.

So one of the main roles of reporting accountants is to undo what has been done by other accountants.

Second, generally speaking in English law, a purchaser will not be able to rely on audited accounts. You would be very wrong if you thought that audited accounts are prepared by independent experts to reassure the outside world on the state of a limited company's finances. Apparently, they are not part of the price of limited liability, there to give information to anybody doing business with the company so they can have some idea of the risk they are taking. Audited accounts most definitely cannot be relied upon. Auditors are not responsible to shareholders, creditors or anyone else who deals with a company. They cannot be held liable in negligence if they fail to prepare or audit financial statements with due care and skill.

The case of *Caparo Industries* v *Dickman* established all of the above. The case went as follows. A UK listed company called Fidelity issued a profits warning in March 1984. Fidelity's share price fell sharply. In May the (unqualified) audited accounts were issued and the directors announced that profits were lower than had earlier been predicted. On 8 June Caparo began to acquire Fidelity's shares. By 6 July it had bought 29.9 per cent of Fidelity's issued share capital and in September it mounted a full bid which was successful.

Caparo subsequently alleged that Fidelity's accounts were inaccurate and misleading. It was suggested, for example, that stock was overvalued and that credit notes due to customers had been understated. The alleged effect was that the accounts should have recorded a loss of around £400 000 whereas in fact they reported a profit of £1.3 million.

Audited accounts had been sent to shareholders on 13 June. Caparo was a shareholder by that time and claimed that its share purchases made after 13 June were based on those (inaccurate) accounts. It claimed that had it known of Fidelity's true position it would not have purchased those shares nor would it have made the eventual bid at the price paid, if at all. It suggested that the auditors should have been aware that Fidelity was vulnerable to a bid following the fall in Fidelity's share price after the March profits warning, that any potential bidder would be likely to rely on the accounts when assessing a bid and that a bidder would suffer a loss if the accounts were inaccurate.

The general rules of the law of tort would look at foreseeability, proximity and fairness before giving a ruling on whether an auditor owes a duty of care to people who rely on negligently audited financial statements. Caparo had proximity. (It was a shareholder.) It argued foreseeability. (Many a company has been taken over following a profits warning and as anybody with even a passing knowledge of how the City really works would know the profits warning would lead to potential bidders taking a closer interest in Fidelity. The first thing they would do is turn to the latest audited accounts.) It probably also had fairness on its side. It would not have paid as much for the bulk of its shareholding if it had known that the accounts were overstating profits by some £1.7 million.

The Court of Appeal and the House of Lords ruled that not only is there no duty of care between an auditor and potential investors in a company, but there is not even a duty of care to existing shareholders. Apparently, (according to Lord Oliver) an auditor's report is not issued for 'the purposes of individual speculation with a view to profit'.

Aims

Until a firm offer is made, the vendor will have controlled information. Anything provided will inevitably have presented the target company in its best light. The would-be purchaser will probably have based its offer on a multiple of last year's profit and will have made a number of assumptions, for example:

- The future performance of the business will be similar to the past.
- The relationships with customers are strong and this will continue.
- Margins are not under pressure.
- Accounting policies have been consistent and reasonably applied.
- There are no looming liabilities such as significantly higher maintenance costs.

This is the acquirer's opportunity to satisfy itself on the assumptions made, not just about the target but also about how well the target fits the buyer's acquisition strategy and the deliverability of its synergy assumptions. It is also the only opportunity a buyer will get to make sure there are no skeletons in the cupboard big enough to break the deal. It presents the ideal opportunity to find as many smaller skeletons as possible with which to negotiate a price reduction. FDD will be important in determining the net debt position at completion and therefore any ramifications for price clauses in the contract. It can also help in structuring the transaction. It may identify some pretty uncertain liabilities which end up being left with the seller. It may identify that tax efficiency is best achieved by leaving debt in the business or that tax losses can be used by acquiring the company rather than assets.

But financial due diligence goes one step further than purely transaction-related enquiries. Its real aim is to look behind the information provided by the target company and assist the acquirer in forming a view on underlying profitability. This will provide the basis for forecasting future performance.

The fundamental building blocks of financial due diligence are therefore strikingly similar to those in the other due diligence disciplines. These can be summarized as:

- Verifying the numbers on which the offer is based
- Identifying any deal breakers
- Providing ammunition for the negotiations/identifying where warranties or indemnities are needed
- Giving confidence in the underlying performance, and therefore future profits.

DEAL BREAKERS

Deal breakers or items for which warranties/indemnities may be needed include:

- Over/under valuation of assets and liabilities
- Adequacy of provisions
- Potential black holes, for example pensions under-funding.

AMMUNITION FOR NEGOTIATIONS

Under the heading of helping to shift the balance of negotiating power would come:

- Highlighting risks
- Highlighting liabilities
- Challenging forecasts
- Challenging accounting treatments
- Down-rating past performance.

MAINTAINABLE PROFIT

Maintainable profit is the underlying profit which the target company is capable of earning. There is no particular magic to the concept but it is much more than taking historical profits and stripping out any 'abnormal' items – although this will be the starting point because underlying profit can be masked by such things as:

- Group and other management charges and expenses
- Owner expenses
- Transfers of business
- Reorganization provisions
- Transfer pricing
- One-off expenditure

- Sale of fixed assets
- Pension accounting
- Insurance claims
- Stock write-offs
- Changes in accounting practices, policies and procedures.

Underlying profit is about understanding the business. It is not a simple, mechanistic, feat of number crunching after working through the target's books. It means making an assessment of the means by which profits are generated, which in turn means understanding the market, customers, production, suppliers and management and identifying factors key to the success of the business. Of course, it is quite possible that the numbers have been cobbled together or achieved more by luck than skill. For these reasons it is also an important function of financial due diligence to review:

- The reliability of the systems generating those profits
- Budgets and projections and the assumptions underpinning them
- The numerical integrity of the budgets and forecasts
- The adequacy of the assumptions underlying them.

Financial due diligence is not the same as an audit

If all the above sounds like what the auditors do once a year, it is not. FDD will not delve into the numbers. Instead it says what the numbers are and why they are what they are. The accountants' engagement letter will probably state quite categorically that financial due diligence and audit are quite distinct. It will have a clause like,

> Our procedures in preparing the presentation and report will not comprise an audit and we will not be in a position to express a formal opinion on the financial information which we will be reviewing.[1]

The differences are summarized in Table 4.1. The aim of an audit is to verify results. Due diligence seeks to explain results. It begins with information supplied by the company and supports this by interviewing key members of the management team and by reviewing the auditors' working papers. It takes reported results and arrives at underlying profitability after isolating exceptional income and costs. It does not normally involve the independent verification of financial information by checking it to source documents. Inevitably FDD uses a lot more 'soft' issues than an audit.

The financial due diligence team will try to speak to the auditors and review the audit files for the last two to three years and, if they are also looking at tax, the tax files for up to the last six years. They will do this at an early stage of the investigation, not to get 'the answer', although there is an element of that, but to try to get a picture of how thoroughly the numbers have been scrutinized. The amount of audit scrutiny can vary enormously. Reviewing audit files is a good starting point, but it is not a substitute for access to the target.

Table 4.1   The differences between audit and financial due diligence

	Audit	Financial due diligence
Aim	Verify results and present a 'true and fair' picture	Establish underlying profit Flush out 'black holes' and negotiating issues
Focus	Past Independent verification of numbers to give assurance as to the reliability of historical financial information	Past and future Understand why the results are what they are Focus on key drivers of a business
Scope	Defined by statute and regulation	Often limited just to key issues
Access	Unrestricted	Might be restricted
Evidence	Substantive and compliance testing	Interview-based

Hold harmless letters

Although giving access to audit papers is something of a professional courtesy, the auditors will lay down a number of conditions. They do this in the form of a letter asking as a minimum, for:

- An indemnity from the acquirer against any legal action which may come their way as a result of allowing access to the audit working papers
- Confirmation from the investigating accountants that nothing can be relied upon and that everything will be kept confidential.

They might also insist on a number of other conditions some of which are sometimes completely over the top and should be resisted if at all possible. However, they have the papers and if the deal goes ahead they are probably going to lose an audit client. There is little incentive for them to cooperate and every risk if they do. If they lay down the law on indemnity a buyer, and an investigating accountant who wants to see those papers, usually has little choice but to accept. Whether a protracted fight is worth the effort is another question because reviewing audit papers is not that important to the investigation.

Terms of reference

If you lack a cure for insomnia, spend as little time as you possibly can on terms of reference. Often the reason why financial due diligence reports are long and boring is that the accountants have not been told what is of real importance, or they have been told and failed to understand. The blame for this can lie on both sides, but you, the commissioner of financial due diligence, should recognize that you reap what you sow. Time spent with the reporting accountants thinking through terms of reference in the early stages will be time well spent. This, remember, is going to be carried out by people who trained as auditors. An audit is very prescriptive. In contrast, there is very little guidance from the profession on non-audit investigations such as financial due diligence. They have to be told what to do so you must be clear in your own mind:

- what must be confirmed
- what must not be true

for the deal to go ahead. Only then can the purchaser and the reporting accountant agree a scope which tests the purchaser's preconceptions of the target company. Until you are absolutely sure what you need, do not let the process start.

Another key is for the reporting accountants to understand the full context in which their report is being prepared. For example if the report is on a company which is being acquired, the reporting accountant should seek to understand the purchaser's acquisition strategy and why it is planning to make the acquisition in question. If it is to gain market share but fold all operations into the acquirer's existing facilities, the investigation will have a different focus than if it is to enter a new geographical market and keep the acquired operation running.

Reporting

The most common type of due diligence report is a detailed written report, known as a Long Form Report, covering almost all aspects of a business. The Long Form Report may be exactly what you want at the end of the financial due diligence exercise. However, remember that communication should not be a one-off event. You must communicate regularly with advisers and not wait for the finished tome to arrive.

The areas typically covered by a Long Form Report are described in detail in the Topics section below, but the important point to note at this stage is that a Long Form Report provides a profile of the whole business, not just the financial aspects of it.

It need not always be so all-embracing. The terms of reference for a report commissioned by a sponsor prior to a flotation or by a private equity investor will be immensely detailed. In these circumstances the sponsor or investor will be trying to protect itself by ensuring that there is almost no limitation on the scope of the report. The resulting reports are therefore legitimately very long and can seem unfocused because of the sweeping nature of the instructions.

In contrast an acquirer of a business, or a bank which has an existing relationship with a company, will very often provide a much tighter brief, asking the accountant solely to focus on those areas which are of particular importance to them. As already mentioned in Chapter 3, it is a good idea in these circumstances for the buyer to work with the accountants, who will often have more experience of financial due diligence enquiries, to establish an appropriate brief. If after starting the assignment it becomes apparent that the scope of work needs to be extended, an extension of the scope can always be negotiated.

Clearly, financial investigation reports which are prepared on the basis of a more focused brief will be much shorter documents than the traditional Long Form Report described above. However, these reports should not be confused with Short Form Accountants' Report. This term is normally used only to describe the summary audited accounts contained within a prospectus and not short due diligence reports.

Facts and opinions given by individuals are usually attributed to that person in the report. A draft of the report, excluding conclusions and recommendations, will usually be given to the directors of the target and they will be asked to confirm in writing the factual accuracy of the report. From a negotiating point of view, however, this may not always be a good idea. If, for example, there is a very conservative policy on, say, warranties that suggest provisions should be released the buyer will not want to tell this to the seller. Make sure the reporting accountant is aware of the planned negotiating tactics.

The approach to financial due diligence

Financial due diligence involves detailed analysis of a business supported by interviews with the key people in the business. It is worth emphasizing again that the approach to due diligence is quite different from that adopted in an audit. Experienced practitioners would say that the more the investigating accountant gets around, asks questions and sees questions through until receiving a satisfactory answer, the better. It stands to reason that if the purpose of financial due diligence is to explain why the numbers are what they are, the investigator should be more concerned with finding and getting to the bottom of anything that looks strange than with crunching numbers given by the target.

Cross-border considerations

Local advice is key. Financial statements may look very similar but despite various directives on company accounts, and more of a willingness to adopt international standards, there remain considerable differences between the accounting policies employed around the world. There are also considerable philosophical differences. In many countries taxation is the dominant influence on the preparation of accounts. This means that, for example, depreciation rates may reflect more what the tax authorities want than what is economically appropriate for the business. In the UK, substance over form is a fundamental premise in financial reporting. As the Enron scandal showed, the approach in the US can be quite different as it is in, for example, France where they take a more legalistic approach.

The quality of management information will vary by country. Some countries are prone to producing large volumes of information, sometimes with little concern about its utility for running the business; in other countries even monthly management accounts are unknown.

Because of the lack of effective harmonization, the analysis of financials can be a long and drawn-out affair if the target has operations in a number of different countries. This will need to be factored into the due diligence timetable. But the thing to remember, always, is not to get carried away with the technical or interesting. The FDD objectives are the same whatever the country and that is to get to a proper understanding of the target's ability to make profits in the future.

Choosing the team

In most cases financial due diligence is carried out by firms of accountants. More often than not, the investigating team will be drawn from the purchaser's auditors, but there are no firm rules about this. There are a number of advantages in using the auditors. Chief amongst them is that it usually makes the finance director comfortable. Auditors usually have the manpower and expertise to carry out financial due diligence and they will know quite a lot about the client and its strategy. The important thing to remember is that financial due diligence is not the same as an audit. It involves a lot more uncertainty and calls for a great deal more judgement than an audit and as such may call for a different type of accountant.

The work

Financial due diligence work relies heavily on the target company for information and especially on interviews with its management team. The FDD team therefore needs to plan the work in conjunction with the target. Investigating accountants need the key people to be available and information they require to be on hand.

It is therefore vital that in planning the work the investigating accountants supply the target company with a detailed list of their information requirements and the people they will wish to see, which is why the process will usually kick off with an information request (see Appendix A2).

The accountants will then start their interview programme. The first port of call will rarely be the finance team. First they should speak to those who are responsible for the company's commercial operations. An understanding of the company's history, strategy, competitive environment, purchasing and sales, marketing and production operations is essential. A proper understanding of the business leads to a much more meaningful interpretation of its financial results. Even if the brief does not call for long 'history' and 'business strategy and activities' sections it is still worthwhile for the investigating accountants to cover these areas.

The main operating locations of the company will also be visited at an early stage so that the reporting accountant gets an understanding of the operating and cultural environment of the target.

Reviewing working papers should be another early activity although because auditors often try to include some extremely stringent clauses in hold harmless letters, it is not always as early as it should be. Working papers should provide a good overview of the financial control and management information systems of a company, together with an understanding of any key judgements arrived at in preparing the audited financial statements.

Next will come a review of financial information provided by the target: management and statutory accounts, managing directors' reports, business plans, budgets, forecasts and so on. The heart of the work is the analysis of the numbers provided by the target and above all interviews to expand on and clarify them. The best reporting accountants do their homework before the interviews, keep detailed interview notes, probe the answers given, check them by speaking to other people and make sure that they are consistent with the results of the business. Very often inconsistencies will emerge after asking different people the same question or through analysis of the records. It is therefore essential that the door is left open for follow-up discussions.

Topics covered in a Long Form Report

The following is a comprehensive list of what could be included in a Long Form Report. How many are covered and to what depth will depend on the specifics of the transaction.

HISTORY

This section is really a run-in to the rest of the report. The questions it addresses will include:

- Origin of the business
- Principal events in the last ten years such as changes in ownership, products and services, management and competition

BUSINESS ORGANIZATION

This section describes how the company is organized and run:

- Share Capital and Ownership
- Nature of share capital, details of shareholders, rights attaching to different classes of shares together with options and warrants
- Legal structure
- Explanation of group structure, details of share capital for main subsidiaries and any minority interest
- Management structure

Much of the factual information here overlaps with legal information. Let the lawyers report on the facts. The advantage the accountants can add from their management interviews is to paint a picture of how the target really works. Changes in management and shareholdings can happen for perfectly understandable reasons. They can also happen because the majority shareholder is a total megalomaniac with whom nobody can work. If your intention is to integrate the business with yours and have him run the combined operation, you might like to know how he really operates. Similarly, entrepreneurial companies are often reliant on one charismatic leader. You know an entrepreneur will not stay for long once the deal is done, but do you know what you need to do to make up for his or her departure? Without knowing just how dependent the target is on one individual the answer is 'no'. Again the accountants will give a view. Of course you do not need accountants to do this but as they are likely to spend a good deal of time on site and speak to most of the management, they do make good spies.

BUSINESS STRATEGY AND ACTIVITIES

The aim of this section is to provide an understanding of what the business does, and of its strategy. It covers a wide range of different areas and is as much concerned with evaluation and opinion as it is with fact-finding. The section will include:

- An overview of the company's strategy. The investigating accountant will not only describe the strategy, for example, but will also want to know who is involved in its setting and how often it is reviewed.

Table 4.2   An example of a business overview

Inputs		Facilities	Sales		Markets	
	2001 £000	110 000 square feet manufacturing facility in Alton (freehold)		**2001** £000		**2001** £000
Material	3824		Big Trucks		Road Transport	58%
Subcontractors	887	109 direct shopfloor employees	Limited	6990		
Direct labour	1736				Refrigeration	36%
Direct costs	6447	4 sales staff	Refrigerated Panels Plc	4411	Commercial	
		64 administrative staff			Fabrication	6%
Production overheads	3492	*Activities*	Bespoke Toilets	697		
Admin overheads	930	Laminating plastic sheeting	Others	52		
Distribution	161			12 150		
Marketing	445	Bonding plastics to ply				
Total recurring costs	11 475	Proofing completed wood/plastic sections				

- An overview of the business. Table 4.2 is an example of how an overview might be presented.

MARKETS AND COMPETITORS

Ideally, in this section there should be as much emphasis on analysis, market dynamics and market drivers as there is on fact-finding. FDD will collect information mainly from management. Many of the headings below may well be the subject of commercial due diligence which will collect information from outside the company This means that with a properly managed programme a buyer can get valuable insights on the most important topics from two completely different sources. FDD headings would include:

- Sales and gross profit by activity and geography
- Overall trends in sales or gross margins with a brief explanation. (The detailed analysis will be given in the Trading Performance review below.)
- Trends in market sizes, shares and growth
- Competitors
- Competitor positioning vis-à-vis the target
- The sustainability of sales and margin in each area of activity and in each geographical market
- Proposed new products and markets
- Barriers to entry for new competitors
- Threats and opportunities

SALES AND MARKETING

The aim here is mainly to probe for vulnerabilities. A heavy dependence on a few customers or long-term contracts can be an obvious cause for concern, as could any long-term agency agreements if the acquirer is planning to integrate the business. Customer dissatisfaction is another obvious area to probe. Credit notes, unpaid bills, invoice disputes and warranty claims can all be evidence of something fundamentally wrong with the business and its inability to maintain market share going forward. Related interviews, say to probe the level of salesforce motivation, may well confirm that customers are voting with their feet. On the other hand special discounting or an exceptional level of advertising/promotion may have massaged recent business performance.

A commercial due diligence exercise once revealed how a business had ramped up its advertising in the months prior to sale. During the sale process the seller claimed there was a lot of potential in the business which could be realized with a good advertising campaign. The truth was quite different. The pre-sale advertising campaign had in fact little effect on sales which was why the owner had put the business up for sale in the first place.

Areas for investigation include:

1. Customer base – profile, dependency on major customers
2. Analysis of sales and gross profit by major customers/customer groups over the previous three to five years
3. Extent of customer dependencies/major contracts
4. Customers by geographic region, industry type and any other appropriate criteria
5. Stability, reliability and sustainability of major customers/customer groups
6. Strategies for:

   - Marketing
   - Pricing – leader or follower, how often prices reviewed, ability to flex
   - Sales
   - Advertising
   - Distribution

7. Organization of the sales and marketing functions
8. Details of selling methods including incentive schemes and the use of agents
9. Standard terms (discounts, credit terms, warranty)
10. Seasonality of sales
11. Effectiveness of the sales and marketing function

PURCHASING AND SUPPLIES

Underlying profit could be severely affected in a business where there are unstable input prices, a dependency on a few suppliers, frequent supply disruptions and no alternative supply sources. The picture could be worsened by volume rebates which have been recognized in the management accounts but are not in fact earned and forward purchase contracts made just as raw material prices peaked. The review of purchasing and supplies would include the following headings:

- An assessment of the effectiveness of the buying department

- Organization and control of the purchasing
- Principal raw materials
- Key suppliers
- Supplier reliability
- Rating versus the alternatives
- Supplier relationships: any disputes?
- Extent of dependence on suppliers
- Terms of trade – payment, contracts, returns, lead times
- Price volatility
- Quality control procedures
- Procedures for receiving, storing and issuing stock
- Are warehousing facilities suitable and adequate?

PRODUCTION

Production management is about solving problems. Investigating accountants will always find plenty of problems to write about. Their focus, however, should be on the future. Are there any constraints on capacity? Is a costly overhaul going to be needed in the near future? How well do production facilities compare with those of the competition? Are lead times under control and on a par with industry standards? Do research and production work effectively together? A full due diligence report would report under the following headings:

1. Key production processes and how they are organized
2. Production statistics, lead times and quality control
3. Main items of plant and equipment, age and serviceability
4. Competitiveness of the company's production capabilities in its main areas of activity
5. Capacity/growth issues. Potential bottlenecks
6. Review of planned capital expenditure
7. Impact of new technologies
8. Stockholding policy
9. Subcontracting arrangements
10. Research and development, an explanation of what R&D is carried out

   - Is it properly controlled?
   - Is it adequate to maintain the future growth?

PREMISES

These days, book values and valuations of premises tend to be in line, but you never know. Dilapidations and environmental problems could be a concern for future profits, as could any expenditure needed to meet business plans. Under the heading of premises, the investigating accountant would include the following:

- List of leasehold/freehold premises
- Planned disposals/redevelopments
- Adequacy to meet growth plans
- Recent valuations
- Dilapidations

HUMAN RESOURCES

This section is not only about collecting facts, and explaining and commenting on organization structure, reporting lines and so on. A valuable by-product of FDD, which should always be requested, is the accountants' view on the management team. After all, having spent a number of weeks in close proximity to management, and having interviewed them extensively, the FDD team should be better placed than most to comment on management's strengths and weaknesses. Accountants also need to take a view on the impact of other human resources issues that can be factored into past and future profitability. The acquirer will want to know whether it is buying a business from a 'fat cat' management which is overstaffed by people paid well over the going rate. There will be softer, non-financial issues too which need to be explained and commented on. High staff turnover and low staff morale are usually symptoms of wider problems in a business, as could be the recent loss of good staff. Labour shortages may make it impossible to achieve planned growth.

Many of the headings below may be the subject of a more in-depth human resources due diligence and the topics are treated more fully in Chapter 7. Typical financial due diligence report financial headings would include:

- Organization chart with comment on any gaps or imbalances
- Overall culture and management style
- Details of directors and management, length of service, responsibilities, other interests, analysis of service contracts, pension and benefit entitlements. Any changes in senior management in the period under review. Any proposed changes. Assessment of management's strengths and weaknesses. Dependence of the company on key individuals, succession plans/policies, compliance with Cadbury and Greenbury
- Employees. Analyse employees between different areas of the business and different functions. Full-time versus part-time. Detail on union arrangements, staff turnover, remuneration policies, pensions, frequency of pay reviews, date of next/last pay review, terms and conditions of employment, use of temporary or part-time employees, recruitment plans, skill shortages, Recruitment and training policies, unfair dismissal or other claims. Assess the strength of the human resource management of the business and the extent to which its workforce provides a competitive advantage to the business.

INFORMATION SYSTEMS AND ACCOUNTING

This section analyses and assesses the key elements of the accounting and management information systems. It is fundamental to the whole financial due diligence exercise not just because of the effect the reliability, or otherwise, of the information can have, but also because of the impact accounting policies and their interpretation can have on reported profits. The target's ability to produce timely and accurate monthly management accounts is one indicator of how well-managed the target is and whether it has its house in order. Report headings would generally include the topics that follow.

Accounting policies and practices

Not only will different accounting policies mean two identical businesses may report very different results, different interpretation of those policies can play a major part too. The FDD team must, therefore, not only be on the lookout for changes in policy but, easier said than done, also be looking for changes in the application of those policies. The potential for 'flexible' reporting is picked up in the next section which looks at some of the profit and balance sheet manipulations commonly encountered. Consistency and comparability may be even more difficult in cross-border transactions where differences of definition can also play their part in clouding the numbers. Typically an FDD team will report on the following:

- A summary of accounting policies and treatments[2]
- Whether the accounting policies and treatments comply with generally accepted accounting standards
- An explanation of any that are unacceptable
- Whether, and to what extent, accounting policies and treatments are consistent with the policies adopted by the purchaser
- Whether accounting policies and treatments been applied consistently during the period under review

Management information

The accountants are perfectly capable of reporting on the facts of the information system, but again here is an area where their judgement is called for. Generally speaking, a poor information system will mean a poorly run business. But poor is a relative term which calls for a comparison with other systems. The accountants should have seen enough other systems to be able to give an opinion. This is what to expect:

- An overview of management information systems
- A description of the main management information reports produced by the company
- A review and assessment of the costing systems
- Management's assessment of whether they have sufficiently accurate and timely information to allow them to monitor and control the business and to react to any opportunities or threats
- Management's views on the future development of systems
- Reporting accountants' opinion on the effectiveness of the information systems
- A summary of weaknesses which need to be addressed

Control procedures

Here again the accountants should be able to form a pretty reliable opinion on the quality of the systems for managing and controlling the main financial functions of the company, for example:

- How well credit control and debtor collection operates
- Whether the books and control accounts (debtors, creditors, bank account and cash) are regularly balanced and reconciled

Computer systems

Computer systems may be covered by IT specialists but, if not, reporting accountants will normally:

- Describe the main computer systems
- Review third-party maintenance contracts
- Report on software ownership and maintenance

- Report on security
- Assess back-up arrangements
- Assess the adequacy of the current systems for present and future needs

Budgets

Budgets are an essential planning and control tool in most businesses, so financial due diligence should show how the process works in the target company and, more importantly, how effective it is. Accountants should also be able to come to a view on the current year forecast from an analysis of performance against budget. The Long Form Report will include the following sub-headings:

- Explanation of the budgetary process
- Comments on its effectiveness and on the historical accuracy of budgets
- Performance versus budget since the last accounts date and its impact on the full year forecast

TRADING PERFORMANCE

This section is the one which analyses the historical profit and loss account for the business for the last three to six years, together with the most recent management accounts. The approach is to take each category of income and expense and do the following:

1. Break down the figures so that their composition can be understood
2. Analyse the trend in results in relation to each item of income and expenditure to understand:

   - any unusual items
   - the relationship between the figures
   - any underlying patterns

3. Above all, get to understand where the profits come from. Which products are most profitable? Do profits come from trading or, at the other extreme, from the sale of second-hand cars supplied at a discount by the parent?

The closer the investigating accountants can get to being able to use the past to understand the future, the better.

Breaking down the numbers

To see what sort of analysis might be carried out to get behind the numbers, it is probably best to go through an example. Appendix B1 does exactly that. As an aid to understanding the cleaned-up numbers the FDD team will also produce tables which explain the numeric basis to the differences between the years. There is an example of these tables too in Appendix B1.

Analysing the trend in results

Getting behind the numbers, as in the example in Appendix B1, is where financial due diligence provides the real value added. The biggest wins, however, tend to come not from

Table 4.3   P&L manipulations and other traps for the unwary

Issue	Consequences
Sales have been temporarily inflated or brought forward by 'channel stuffing' Management have resorted to inappropriate revenue recognition in seeking to drive the numbers rather than the business	• A significant increase in the number of credit notes • Sales drop off rapidly, for example because major customers do not re-order or do not re-order for some time • There is a need to reverse sales (and profits) booked (especially applicable to work carried out on contracts which span more than one accounting year)
Generally sales are dependent on sales effort rather than long-term contracts or commitments	If management have taken their eye off the ball during the sale process, post-deal sales may fall off because of a lack of pre-deal sales effort
Attempts to increase sales pre-deal have failed	Increased advertising, for example, has failed to stimulate sales. Potential of the business is less than originally thought
Sales and cost of sales not matched	This is more common in some industries than others. Where actual payments and/or costs are spread over a long period, it is clearly much easier than with a cash business to recognize sales ahead of costs. Similarly it is quite common, for example, in the construction industry, to find large and complex projects spread over more than one financial year, and, with many of them, a chance that there will be claims some years after completion. Again, the scope for taking profits early by mis-matching sales and costs is high
Costs are unsustainably low because current depreciation policies are inappropriate for the future	In some industries, for example computer software, assets lose their value quickly and need replacing on a regular basis. If assets have been fully written off, recent depreciation will have been low. However, if those assets need replacing in the near future, depreciation will soon be back to much higher levels and profits will suffer accordingly
Costs deferred by carrying them forward in closing stock	See under stock, Table 4.4
Costs deferred/reduced by being capitalized	Interest on borrowings used to finance the construction of fixed assets R&D capitalized. Not only is the charge to profits reduced but also deferred as the capitalized costs do not need to be amortized until the programme comes into commercial production. Will hit the P&L eventually
Material costs dependent on a few suppliers	The buyer should be concerned about special pre-sale deals and the possibility that suppliers will take advantage of a change in ownership to increase prices
Labour costs kept artificially low	• Pre-sales promises made about pay increases or bonuses which the buyer will have to honour • Cash payments made to avoid national insurance costs have to cease • No accruals made for holiday pay/bonuses means a P&L hit
Cost of sales kept artificially low	If inter-group transfer prices or related party transactions have been used to keep cost of sales low, post-deal profit will suffer 'Normal' quantity discounts from suppliers over-estimated and over-accrued means a P&L hit
Looming liabilities not provided for	The basic rule which runs through accounting is that losses should be recognized and provided for as soon as they are discovered while profits should only be accounted for when they are realized. It is a rule which is often broken. The uncertainty around losses crystallizing allows them to be fairly easily dismissed, especially when crystallization may be some way off. Post-acquisition will lower profits

isolating non-recurring items but from unearthing a profit figure which is higher than it should be where price is based on a multiple of profit. Changing accounting policies is one way to massage profit, but most investigating accountants should be alive to that sort of manipulation.

More subtle are the 'judgements' which go into constructing a profit and loss account. Imprudent revenue recognition or the deferral of costs by including them in balance-sheet items like stocks, fixed assets or prepayments are the most frequent means of pushing up reported profitability. Generally speaking these will lead to differences between profit and cash flow. Sadly cash flow is often neglected when analysing financial statements. Any serious discrepancies between profit and cash should arouse suspicion and be explained. Gross margin is another figure to analyse very carefully and an explanation for any changes needs to be pursued until there is a satisfactory explanation.

Table 4.3 shows the areas of risk to the profit and loss account which FDD should watch out for.

Accounting 'judgements' are one thing, but there are other means by which short-term profits can be manipulated, especially if a target has spent the last few years grooming itself for sale. It is possible, for example, to increase short or medium-term profits at the expense of the long-term health of the business. Financial due diligence should seek to identify any such manipulations. The most common is cutting back on investments accounted for as costs such as research, development, marketing and training.

The consequences of short-term profit improvement also need to be understood. Cutting the cost of a branded product by using lower-quality raw materials or switching production to low-cost countries may be perfectly acceptable to customers. On the other hand it is just as possible that once they discover the poorer quality they will lose confidence in the brand and take their allegiance elsewhere. This is where commercial due diligence takes over from financial and provides yet another example of why advisers must be made to work together. The financial team can identify profit improvements which are possibly detrimental to the long-term health of the target business and the commercial team can assess their likely effects.

BALANCE SHEETS

The approach to the balance sheet section is similar to that for the profit and loss analysis, in that each significant asset and liability is examined to ensure that:

- The basis of values appears to be reasonable
- There has been no distortion in the trend
- Assets and liabilities are properly recorded. It is not unknown for crucial assets not to be owned by the business or for liabilities not to have crystallized yet.

Some of the issues which might be considered under each of the balance sheet headings are covered in the following sections.

Fixed assets

The aim is to assess whether the fixed assets are consistently and reasonably valued and whether they are adequate to support the projected future earnings of the company:

- Are intangible assets reasonably valued?

- What is the composition of fixed assets and how have their values been arrived at?
- Are there detailed registers and analyses?
- Have there been any recent independent valuations?
- Are the depreciation policies reasonable and consistently applied?
- Does the company have clear title to its main assets?
- Has the company capitalized interest or own labour within fixed assets?
- What capital commitments are there?
- What capital expenditure is required?

Even this seemingly mundane area can have a bearing on negotiations. There have been cases where the indicative offer for a target company included a minimum net assets figure – based on historic numbers – that was quite low. The target was in the middle of a large modernization programme that would need a few more years of sustained capital expenditure. The modernization was key to future profitability, but the low minimum net assets figure in the Heads of Terms gave the vendor every incentive to stop the capital expenditure. The sale and purchase agreement therefore contained a minimum capital expenditure figure in addition to a minimum net assets number.

But the crunch is the second half of the sentence above: are [the fixed assets] adequate to support the projected future earnings of the company? It is not unknown for companies to be groomed for sale. Reducing investment is a good way of flattering both profits (by reducing depreciation) and cash flow. Trawling through the investment numbers over several years may reveal a fall off in investment, but just as effective will be the accountant's interviews with production, operational and technical management.

Stock and work in progress

Stock is the only item which appears both in a company's profit and loss account and in its balance sheet. Given the amount of discretion used in stock valuations, the scope for short-term profit manipulation and the number of times significant misstatements of accounts turn out to be due to inflated or deflated stock, this is one of the most critical areas for investigation. Relatively small errors in relation to stock and work in progress can significantly distort the overall trend in the results of the company, and the margin for error is vast.

The key is to ensure that the approach to stock and work in progress is acceptable and has been consistent throughout the period under review. This means looking in particular at the basis of valuation, particularly where overheads are included, and at how slow-moving or obsolete stock is identified and provided for. In the UK, the basic rule is that stock should be valued at the lower of cost or net realizable value. Cost, according to the rules set out in SSAP 9, is:

> The expenditure which has been incurred in the normal course of business in bringing the product or service to its present location and condition. This expenditure should include, in addition to the cost of purchase, such costs of conversion as are appropriate to that location and condition.

The importance of 'seeing things through' in due diligence is particularly important here. For example, it might be wise to pin down the extent to which movements in gross margin have been influenced by stock values. In particular, the words 'costs of conversion', in the above definition, can hide a multitude of sins. It is probably acceptable if those sins have been committed on a consistent basis but, as any stock carried forward at the year-end could effectively contain an element of deferred expenditure, the danger comes when the many grey areas are exploited to manipulate stock values and hence profit.

Other, more predictable enquiries would include asking about the level of stock losses in recent stock counts, whether the physical condition of stock has been verified, and how any third-party stocks are valued.

Apart from the alarm bells that should ring over recent changes of accounting policy, the areas of risk are summarized in Table 4.4.

Table 4.4 The reasons why stock values could be wrong

Issue	Consequences
Conversion costs	Direct labour costs, direct production expenses and production fixed overheads are all part of the conversion process. If the actual costs for any of them are going to be charged at a significantly higher rate post-acquisition, for whatever reason, gross profit levels will not be sustainable.
Overhead costs	The more overhead which can be included in stock, the higher the profits for the year. The basic rule is that overheads should be classified according to their distinguishing characteristics. The salary of the production manager is therefore a cost of production while that of the marketing manager is not. Overheads should be based on 'normal' activity levels. There are many grey areas which may, or may not, be treated consistently.
Year-end stock	Year-end stocks may be built to artificially high levels to boost the level of deferred expenditure carried forward to the next accounting period.
Production inefficiencies	Production problems and stock spoilages should be written off to the P&L but in the interests of window-dressing could be carried forward in the stock valuation.
Obsolete/slow-moving stocks	Regular provisions can be too low, thus inflating profits. One-off provisions can be delayed. Excess provisions made in order to defer tax may be released before sale of the business, artificially boosting profit. Stock being purchased may not be usable or of the required quality. Detailed reviews of usage, purchase dates and so on coupled with a walk-through of the plant should help determine its physical state as well as give a rough idea of quantity (see next point).
Non-existent stocks	The book position is much higher than reality due to fraud, deterioration or bad recording. Past profitability is overstated. It is surprising how accurate an idea of stock levels can be gained just by walking through a plant.

Debtors and receivables

Debtors and receivables is another area for careful investigation. Review the credit control procedures, the analyses of aged debtors, the provisions and bad debts written off. Again, it is important to establish whether the approach has been consistent and whether the making and release of provisions or the writing off or writing back of a bad debt could have distorted the trend in the results.

The recoverability of the debtors in the most recent balance sheet will be of key importance to the acquirer

- Is the debtor age profile acceptable?
- What is the trend?
- Is there an acceptable system for establishing and enforcing credit terms?
- Are bad debt reserves created on a reasonable basis?
- What is the past experience with bad debts?
- Is the business vulnerable to large debtors defaulting?

Financing and bank arrangements

The investigating accountant will wish to establish whether the cash and bank accounts are properly controlled and whether the company's facilities are adequate and secure. When reviewing the accounting systems the investigator will have established how bank reconciliations are carried out, what the cheque signatory and authorization limits are and how the treasury function (if relevant) operates. With the bank facilities, the accountant will wish to establish what the terms, conditions and covenants relating to borrowings are and whether the company is likely to have adequate facilities for its foreseeable requirements.

Creditors and other liabilities

These should be analysed in order to identify any liabilities which have not been disclosed or any unusual items or trends in relation to the company's creditors.

- Does the company receive any special credit terms?
- Is the business under creditor pressure?
- Are there any long-term liabilities such as hire purchase and finance lease obligations?
- Are there any loans from shareholders that could be repayable in the short term?
- The completeness of the liabilities reported in the latest balance sheet? As mentioned above, this will be a key issue. Every business has liabilities which are not recorded in the balance sheet and for every long-term or contingent liability that is recorded, there is a large dose of subjectivity. Are provisions properly made and appropriately calculated? For example, is the warranty provision in the balance sheet in line with what might be expected from warranty terms and product performance?

However long or thorough the investigation, no accountant can be sure of finding every relevant unrecorded liability, but the more experienced will get pretty close because they will know how to look. They will make a point of reading Board Minutes or the minutes of other management meetings for signs of trouble: managers are usually quick to report anything which may come and bite them so as to head off accusations of poor performance. They will rely heavily on their interviews, where they will make a point of speaking to non-financial as well as financial staff and junior managers as well as senior managers, and on their 'nose'. For example, a slow-paying, stroppy customer may be more than a simple bad-debt risk. This could be the source of the next legal claim for non-performance.

Share capital and reserves

Details of the share capital together with any options or rights attaching to the shares will have been covered in the first section of the report. Therefore in this section it is necessary to explain any changes to the share capital and reserves during the period under review and whether there are any unusual reserves or restrictions on distributions to shareholders.

Cash flow statements

Cash flow is as widely used in valuation as profit. The relationship between profit and cash generation is a vital piece of knowledge which FDD must report on as thoroughly as possible. There may be perfectly good reasons for differences between profit and cash. A heavy investment programme may be one, as may sales growth. On the other hand it could be down to poor cash management which, for example, could manifest itself as frequent breaches of overdraft limits.

Taxation

Tax is a subject all of its own (see Chapter 10). Tax due diligence is best carried out by a tax expert. He or she will carry out a detailed review of the tax affairs of the company and assess whether the tax provisions are adequate and whether there is a risk of additional tax liabilities emerging.

The financial due diligence team and the tax due diligence team will have to work closely, and indeed the investigating accountants may be best employed as information-gatherers for the tax specialists. This leaves them with the general tax role of commenting on how up-to-date the target's affairs are in the various areas of taxation and whether there are disputes, taxes overdue or investigations pending. They should also give an assessment on how aggressive the target company has been with its tax planning.

FUTURE PROSPECTS

Not every piece of FDD includes a section on forecasts. It is not necessary where the intention is a fundamental change in the way the target does business. For the rest in many ways this section is the nub of the whole exercise. What does the future hold? Sadly, it is a topic which makes reporting accountants very nervous. The further forward the forecasts go, the more nervous they get. Depending on the industry, they will take the view that a twelve-month period is reasonably forecastable but are loath to go much further.

Left to their own devices, reporting accountants will confine their findings to a pretty clinical review of the target's forecasts. Typically they will set out to answer the following questions:

- Have the forecasts been correctly compiled on the basis of the stated assumptions?
- Are those assumptions reasonable?
- Are they clerically accurate?
- Are the accounting policies used consistent with the usual policies?
- How accurate has forecasting been in the past?
- Are the forecasts consistent with the trends in the management accounts?
- What are the vulnerabilities?
- What are the key sensitivities in the forecast?

The typical forecast for any business is a 'hockey stick' a couple of years out. Where a business is being sold, an even brighter picture of the future is painted. Accountants should always seek to separate the concrete reasons why the future is going to be so much better (for example, new products and new customers in the pipeline, new cheaper supply sources) from management's wish list, but they will rarely go further than giving comfort on the level of care that has gone into preparing the forecasts.

As worthy as the above work may be, it is not exactly rolling back the frontiers of knowledge. If ever there was an area ripe for two of the due diligence advisers to be made to work closely together it is in this one. The financial due diligence team will have built up a detailed picture of the workings of the business while the commercial due diligence team will know all about market prospects and the target's competitive position. Do not let them work in splendid isolation. Put the two together to review the projections and to come up with longer-term forecasts!

The value of this approach even for relatively short-term forecasting was demonstrated during due diligence of a company that makes 'big-ticket' products used in large construction projects. The target's forecasts were basically the sum of the value of all contracts bid multiplied by their assessment of their chances of winning the work. So, for example, a contract worth £2 million that the target estimated it had a 50 per cent chance of winning would go into the forecasts at £1 million. The due diligence team was able to speak to a large sample of people responsible for awarding those contracts and get a pretty good handle on forecasts for the next couple of years. For longer-term forecasts, the traditional commercial due diligence topics take on an increasingly important role. Market growth, the target's ability to win share and pressure on prices will have a much bigger influence on the bottom line than the minutiae of accounting such as trade creditor reversals or provisions for slow moving stock.

No forecast is ever 'right'. Due diligence is more about understanding the range of possible outcomes and the risks inherent in the business. Again, the financial and commercial teams should be working together on sensitivities. If you leave sensitivities to the typical due diligence accountant what you will get is the near mechanical application of what-ifs: 'What if prices decline by 5 per cent?', 'What if the market turns down by 10 per cent next year?'. On the other hand, if you leave the average commercial due diligence team to comment on forecasts you will get no numbers but trend lines and ticks in boxes instead. What is called for is a bit of synergy from the advisers.

In short, two plus two does equal five if the commercial and financial due diligence teams can be made to work together on forecasts and sensitivities. The seasoned opinion of the commercial due diligence expert, armed with first-hand knowledge of market drivers and competitive position, and the analytical prowess of the accountants, armed with a financial model of the business, ought to be a devastating combination. As well as getting the commercial and financial teams to work together on forecasts, it is also a good idea to involve those managers who are going to be running the business.

Critical for the buyer is to know the odds of forecasts being achieved. Press for opinions. And do not wait for a bland, descriptive, assessment of forecasts or 'negative assurances'.[3] Get across during the selection and/or briefing of investigating accountants that you want opinions, and opinions is what you will get. Finally, if the plan is to reorganize the target post-acquisition, or to merge it with other operations, the buyer might be just as interested in the accountants' opinion on the post-acquisition/post-reorganization forecasts as on the target's.

OTHER MATTERS

This section is really a collection of items that have come to light during the financial investigation. For example, here might be noted whether there is any litigation going on or about to start, whether there are any contingent liabilities, any capital expenditure committed and a summary of employee pension arrangements.

Conclusion

You are not going to feel comfortable if you do not commission financial due diligence. The challenge is to get good value. The term 'reporting accountants' is a good one because left to their own devices they will only report. This is not all bad. You need to understand the routine accounting issues, you need to understand underlying profit, you need an assurance that the balance sheet is clean and that the profit and loss account has not been overly manipulated. If you employ accountants to cover pensions and tax, you will certainly want to make sure that there is nothing which is going to come back and bite you.

But you should want more. You want to understand the quality of the target and the extent to which it meets your strategic objectives. This means that you want firm opinions from the accountants on non-financial as well as financial issues. More than any other adviser, these are the people who will spend most time closely observing the target and its management. Make sure they understand the importance of their 'intelligence' role and make sure their team is capable of performing that role.

5 *Legal due diligence*

This is a surprisingly short chapter given that the words 'lawyers' and 'due diligence' are almost synonymous. The reason is simple. Many of the specialist legal issues are covered in subsequent chapters. Legal due diligence is central to the entire due diligence programme because it forms the basis for the sale and purchase agreement. Given this, it is doubly important that legal advisers work closely with the other due diligence professionals and focus on the commercial implications of their findings. Lawyers are trained to spot problems but what is needed is for those problems to be put in their proper commercial perspective.

Objectives

Legal due diligence is undertaken to achieve three objectives. These are to:

- uncover potential liabilities
- find any legal or contractual obstacles
- form the basis of the final agreement.

Each of these is covered in turn below.

UNCOVERING POTENTIAL LIABILITIES

In an asset sale, purchasers do not normally take over liabilities. They are only responsible for liabilities (although employment liabilities and obligations are an exception here) if they specifically contract with the seller to take them over. A company, on the other hand, is a separate legal entity and as such normally comes with liabilities as well as assets. In other words, if the buyer buys the company, it will continue to be responsible for the liabilities of the company. Liabilities come in three guises:

- actual
- future
- contingent.

Some liabilities will be quantified, recorded and provided for. Others will not. As well as verifying the size of known liabilities, the purchaser of a company should make as certain as is possible that there are no sizeable unforeseen liabilities lurking in the background. At the very least these will mean the buyer has paid more than it should have. At worst, as for example in the case of Atlantic Computers (see Chapter 3), they can bankrupt the buyer.

Liabilities that are not recorded in company accounts can come from a whole host of sources, many of which are dealt with in subsequent chapters, and, as far as the lawyers are concerned, sometimes from other specialists. Pensions (Chapter 9) is perhaps the biggest worry in this area with tax (Chapter 10) not far behind. Depending on the post-acquisition plans, human resources (Chapter 7) can be a legal minefield. Any would-be US acquirers in Europe would do well to pay particular attention to this subject in due diligence. Unlike back home, European labour laws, especially outside Great Britain, can be very tough. If part of your post-acquisition plan is to close that expensive Paris head office, take local legal advice and look very carefully at how much it is going to cost (and how long it is going to take).

The overlap with other disciplines does not stop there. Legal investigators need to understand the financial and accounting position of the target company and should also be concerned with the contractual issues in the financial area such as loan agreements, charges, guarantees and indemnities given by the target company and any other banking arrangements that may be in place.

Environmental due diligence is another area where lawyers tend to get involved. Most of the big law firms will have environmental practices. As discussed in more detail in Chapter 11, the purchaser will need to find out whether there will be a responsibility for cleaning up polluted land, whether environmental permits are needed and are transferable, whether the target (and its predecessors) have complied with environmental laws and regulations and whether the target has adequate systems and procedures for complying with environmental regulations.

Intellectual property is a highly specialist legal area, although there is more to it than the purely legal, as we shall see in Chapter 14. The intellectual property rights of the target company need to be identified, their ownership verified, their validity established and, perhaps most important of all, their sufficiency confirmed.

Contracts could also be a source of unforeseen liabilities. Lawyers will review major contracts and agreements, first to make sure they contain no nasties and second to confirm they can be transferred to the purchaser. Change of control clauses are Jekyll and Hyde characters. On the one hand they are useful for certainty and stability, on the other they present the perfect opportunity to renegotiate the original contract.

Another source of potential liabilities is litigation. One of the main tasks of legal due diligence is reporting on any litigation or disputes affecting the target company. What the buyer does not want here is a list. Anyone could provide a list of pending or threatened litigation and there is no need to hire expensive lawyers for that. Where the lawyers come in is in assessing the likely damage litigation will cause. One element of this is gauging the chances of success or failure and likely cost. The other is bringing streetwise judgement and experience to a list of outstanding litigation in order to spot the danger signs. In the scheme of things, a few claims for industrial deafness against the target are neither here nor there. The same number of claims for lung damage allegedly caused by exposure to asbestos should set all sorts of alarm bells ringing.

The lawyers will also look closely at legal structure. Legal structure is important because there can be all sorts of problems which arise when a company leaves a group. There are obvious ones like capital gains tax liabilities being triggered because of inter-group transfers of assets or change of control clauses in licences and distribution agreements. There are less obvious ones like the target company no longer being able to benefit from group discounts. And there are totally off the wall ones (and this is a true story) like the seller having already sold the target's intermediate holding company to somebody else without realizing it.

Given the degree of overlap with other specialisms, it hardly needs saying that due diligence lawyers must liaise with other due diligence professionals.

LEGAL AND CONTRACTUAL OBSTACLES

Title

Buying a company means buying its shares. Shares in the target will have owners. The lawyers need to check that those from whom the shares are to be bought actually legally own them and that the new owner is not going to be responsible for any liabilities attaching to the shares which were entered into by the previous owners. This means:

- Inspecting documents relating to the allotment and issue and transfers of shares, the approval of transfers at board meetings and registration of the various transfer documents.
- Checking that former shareholders have returned their certificates and that current shareholders, or at least those who are selling their shares, have certificates.
- Verifying that the shares to be sold are not subject to any charges or other encumbrances.

In a similar vein, the legal investigators need to verify good title to, that is that the target actually owns, any freehold or leasehold property and any other major assets. As with their investigation of shares, they should also investigate whether there are charges or other encumbrances over property or assets. The effect of a charge on the value of land, property or assets is fairly obvious. Encumbrances can affect the value of the land in a number of more subtle ways such as its marketability or even the right to continue using it for purposes of the business.

The purchaser will also be interested in finding out about any breaches of covenant and, for leasehold property, any breaches of the lease(s).

The right to domain names also needs checking. Just because a company owns a trademark does not give it the right to own the domain name as well. People have been registering Internet domain names which include the names of well-known companies. This probably counts as passing off or infringement of trading names but, nevertheless, a buyer should check that the target has taken steps to protect itself from this sort of activity. Registering everything could be expensive and unnecessary. It is therefore important to decide which names could be useful in the future and which are irrelevant.

Consents and releases

These days the sale of a company or business is likely to require a number of consents or releases. For example, a target company's shares may need release from a parent company debenture, one group of shareholders might have pre-emption rights, the deal might need merger control clearance (Chapter 12) or there might be a need to consult with the target's works councils or joint venture partners. The legal due diligence advisers should help identify what needs to be done so that consents and releases do not delay the transaction.

Regulatory issues

The purchaser needs to see any licences, permissions and registrations which are necessary for lawful conduct of the target company's business. For example in the UK any company carrying on a financial services business needs authorization from the Securities and Futures Authority (SFA). Regulatory bodies such as this usually keep lists of companies registered to act under its auspices.

If the target company does require a special licence to carry on business then it should be verified that this is in force and not about to be taken away. At the same time it should be checked whether the acquisition would affect the licence in any way. The buyer's legal advisers should look at three different, but related, licensing issues:

- Which licences does the target not have which it *should* have?
- Whether the licences are transferable. If you are buying the company which holds the licences this is not an issue. Where it becomes an issue is where you are buying assets or where the licences are held by another entity, by the parent company for example.
- If licences are not transferable, will new licences be forthcoming?

Due diligence is always carried out at a breakneck pace whereas dealing with licensing authorities can be a tortuously slow grind. If the lawyers cannot satisfy you on the above in time, it could be a case of making completion conditional upon a licence being granted. The importance of authorizations differs by industry. In the food industry in the UK, for example, it is difficult to do very much without authorizations.

Alternatively the target may be part of an elite 'club' or trade association which confers prestige and respectability. Its standing in important organizations needs to be checked. Industry bodies very often police industry codes of practice. Has the target been complying with these?

Special accreditations may be central to a target company's profitability. For example it may be accredited as being able to test safety critical equipment to relevant health and safety standards. This should be checked as standards have a habit of changing.

THE FINAL AGREEMENT

The sale and purchase agreement records the legal understandings of the buyer and seller about the transaction. The document has three basic goals. These are to:

- bind both parties to completing the transaction
- ensure the seller does not change the company in any significant way before the deal completes
- govern what happens if problems appear that should have been disclosed

Most of the negotiating effort that goes into the agreement is about who picks up the bill for company defects that appear after the deal is done. This means that, in one form or another, information from the due diligence programme will be included in the disclosure letter and a good deal of it will end up being included in the agreement. Both sides will be happy with this. For the seller, the contents of the disclosure letter will qualify the warranties. The seller will not be liable for the matters disclosed. The purchaser gets peace of mind because the contents of the disclosure letter, including a lot of the due diligence information, will be warranted as accurate. This in turn explains why lawyers play such a pivotal role and why it is often the in-house lawyer who usually ends up coordinating due diligence.

Choice of advisers – local advice

Chapter 3 discussed the choice of advisers. There is one further consideration when it comes to choosing legal advisers and that is that different due diligence topics could be governed by different laws. For example, the law under which the target company is incorporated will govern the constitution of the target and the rules about the ownership and transfer of its shares, whereas its interests in land or property will be governed by the laws of the country in which that land or property is situated and employment issues are likely to be governed by the laws of the countries in which the employees are based. Although the most obvious differences are between common law systems (such as in England and all of the USA except Louisiana) and civil law systems (for example in continental European countries), there are significant differences even between systems that have the same origin.

For all of these reasons, it is very important to take local advice where foreign law issues are involved. Sometimes local can mean very local indeed:

> If we made a mistake in our choice of lawyer, it was only that we chose a New York attorney to fight a case in Chicago, thereby opening ourselves up to suffer by the enmity between the two cities.[1]

It is also worth remembering that in some countries the law is not the law, but a goal. Be realistic about what local legal advice can sometimes achieve.

Briefing lawyers

A theme which runs throughout this book is the very strong relationship between the quality of the due diligence and the buyer's management of the process. Briefing advisers is an important part of due diligence management, and a good briefing is doubly important in the case of legal advisers. They are central to the deal so they must know everything there is to know about it. Many lawyers will privately tell you that they find due diligence an impossible exercise and the reason they find it so difficult can be traced to the quality of the briefing they are given. Typically they will suddenly be confronted by a very large volume of information in the form of copies of documents. They must read all of them and assess their consequences. How, without a proper understanding of the context of the deal or the buyer's concerns, can this be done? How can any lawyer know whether a change of control clause in a contract is significant without a proper briefing?

The process

Data rooms apart, the normal starting point for the purchaser is to kick off a number of searches and at the same time to send the seller's lawyers a request for information (see Appendix A2). This is a very detailed questionnaire, normally drawn up by modifying a standard, comprehensive form by deleting inappropriate questions and adding questions which are specific to the nature of the transaction, the nature of the business or need to be answered following initial investigations. For example, commercial due diligence or industry knowledge may have revealed that although the target's UK market position is deteriorating rapidly (and is perhaps being kept artificially high) there is tremendous scope for expansion in Germany. However, the official German distributor is hopeless and much of the demand in Germany is being satisfied by unofficial parallel imports. In this case, legal due diligence should be very concerned about contractual terms between the target company and its German distributor because clearly this is going to be a major issue once the deal is done.

Getting the questions right is a must. Be focused and show that you are focused and you will get the best results. There is nothing worse for a seller than receiving a long meandering list of questions which are irrelevant to the target. Would you be convinced of the need to put yourself out to provide accurate and pertinent information quickly if you think that the buyer's advisers, and therefore by implication the buyer, are robotically going through the motions, through a checklist, rather than focusing on the real issues and appearing to know what they are doing? Nevertheless, as ever, there is a balance to be struck and questions do have to be framed in sufficiently broad terms to elicit all the information required.

Carrying out the investigation

In many cases there will be other advisers specializing in one or more of the areas legal due diligence needs to cover. If specialists do need to be commissioned, remember that extra time is going will be required for them to finish their work and for their findings to be incorporated into the process. Some may also need much more access than the seller had initially contemplated.

Similarly, the odds are that more time is going to be needed if there are subsidiaries or significant assets in overseas jurisdictions. Some local due diligence will have to be carried out by local lawyers. Local law may also have timing implications for the transaction. Language barriers and time differences will do little to speed up the process and cultural differences, including fundamental misunderstandings of what due diligence is about, can stop a transaction dead. By no means all the world is steeped in the sacred Anglo-Saxon tradition of *caveat emptor*. In many parts of the world a request to carry out due diligence is very likely to be responded to with 'if you don't trust me, push off'.

Getting the information

Most of the information for legal due diligence will come from the seller. The seller's lawyers will normally coordinate the preparation of responses to the questionnaire and the collection and distribution of any documentation requested.

The buyer needs to be sure that someone on his or her side keeps a careful record of what is received when and to whom it has been circulated. There are a number of software packages around to assist with this tedious but necessary task.

Once the buyer's legal advisers start receiving replies to their request for information, they will start to review them. It is normal for this information and documentation to be reviewed in a fairly mechanical way. This has a number of advantages, not least that it is a cost-effective way of getting through large amounts of detailed information in a relatively short time. It should also leave partners and more experienced practitioners more time for supervision and to investigate the most important items. This is also good. It cannot be said often enough that there is no substitute for large amount of streetwise detective work by experienced professionals.

Other information sources

DISCLOSURE LETTER

The disclosure letter is itself a source of due diligence information. Sellers often deliver the disclosure letter at the very last minute possible so that you do not get the chance to go through it properly. The motive? Simple: the less time you have to comb through reams of information the lower the odds of you noticing the odd controversial (and no doubt potentially expensive) item slipped in.

The purchaser should always insist that the seller delivers an early draft so that the due diligence process can get underway in a meaningful fashion. You should not however expect it to be the final version of the disclosure letter which is submitted first. Disclosure letters will go through a succession of drafts. Each draft will disclose more information especially since the purchaser and its advisers should be asking questions about the information disclosed and seeking further and better particulars.

OTHER ADVISERS

More often than not other advisers will complete their due diligence before the legal due diligence is finished. It has already been stressed that legal due diligence cuts across many other areas. Other advisers should be encouraged to highlight any concerns which may need special attention for the legal advisers. Similarly, the legal advisers should make a point of speaking to the other advisers to make sure nothing falls between the cracks Atlantic Computers style (see Chapter 3). Better still, the buyer should do it for them and make sure all points of concern are communicated to the legal advisers. This helps with the documentation as well as the legal due diligence.

PUBLIC INFORMATION – GENERAL BACKGROUND INFORMATION

The process of information requesting and reviewing goes on until the purchaser is satisfied, everyone gets fed up, or one of the principals presses the button for completion. While the legal advisers are waiting for a reply to the request for information or the first draft of the disclosure letter, they will probably build up a profile of the target from published information. There is an enormous amount of company information in the public domain.

Databases

The internet and subscription databases are probably the first stop, although as part of the initial briefing the purchaser should have given the legal team enough general company and industry background to short-circuit this stage. The investigating lawyers need to start with a good idea of the nature of the target company, its business and its affairs over the past three to five years to use as a guide to where to concentrate their efforts.

Credit reference agencies

Credit reference agencies will provide a credit risk assessment of the target company and give hints as to how it is regarded by the wider business community.

PUBLIC INFORMATION – SPECIFIC INFORMATION

As well as using public information as a means of building up a general profile there is much which can be used for more specific enquiries.

Property

In the UK, if property is registered, a search of the Land Registry will reveal the owner, the benefits attaching to the land and any encumbrances such as mortgages and restrictive covenants. It will also have a plan showing the boundaries of the property.

If the property is unregistered, its ownership can only be confirmed by inspecting the title deeds. However, a search at the Land Registry will reveal that it is unregistered and a search at the Land Charges Department in Plymouth will show details of mortgages, restrictive covenants, adverse easements, matrimonial land charges and so on. (The search is made against the name of the owner of the property rather than the property itself.) In the case of Limited Liability companies, Companies House information will also give details of charges against property, registered or unregistered.

In the UK, Local Authority searches will show planned changes to the area, for example whether a motorway is planned to go through the property. The local land charges registry will say whether a building is listed or in a conservation area or whether it has to comply with local planning enforcement notices.

Especially now that new developments are being encouraged on brownfield sites it is not unusual for modern premises to be built on reclaimed land. A buyer would probably want to know if a factory has been built over, for example, old mine workings. It is possible to search specialist registries to find, for example, where the coalmines once were. Chapter 11 on environmental due diligence makes the point that it is not just the obvious industrial sites that could cause concern. A brand new building on a brand new office park could be a considerable burden if built on an old rubbish tip which is still giving off large quantities of methane.

Companies registration office

In some countries there is a system for filing company documents. In a place such as Companies House in the UK, there is a central registry which contains the target company's latest filed accounts, and details of its constitution, shareholders, officers, changes in the directors and secretary and notices of appointments of receivers, liquidators and so on. There is usually a short delay in documents actually getting in the files so in the UK, for example, changes made in the last 21 days will not yet be recorded.

The Register of Disqualified Directors at Companies House will show if a person has been disqualified as a director. The Land Charges Registry will reveal whether any individual sellers or directors have any bankruptcy proceedings outstanding or pending.

As well as conducting a search on the target and its subsidiaries, the legal advisers will probably search the seller too, just to check it has the powers to sell the target company.

Courts

Where the buyer wishes to verify the status of any pending litigation disclosed by the target or where searches need to be made to ensure that no steps have been taken to put it into receivership or administration or to wind it up altogether, searches can be made at Court.

Restrictive trade practices register

In the UK, details of any registered agreement under the Fair Trading Act have to be registered. There may be restrictions registered which benefit, or which may bind, the target.

The report

Lawyers more than anyone else know they are not going to be sued for reporting too much so, without a proper briefing from the buyer, the legal report will tend to be a long, incoherent, rambling affair, stuffed full of every detail. This will be supported by a mountain of copies of the documentation supplied by the seller.

The challenge is to manage the lawyers properly. Insist on:

- Drafts of the report
- A commentary on issues as they turn up
- An executive summary at the start of the report which identifies the major issues and gives an opinion on how they should be addressed in the sale and purchase agreement
- A presentation of findings, again covering the highlights and how to deal with them

And when you say 'major' or 'highlights', make sure the meaning of the term is properly understood. A leading in-house lawyer recounts the story of the time he asked his legal advisers to set out the *highlights* of a long and complex global merger for the board. He got 63 pages.

Conclusion

Legal due diligence covers a multitude of specialities as well as the more obvious legal areas such as title, consents and releases, and regulatory issues. The same firm of lawyers could well cover some, or all, of these. If other specialists are involved, the lawyers must liaise very closely with them because what they find could be an important input to the final agreement. For the same reason even where the lawyers cover all the 'legal' disciplines, they still need to work closely with other advisers and with overseas lawyers where local advice is needed on cross-border issues. When it comes to reporting, you should make sure they liaise with you throughout the transaction and make sure they give you an executive summary which highlights the key *commercial* issues. Insist on a presentation of their findings. Above all, ask for, and get, opinions. You are paying for opinions, not paper.

6 *Commercial due diligence*

A company is acquired not for its past performance but for its ability to generate profits in the future. Commercial due diligence (CDD) is all about estimating future performance. In contrast to most other forms of due diligence, it looks outside the target for its information. CDD gets its information from published sources but, more importantly, by talking to knowledgeable people in the same market as the target. As well as being an important activity in its own right, this can make commercial due diligence a complementary activity to other forms of due diligence, especially financial, technical, cultural and intellectual property, and sometimes even antitrust, due diligence.

In its traditional form, commercial due diligence is the investigation of a company's market(s), competitive position(s) and, putting the two together, its future prospects. It fits into the deal evaluation process as shown in Figure 6.1.

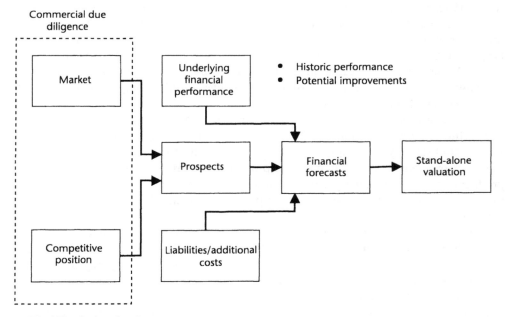

Figure 6.1   The deal evaluation process

Aims

Traditionally commercial due diligence has had three aims:

- Reducing risk. Purchase price is normally a ratio of current profit but if future profit is under threat, say because customers are about to desert the target, the buyer needs to know this and negotiate the price down accordingly.
- To help with valuation. Projecting a business ten years out is not easy, yet this is exactly what a discounted cash flow demands. It certainly cannot be done using just historic financials.
- To help plan integration. Bad integration is a major reason why acquisitions fail. Commercial due diligence examines the target's markets and commercial performance. In so doing, it identifies strengths and weaknesses which should be addressed as part of the integration process.

These are perfectly valid roles for CDD, and probably exactly what is needed on some smaller deals. Ideally, however, CDD should go much further.

If approached from a strategic angle, commercial due diligence will go beyond simply evaluating the risk that the future performance of the company will fall below the forecasts on which the price of the business is calculated. Giving comfort on the immediate top line, and maybe gross margin, is an important output of CDD and it would be a waste of a good investigation if the output from CDD was not fed into financial forecasts. Ideally, though, the aim of commercial due diligence should be to give comfort that the deal will actually work. This is true even where the buyer is a financial buyer and the acquisition is going to stand alone. There is going to be no integration, and no synergies, but the financial buyer will probably be looking for an exit in three years or so. It is here that strategic CDD comes into its own. Buying now with a view to exiting requires a strategic understanding of the target and its market in order to understand the prospects of selling the business.

CDD, then, should be seen as much more than a market review or customer referencing. It should instead be seen as a mini strategy review – 'mini' only because of the tight timescales in which the work is done.

Many acquisitions are carried out for the wrong reason, which perhaps goes a long way to explaining why the failure rate is so high. To succeed, they should be used as a strategic tool. The point of strategy is to improve returns – or at least to stop them deteriorating any more than they otherwise would. This means improving profit. Profit is sales *less* costs. Sales are the product of price and volume. Costs come in two varieties – fixed and variable. This is shown in Figure 6.2. It is worth bearing this simple picture in mind as we discuss the strategic benefits of commercial due diligence.

There is really only one strategic benefit on the cost-saving side available from acquisition: economies of scale. These can derive from nearly every function of the business. In mature industries they will come from cutting underused capacity, say by folding two factories into one and reducing duplicated overheads so that base costs are reduced. Or scale economies could be about building R&D and sales and distribution capability as, for example, in Glaxo's acquisition of Wellcome in 1995. Drug prices were being forced down as central buying authorities took over from doctors as the main buying influence. Fragmented and relatively price insensitive buyers/specifiers gave way to much more powerful and price-conscious buyers. At the same time, a record number of patents were expiring. Suddenly drug companies needed to be very big to be able to afford the R&D which would lead to the patent protection which in turn would mitigate the price pressures. Getting patented solutions specified by doctors also called for a big salesforce to get the coverage. The more drugs it had to sell, the more cost effective would be the salesforce. Another source of economies of scale could come about by bigger purchases and therefore variable cost savings.

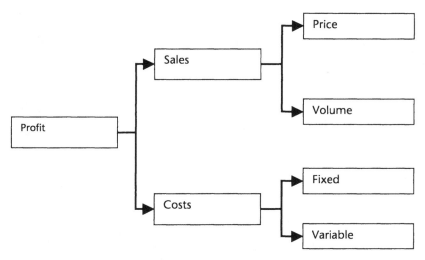

Figure 6.2   The components of profit

The point of all the above examples is that cost per unit is now lower, and competitive position improved – because any competitors without the same scale now either have to reach the same scale or stay at a small scale and risk cost disadvantage. But the critical thing is the mathematical implication of the phrase *cost per unit*. The assumption is that the number of pre-merger units at least stays constant, otherwise cost per unit is likely to go up compared with the pre-deal position. In other words, a company could achieve all sorts of cost savings through acquisition but still be worse off if the sales of the combined entity fall. Sadly, the evidence (see for example *McKinsey Quarterly 2001* Number 4) seems to point to sales being lost in acquisitions! According to the *Financial Times*,

> Most mergers that fail do so because revenue growth stalls during integration and fails to recover.[1]

This is not good news because sales tend to hit the bottom line much harder than costs. A simple illustration will serve to show this. Company A and company B both have a 25 per cent gross margin and make 10 per cent profit on sales on £100m. Both are growing at 2 per cent in real terms. Company A buys company B for a 30 per cent premium over its cash flows for the next 10 years discounted at A's cost of capital. The graph in Figure 6.3 shows the trade-off between sales growth and costs for the shareholders in company A to be no worse off after the acquisition.

If growth continues at 2 per cent, costs must be cut by just over 1 per cent for value not to be destroyed. In other words, by cutting costs by just over 1 per cent, in year 10 company A will be earning the same as both companies would have earned had the acquisition not been made *plus* it will make an adequate return on the premium it paid to buy company B. Combined costs in the first year of acquisition are £183 million and must be cut by what looks like a fairly modest £2 million.

Look what happens, though, when growth is zero. Now fixed and variable costs have to be cut by £13 million or six and a half times the 'with-growth' amount – and this is after variable costs have fallen by £3 million because of the lack of sales growth.

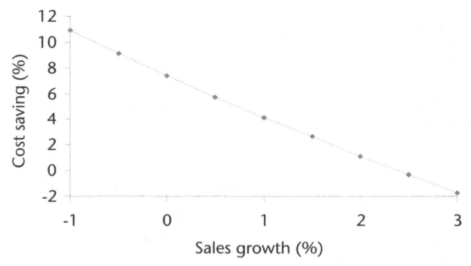

Figure 6.3   The trade-off between cost savings and sales growth

It gets worse. Up to 40 per cent of all mergers fail to capture identified cost synergies[2] and on top of this, cost savings have a nasty habit of being short-term, one-off gains or of leading to a downward spiral of low motivation and falling performance. As the old saying goes, 'downsized, right-sized, capsized'.

And all of this is just to stand still. From the above it is clear that if profits are to grow, then sales are going to have to grow more than they otherwise would have. To do this the acquisition must bring a strategic advantage. In other words, the acquisition must be aimed at taking the acquirer to a new level relative to the competition. Even if the only strategic advantage an acquisition brings is economies of scale, sales are going to have to increase more than they otherwise would have done for that advantage to be realized.

In many cases, the reality is that,

problems often result from transactional myopia and strategies based on optimism, rather than reality. The focus becomes the nuts and bolts of the transaction. Forgotten are the sources of its profitability and cash flow, an understanding of its market and the need to maintain a close relationship with the customer.[3]

Topics

The conclusions from all this are straightforward:

- First of all, commercial due diligence must focus on the ability, post-acquisition, to achieve sales growth, that is to win price increases or sales increases, or both.
- Second, it should not just concentrate on the pre-acquisition position of the target but should assess the likely strategic position of the combined entity – unless the target is going to run as a stand-alone business.

Table 6.1 The headings for a commercial due diligence exercise

	Market	Competitive position of the combined entity
Price	Degree of industry rivalry: • Number of firms • Relative shares • Degree of differentiation • Stage of industry life cycle • Demand/supply balance • Fixed cost intensity • Height of exit barriers Buyer power: • Relative size of customers • Degree of customer concentration • Profitability of customers • Cost of product relative to buyer's total costs • Importance to performance of customer's product • Ease of backward integration • Ease of switching/cost of switching/ availability of substitutes Threat of new entrants: • Cost of know-how • New technology • Cost of plant and equipment • Importance of experience • Economies of scale Degree of commoditization	Relative share Rationality of competitors Performance relative to the competition against customers' purchasing criteria Product strengths relative to competitors': • Performance • Differentiation • Innovation Relative distribution strengths: • On-time deliveries • Distributor network • Salesforce • Back office • Location/access to markets • Strength of customer relationships Brand strengths Costs relative to those of the competition: • Cost base • Proprietary technology or know-how
Volume	Existing market share Market growth Stage of product life cycle Threat of new products Shifts in technology Cyclicality/stage of cycle Change of regulations	Segments served Segments not served New territories New applications New products

Once this is understood, the subject headings for CDD fall straight out of a strategy textbook, as is shown in Table 6.1.

To make the point once again, doing commercial due diligence properly means looking not just at the market. It must be concerned above all with the post-acquisition competitive position within it. Just because a market is big and growing does not necessarily mean the acquisition is well placed to benefit. A deal to buy a niche manufacturer of construction equipment in a market growing at 20 per cent a year was halted when due diligence pointed out that this particular manufacturer's niche was never going to grow at the same rate as the overall market.

Scope

The above is CDD in its full form. CDD is not always carried out in its full form, especially on smaller deals in familiar markets. What is done is very much up to whoever commissions the work. Whether or not to conduct CDD, how much to do and where to concentrate resources is a business judgement based on the balance of risk and knowledge. Factors to be considered would include:

- The buyer's existing knowledge: companies which are already active in a market should know their market well. All too often, though, when companies think they know about markets they do not, or rather their knowledge is of the wrong kind to assess future prospects. Also, deals where the overlap between two companies is total are rare. There may be competition between acquirer and target in certain areas, but there are also likely to be activities, market segments or geographical markets about which the buyer knows next to nothing.
- The perceived level of risk: if you are buying a small company, in the same market as yours, where the consequences of the deal going wrong are minor and there are no unanswered integration questions, the level of perceived risk is low.
- The size of the deal: deal size and risk are often related in the minds of buyers.
- The need for 'political' justification or to convince potential investors, lenders or a sceptical board.
- The audience: a full PLC board is going to want much more than say an owner-manager who has been in the business a long time. Banks will need even more.
- What claims the seller has made that sound peculiar or are critical to valuation and/or the target's future.
- The information and analysis needed to get the deal done, for example to justify the price being paid. Here again, though, it is important to look at the target's competitive position as well as examining the market. Market due diligence alone is not enough to answer the questions that need to be asked just to complete the deal. Questions like 'Is this company any good?', 'Am I paying too much for it?' need to take into account competitive position as well as market factors. The competitive position of the target is fundamental to its future performance and therefore its value. A target market may well be attractive, but there is no guarantee that an acquisition candidate will perform in line with the market and although competitive positions can be changed with investment and new management, the competitive position now is going to give a good indication of where the weaknesses are, what needs to be done and, therefore, the time and resources needed to improve the target's position.
- Any other particular areas of concern.
- Whether a proper strategic review (of the buyer) was felt necessary as an underpinning of any proposed acquisition.
- The reasons for the deal. If we go back to Table 2.3 in Chapter 2, the focus of CDD might be different according to the reasons for the deal, as shown in Table 6.2.

Table 6.2   The commercial due diligence focus will vary with the type of deal

M&A type	Strategic objectives	CDD focus
The overcapacity M&A	Eliminate overcapacity, gain market share, achieve scale economies	Ability to retain market share, market growth, competitor reaction, relative strategic advantage post-deal
The Geographic Roll-up M&A	A successful company expands geographically; operating units remain local	Strength of local operations and local management, target's ability to continue meeting customers' key purchase criteria, market growth
Product or market extension M&A	Acquisition to extend a company's product line or its international coverage	Strength of product relative to competition, strength of customer relationships, target's ability to continue meeting customers' key purchase criteria, market growth, competitor reaction, cross-selling opportunities, distribution/marketing synergies
The M&A as R&D	Acquisitions used instead of in-house R&D to build a market position quickly	Target's relative market position, industry and technological trends, customer acceptance of the product/technology, target management ability, originality of the technology being acquired, assessment of competing technologies
The Industry Convergence M&A	A company bets that a new industry is emerging and tries to establish a position by culling resources from existing industries whose boundaries are eroding	Industry and technological trends, target's product/technical capability

All of this means that commercial due diligence can be highly tailored and, as well as the general headings of market and competitive position, could include some very specific topics such as:

- Management
- Cross-selling opportunities
- Customers' immediate sourcing intentions
- Ability to penetrate new geographical or product markets
- Intelligence on the market or a target before an approach
- Future legislation/regulations
- Trading conditions in important parts of the market
- Imminent technological changes which might threaten the demand for one of the company's major products or services
- Whether a major new competitor is considering entering the market

- Degree to which the target is vulnerable to loss of large customers
- Degree to which a new product or service can be rolled out nationally
- Whether or not the target has been damaged by the sale process
- Analysis and forecast of the prospects for individual product lines

To sum up, the problem with many CDD investigations is that they easily become pieces of marketing due diligence looking, for example, at the ability of the target's salesforce and other detailed day-to-day sales and marketing issues. While this is important, much more important are the strategic issues – the strategic issues behind the deal, not just the strategic position of the target. Marketing issues can be fixed; strategic issues often cannot.

Overlap with financial due diligence

Some would argue that financial due diligence will provide much of the information and analysis needed to form a view on commercial prospects so why go to the trouble and expense of conducting detailed commercial due diligence? The reason is that financial due diligence tends to be internally focused. It collects its market and competitive information from management. This is one way of reaching an assessment of future prospects. However, by itself it is often not enough. At the very simplest, if management say their products are the most highly rated by all the big customers in the marketplace, due diligence needs to check with those big customers that this is in fact the case – and that it will continue to be the case. In one investigation of a tired UK brand, CDD very quickly discovered that all the major supermarkets wanted to stop stocking the product. Those that did so quickly found themselves bombarded with telephone calls from out-of-work actors, hired by the target, expressing disappointment that they could no longer find the product. Faced with this buying interest, the product was quickly given back its shelf space.

On a wider level, understanding the future needs an input from more than one perspective and it needs to be up-to-date which means talking to a wide range of relevant people operating in the market. This, financial due diligence does not do. For example, just because an industry has been price-based in the past does not necessarily mean it will continue that way. Even the construction industry is moving towards a mentality that puts service and just-in-time delivery at least on a par with price. It is only by talking to customers that this trend would be confirmed. Similarly, customers' buying habits have a tendency to change with time. For example, personal computer distributors are now having to change to offer much more than just the traditional supply and install. By getting most of its information from sources outside the target, CDD attempts to come to a view of the future by a completely different route.

FDD and CDD, then, should be seen as complementary. This complementarity should be recognized by ensuring the two teams work together. Both financial and commercial due diligence teams have access to sources and to information which can be valuable to the other. The financial due diligence team will have access to debtors lists for example. These will contain the identities of ex-customers. For obvious reasons, the CDD team will want to talk to ex-customers. In exchange, the commercial due diligence team can find and provide a wider range of estimates of market size and future growth rates which the financial due diligence team can plug into their forecasts and scenarios.

Timing

Commercial due diligence does not have to be carried out after Heads of Terms have been negotiated. In many deals, there is a lot to be said for carrying out CDD early on:

1. CDD can confirm or otherwise the buyer's acquisition strategy.
2. CDD is the least expensive type of investigation to commission from specialist consultants and can provide a clear pre-acquisition stop-go decision before more expensive investigations are started. If there are fundamental problems with a company or its markets, you can save a great deal of time and money by discovering them early.
3. As CDD can be conducted without the knowledge of the target it:

    • can avoid raising the seller's expectations
    • avoids any embarrassment if the acquisition is not progressed
    • allows enquiries to be made without the restraints imposed once confidentiality agreements are signed or by the target's management once a deal is in progress

Timescale

Commercial due diligence takes three to four weeks. Any more time and the investigation tends to lose focus. It can be done in less time but if it is, there is a risk of not getting to speak to the best contacts and the quality of analysis tends to suffer.

Choosing the team

The choice of who to do the work is perhaps less obvious than it is for legal and financial due diligence. Commercial due diligence is carried out by a bewildering range of organizations and who to use may differ according to the nature and requirements of the acquiring company. The main options are:

• The buyer itself
• The transaction services arms of the big accountancy firms
• A strategy consultancy
• A market research firm
• An industry expert
• A commercial due diligence specialist

Industry experience may also be a consideration, although as argued below, it should not have an overriding influence on who to use.

THE BUYER

Many buyers carry out commercial due diligence possibly without recognizing it as such. There is usually a lot of knowledge in-house and it is natural during an acquisition to tap this. In other companies the process may be more formal. The major constraint will be the ability to deploy sufficient resources of the right calibre at a moment's notice. However, carrying out any form of due diligence in-house obviously develops a capability. Frequent acquirers tend to have teams of professionals who build up a great deal of expertise. Some of these companies carry out most or all of the various due diligence procedures in-house. This can be a very cost-effective means of doing the work. It should also, in theory, be pretty easy to maintain confidentiality although that is far from guaranteed. Industries tend not to be leakproof and of course a company making enquiries on its own behalf is not going to be able to maintain anonymity in the same way that a third party could. Finally, operators, as opposed to acquisitions specialists, within buyers tend to become distracted by detail when carrying out this type of work.

ACCOUNTING FIRMS

Commercial due diligence is an adjunct to the activities of due diligence accountants – and from their point of view more lucrative than financial due diligence – so it is only natural that they should offer CDD as one of their services. They may argue that the financial and commercial due diligence teams will work together more effectively if they are both from the same firm. This is not much of an argument. Outside professionals can work with the accountants just as well as consultants who are members of the same firm. In fact, in large firms internal politics can often inhibit effective internal cooperation and it is not unknown for staff in a large accountancy firm to be just as unfamiliar with the financial due diligence team as outsiders. The downsides of using accountancy-based firms are:

- Their fear of litigation. This means that they have a page and a half of disclaimers to negotiate before they start work and that they may not express opinions unless they have rock-solid evidence to back them up. This can be a bit difficult in a discipline that relies on analysing and reporting facts and opinions gathered from third parties.
- The accountant's mentality. Accountancy prefers to be precisely wrong than roughly right. A commercial due diligence exercise is all about putting together information from a variety of sources much of which is conflicting or incomplete. Absolute precision, like rock-solid evidence, is a dream.
- Following regulatory pressure, from the American SEC in particular, and high-profile conflicts of interest between audit and advice, audit firms will find it increasingly difficult to continue giving general consultancy advice.

The big advantage they have, although again it might be more apparent than real, is that they have worldwide representation. However, as most commercial due diligence is done by telephone these days worldwide representation probably does not count for so much, especially since their representation outside the Anglo-Saxon markets is likely to be audit-based. Auditors do not generally make good commercial due diligence consultants. Spending a lot of time talking to market participants is not part of their ethos and, in addition, the accountancy firms struggle with the concept of 'platform' based research (i.e. when you cannot tell the respondent the whole truth about the reasons for your enquiries).

STRATEGY FIRMS

Some of the big strategy firms actually started in CDD and some continue to carry out commercial due diligence work on the bigger deals, especially for financial investors. Like the audit-based firms, the strategy firms have strength in both breadth and depth. They also bring great rigour to their work, which is something often missing from CDD. Their main drawback is that despite their incredibly talented staff and superbly crafted processes, they may not actually provide a good answer – and they are expensive. Strategy consultancies are best when working on long-term, leading-edge business problems calling for high levels of creative input. CDD is quite different. It is a fastmoving, cut-and-thrust, information-based activity.

MARKET RESEARCH FIRMS

In contrast to strategy firms, market research firms do collect information – lots of it – and that is their main drawback. They do not shy away from talking to large numbers of people in the market but they tend to lack analysis and understanding. Even qualitative market researchers will tend to think of information-gathering as their primary focus rather than its synthesis into an answer. Furthermore, The Market Research Society in the UK actually forbids members to contact competitors of clients during projects, arguing that it is unethical. However, if the buyer knows what questions to ask and has the resources to assimilate a lot of data quickly, using market researchers to collect data and opinions may be an entirely reasonable means to an end.

INDUSTRY EXPERTS

Industry experts claim their knowledge is more pertinent and detailed than that which can be developed by an industry outsider. They also have a shallow learning curve, lots of contacts and should know where to delve for information. There are, however, downsides. Some have been out of the industry for so long that they have lost touch with it. Others may lack necessary skills such as the ability to obtain and analyse information in the context of an acquisition. If industry experts are to be used, it is important to address the issue of confidentiality in detail. The last thing the would-be buyer wants is some industry expert gossiping with contacts and giving the game away.

COMMERCIAL DUE DILIGENCE SPECIALISTS

There are specialists in commercial due diligence. They claim to offer the best of both worlds by combining the research capability of market research firms with the analytical skills of strategy firms. There is considerable truth in this, although on the whole they tend to fall into one of two camps. Some do not have the analytical horsepower of the strategy consultants while others do not have the research horsepower of the market researchers. However, in most cases they will be the most cost effective means of carrying out commercial due diligence.

Industry experience

With commercial due diligence, probably more than anywhere else, the question of relevant previous industry experience crops up as a factor in the choice of supplier. The same argument as mentioned in Chapter 2 applies, namely that the experience required in order of importance is as follows:

1. Experience of carrying out due diligence
2. Experience of the purchaser
3. Experience of the target company's sector

Commercial due diligence is a process which can be applied to industries almost universally. What counts is the skill of the team in carrying out commercial due diligence, not its industry knowledge or industry contacts. Indeed both of the latter have a habit of being irrelevant and out of date. Instead the buyer should look to the commercial due diligence team to bring highly developed information-gathering and analytical skills and a good dose of solid commercial experience. Even in very specialist industries there is a lot to be said for not using industry experts but instead seasoned specialists who know what they are doing and can therefore bring a fresh perspective.

This last point is a theme that crops up time and time again in all areas of due diligence. It is obviously good to have first-class minds working on an acquisition but by their very nature due diligence exercises do not yield perfect information on which to base decisions. There is no substitute, therefore, for having someone on the team who has the hard-bitten commercial experience to know what to look at and who can recognize trouble from 50 metres. For example it is easy for an inexperienced consultant to come to the conclusion that a market has a huge potential simply because the massive installed base is well past its design life and in need of urgent replacement. However, if the buyers are cash-strapped local authorities it is highly unlikely that demand will ever reach its full theoretical potential. Similarly, a potential turn-round in a pretty basic, mature, process industry may have a previous management who lost a lot of opportunities because of their attitude to customers. Customers may confirm this and hint that new management could win extra business. But in a mature industry that business has to be taken from the competition. In a high-fixed cost process industry where products are by and large undifferentiable, competitors' response will be through price. What chances, then, of a turn-round?

It was pointed out in Chapter 2 that senior due diligence advisers will often 'sell' the work then leave more junior members of staff to complete it. This is something to beware of, especially with commercial due diligence. Securing adequate attention from the experienced practitioner is doubly important because there is often a basic division of focus amongst individuals who carry it out. Good commercial due diligence researchers are second to none at finding out just about anything that is required, especially from primary sources. However, they are rarely good at drawing all, and sometimes even the right, conclusions from the first-class information they collect. This is where the skills of the experienced project leader come in. The leader's role is to stand back from the detail and make sure the research answers the question. Without good, analytical, commercial, project leadership, commercial due diligence exercises too easily degenerate into semi-focused collections of 'interesting' market and competitor information.

Briefing the team

The quality of briefing has a significant impact on the quality of the consultant's report. The reasons for acquiring will, to a large extent, determine what questions need to be asked. If the acquisition is intended to gain market share, stabilize market prices by knocking out a troublesome competitor or acquire a new growth product then it helps greatly if the CDD team know this so that they can determine whether the proposed acquisition will deliver the desired result.

Market and competitive investigations can take place at a number of levels. As already discussed, CDD is best carried out at the strategic level but it does not have to be. As it is difficult to satisfy a mixed audience, the level of the inquiry needs also to be specified right from the start. To an extent this will be self-evident from the buyer's articulation of its concerns, but nonetheless the Chairman is going to have a different perspective to a subsidiary MD and it is as well to be clear from the start who the audience is. It is quite common for the person with responsibility for M&A to brief the team from one perspective only to find that it is the person charged with running the combined entity, and who has a completely different perspective, who asks all the questions at the final presentation.

Buyers have three approaches to sharing information with the CDD team:

- share nothing
- provide selected information
- share everything.

Share everything is best: it is cheaper, quicker and augments what the buyer and target management already has. It also helps to avoid distractions by alerting the due diligence team to projects already underway. For example, the buyer's subsidiary management may have initiated a sales drive in one sector of the market with a great fanfare internally. The chances are that this will have no bearing whatsoever on the CDD exercise, but it is as well for the CDD to include some mention or even evaluation of this, otherwise local management have a nasty habit of rubbishing the whole report.

Tempting though it might be to tell CDD advisers nothing, the right reason for providing commercial due diligence consultants with only the most basic profile of the assignment is that a fully impartial study is required either because there is a high level of internal debate and uncertainty or conflicting reports from the market.

CDD is a bit like peeling an onion. However carefully the acquirer has thought about what questions CDD needs to answer, once the first layer of uncertainty has been bottomed out, there is another then another followed by another. New questions arise as old ones are answered. The questions set at the beginning of a CDD exercise can therefore be very different from those which need answering at the end. There is no real way around this except to stress once again the benefit of staying close to the CDD team as they carry out their work.

Getting access

Sometimes sellers, or their advisers, try to restrict access to customers and management. They may even attempt to discourage the CDD team from talking to competitors. It is amazing how many companies claim to have no competitors! If a seller is reluctant to cooperate with a CDD exercise or uncertain about its consequences, the following are useful arguments in its favour:

- Customer research is a normal part of the acquisition procedure.
- The work will be carried out as a customer care programme. Customer care programmes have a positive PR benefit with customers.

- The researchers know what they are doing and will not upset trading relationships. It clearly helps to be able to point to a solid track record of successful projects in the past.
- The research will not include customers where the relationship with the target is particularly sensitive.
- Change of ownership will not be mentioned or even implied. If pressed, the researchers will say they are doing a customer care survey and know nothing about the company.
- If necessary the seller can agree the question set.

If these fail to win the seller over, it is not the end of the world. It is better to have full access obviously, but it is not impossible to conduct CDD without it. It just takes longer. Sellers too should bear this in mind and be on the look out for any unusual approaches, no matter how innocent and plausible they appear to be, during the negotiating period.

In some cases sellers include a clause in the confidentiality agreement forbidding the purchaser from contacting customers. Buyers should resist this condition. The suspicion has to be that the seller has something to hide.

Getting the information

There are four sources of information in a commercial due diligence programme: management, the buyer's own organization; desk research (known as secondary sources); and primary sources.

MANAGEMENT

Management interviews perform two roles: opening a line of communication and collecting basic information. Most commercial due diligence projects will start with discussions with the target's management.

One of the main points of meeting the target's management is to reassure them that this is not going to be a painful, time-consuming process that will damage customer relationships. Management will naturally be concerned about strangers talking to its customers. They will still have to run the business if the deal does not go ahead and will therefore worry about any damage to trading relationships as a result of the enquiries. That is why it is best to frame the enquiries as a customer care survey.

The other reason for talking to management early on is to collect information. Target management can provide:

1. A thorough briefing on the business and its markets
2. An agreed way to approach customers and other contacts. Whatever access to customers the seller grants, one thing the researcher on a commercial due diligence programme cannot say is 'Hello, I am working on such and such a deal'. The researcher needs a cover for the enquiries (a 'platform'). As mentioned above, one of the most common platforms is a very slight variance of the truth, namely that the study is a market review commissioned by the target. This, of course, requires the full cooperation of the target's management. Management must also go along with the platform if anyone calls to check (which they will). It also has the benefit of giving:

- the researcher a legitimate excuse for calling in the eyes of the person on the receiving end of the call. This helps minimize suspicion and therefore improve the quality of the responses.
- a PR benefit to the target. Customers do appreciate being asked their views.

3. Contact details of key customers and other contacts. Ideally the target should provide names and telephone numbers of customers and others in the market it is worth the CDD team contacting.

One of the key issues in CDD will be customers' key purchase criteria (KPCs) – the criteria used (either consciously or subconsciously) by customers in selecting one supplier over another. Talking to management is the first step in understanding what they are. Questions to ask management will be:

- How does the market segment?
- What are the top five KPCs used by customers in each market segment?
- What is the relative importance of each KPC?
- Are KPCs or their order of importance likely to change in the future?
- What is the management's strategy (value proposition) for each segment?

How confidently they answer these questions (and how robust their answers subsequently prove to be) can also contribute to management assessments.

THE BUYER'S ORGANIZATION

The CDD team should be encouraged to talk to relevant internal contacts at an early stage. Confidentiality is an issue, but again the discussions can be dressed up as something else. Salesmen and others with day-to-day contact in the market can be invaluable sources of information and can assist greatly in framing the overall direction of the study. Furthermore, companies often recruit from their competitors so it is entirely possible that there are former employees of an acquisition target on the payroll.

The greatest danger of relying on internal sources for information and opinions on acquisition targets is that knowledge is at the wrong level of detail.

SECONDARY SOURCES

'Secondary' sources are published or publicly available. There is no comprehensive list of what these might be. These days, the Internet is the usual starting point. Trade journals are a must in most cases, brokers' reports can be very good, if a little broad-brush, published market reports (for example, Keynote, Mintel, Frost & Sullivan, Datamonitor and so on) are a good means of getting a broad outline of a market, its size, growth and the relative market shares of its participants.

The problem is that secondary sources are general, seldom up-to-date and often wrong. They rarely cover specific niches in enough detail and will almost certainly not cover target companies in the level of detail required to get a proper understanding for due diligence purposes. Almost by definition, published sources are always out-of-date even though updating is now a lot cheaper and easier than it used to be. As soon as information appears in print, it is out-of-date. Finally, it is surprising just how often even highly respected market research organizations, who charge a small fortune for their reports, appear to be wrong. Often the problem can be traced to definitional issues, but just as often there has to be a lingering suspicion that they have not been as thorough as perhaps they should. Talking to the authors may help to clear up any inaccuracies, misunderstandings or definitional points, but as a general rule secondary data should be cross-checked.

Despite their drawbacks, secondary sources do have a number of invaluable uses.

Background information

Secondary sources can give the commercial due diligence team valuable background information about the industry – its vocabulary, its size, who is in it, market shares and maybe some basic segmentation. The more researchers know about an industry – or the more they know what they do not know and therefore need to find out – the better the questions will be. The better the questions, the better the final result. Also, talking to people in an industry is far easier if the industry participants think they are dealing with someone who has made an effort and does at least understand the basic issues.

Contacts

The main drawbacks of secondary information – timeliness and specificity – are countered in CDD by talking directly to people operating in the target's market. We will come to the relative merits and demerits of each type of industry contact in a moment. Inevitably many of the people the CDD team want to speak to will be customers and in most cases management will provide a fairly comprehensive list. However, the question the due diligence team should always bear in mind is how representative this list is going to be. Do job candidates give the names of people who do not rate them as references? Not if they can help it. The same goes for target management. They will hand-pick the contacts to be interviewed.

For this reason a good CDD house will go out of its way to find alternative contacts to supplement those provided by management. Secondary sources can play an invaluable role in finding these alternative sources of information. One piece of commercial due diligence in a fairly specialist sector of the packaging industry benefited greatly from talking to ex-employees of the target, all of whom were found through technical articles they had written in the packaging trade press. Furthermore, approaching them on the basis of 'I saw your article on such and such and just wondered how the various companies in that part of the market differed' yielded a much better response than the alternative approach of, 'You used to work for target company. Please can I talk to you about them?'

What target management never realizes when picking only 'friends and family' for interview is that friends and family usually have a pretty secure relationship with the target. This makes them talk much more freely than other contacts with a less secure relationship.

Platforms

As mentioned above, the CDD consultant can never pick up the phone and say, 'Hello I am working for company A who is buying company B'. Some form of subterfuge, or platform, is called for and secondary sources can be good for platform ideas.

PRIMARY SOURCES

Obtaining information from primary sources is the core of CDD. It is the only way of getting relevant up-to-date information on the target and the market in which it operates. This means talking to people operating in the target's markets. Teasing out the best from industry participants requires semi-structured and free-flowing discussions rather than highly structured questionnaire-based interviews. This in turn calls for a lot of planning and skilled researchers who:

1. Can get to the right people
2. Have the experience and nous to build on previous discussions
3. Are prepared, and confident enough, not to stick to the script because:

   - They already know what is being said and therefore need to alter the direction of the conversation to get the most out of the contact
   - They are experienced enough to recognize when an unexpected avenue is worth pursuing

4. Ask intelligent, stimulating questions
5. Can keep the discussions focused

There is really no need to be frightened of asking for information from other people. There is a huge amount of free information available for the asking. If approached properly people are usually only too glad to help.

Unfortunately, there is not one proven ideal information source. Information should also be cross-checked. The researcher therefore has to speak to as many different sources as possible in the time available. It is a question, therefore, of 'surrounding' the target company by speaking to anyone and everyone who might be able to shed some light on the target and its market. Talking to as many people as possible also eliminates bias and helps in finding a consistent message. The types of respondent typically spoken to (in rough order of importance although this tends to vary with industry) are:

- customers
- competitors
- former employees
- industry observers
- corollary suppliers
- distributors
- specifiers
- regulators
- suppliers
- market leavers
- pressure groups
- new entrants.

Customers

Customers are quite possibly the most important group of people to talk to. Talking to enough articulate customers will give the researcher a pretty reliable idea of their purchase criteria and how the various competitors measure up. From this comes a pretty good first cut at the target's strengths and weaknesses, and the opportunities and threats it faces going forward. The main objective with customers is to make sure they concentrate on the big picture rather than with more mundane issues like problems with last week's deliveries. Therefore, usually, the bigger the company and the more senior the interviewee, the better.

Customers come in three varieties:

- past
- present
- non-customers.

And it is important to speak to a good mix of all three.

- *Past customers*   The goal with past customers is to understand why they are no longer buying from the target. It may be completely understandable, like they no longer have a need for the target's products, or it may be something much more serious, for example they may have migrated to some new technology offered by the competition but not by the target. On the other hand, ex-customers may be ex-customers because they have been on the receiving end of appalling service, high prices, poor quality or any number of the other things a company can do wrong – in other words the target did not meet key purchase criteria (KPCs).
- *Present customers*   Present customers will be able to talk in depth about the target's current performance, how it rates against the competition on the KPCs, whether it is improving or getting worse, whether the KPCs are changing, how well the target is keeping up and so forth. But they are customers and, as customers, usually have a choice. They have not chosen to buy from the target because they think it is useless. On the contrary, they have chosen to buy from the target, they are likely to be favourably disposed towards it. For this reason, customer referencing alone is not usually good enough. CDD must involve past and non-customers as well as a wide cross section of other market participants.
- *Non-customers*   Some of these will be the objects of the target's marketing efforts. These prospective customers will give yet another perspective on how the target rates against competitors. Others will never be customers because, for example, the target operates in a different market segment from the one which supplies them. They can provide invaluable insights into how the market really works. Any business-aware researcher who conducts enough good interviews with a cross-section of customers can be confident of coming away knowing at least as much as target management about the way the market works.

One important objective of discussions with customers is to get a rating of the target relative to the competition on key purchase criteria. The starting point is to get confirmation of the key purchase criteria, by segment, both now and in the future and how well the target performs against them, relative to the competition. Market share gains will come about if the target is better than the competition at meeting KPCs.

In the first few interviews, it pays to ask interviewees to validate the list of KPCs offered by management (they may not be the same) and amend as necessary. Thereafter it is a case of asking each interviewee, in a consistent manner, to weight each of the KPCs and to rate those competitors with which they are familiar.

Table 6.3   An example of the output of a KPCs interview

KPC	Weighting	Target		Competitor A		Competitor B	
		Score	Weighted score	Score	Weighted Score	Score	Weighted Score
1 Price	50%	5	2.5	10	5.0	4	2.0
2 Quality	10%	5	0.5	5	0.5	7	0.7
3 Performance	20%	5	1.0	5	1.0	7	1.4
4 Design	10%	5	0.5	5	0.5	9	0.9
5 Reliability	10%	10	1.0	5	0.5	3	0.3
	100%		5.5		7.5		5.3

The results for each interview will look something like those in Table 6.3. As well as helping to rank the target against its most important competitors, customers are also usually knowledgeable about overall market trends so, for example, they can shed light on market growth, technological trends and so forth.

Competitors

Competitors are the second most important source of primary information. They will tend to have pretty forthright opinions on the strengths and weaknesses of the target company. They will usually know management pretty well and in some cases may be ex-employees of the target company. They will also have views and information on the market, the way it is going and what the future might hold.

Approaching competitors is always problematical. Some researchers will not do it at all, while others resort to pretext enquiries, such as 'We are a firm of consultants reviewing this industry', even where the target has agreed to the 'market study' type platform. Competitors' willingness to hold a discussion with someone who says they are working on behalf of a competitor is usually one of two extremes. Reaction is either a straightforward 'no' or an eagerness to talk. One of the reasons people talk to researchers, as we will see below, is in the hope of learning something. This is the card the experienced CDD researcher will play in attempting to talk to competitors, and it is one that works. It has even been known for a firm 'no' to metamorphose into a willingness to talk bordering on the enthusiastic in the space of around 24 hours.

Given their proximity to the target and its markets, discussions with competitors simply have to be a feature of CDD.

Former employees

Former employees are another invaluable source of information. They can be hard to find, and their responses sometimes need a hefty truth filter applied – a well-balanced ex-employee can turn out to be one with a chip on both shoulders. They are well worth tracking down. A former employee can be the single most valuable source of information in a commercial due diligence exercise.

Any former employees of the target currently in the buyer's organization are obvious sources of information. Otherwise industries tend to be fairly small worlds and ex-employees will usually be found working for competitors. They can normally be found by looking through the trade press. In the UK, the names and addresses of all current and former company directors are available through Companies House. In one CDD project a search through the relevant trade journal unearthed three former senior executives of the target company who had set up in business together. They talked at length about their old company, the expertise they had gained there, and their reasons for leaving.

Interviewing former employees is even more valuable where the seller has limited access to customers and other outsiders who deal with the target business. The seller rarely remembers to include them in the confidentiality agreement, although it is not unknown for recent ex-employees to be bound by confidentiality agreements anyway.

Industry observers

The most frequently consulted industry observers are trade journalists. They usually have a tremendous knowledge of their own sector and the players within it which they will gladly share with anyone who is interested.

Other industry observers include trade association officials, academics, and consultants. These people often follow developments in an industry closely and are familiar with many of the major players. Talking to them can provide a good introductory briefing to an industry or an issue within the industry, and can also provide other contacts.

Consultants usually want payment and it is sometimes worthwhile buying their time. A fairly modest sum once secured a couple of hours from a well-connected consultant in the advertising industry who was able to say a lot about a client's use of media auditors to get full value from their advertising spend and, just as important, give the inside track on the agencies' views of them.

Academics are rarely useful sources in a commercial due diligence enquiry, although they may be of help in understanding technical aspects of a product or service. They tend to focus on their pet topics rather than the bigger commercial picture. For example when interviewing a knowledgeable-sounding Dutch academic with years of experience in a fiercely competitive commodity market it soon became apparent that he was unable to talk about anything other than a rather obscure, but revolutionary, new product which was about to be launched but which was relevant to about one-fiftieth of the market and was probably too late and too expensive ever to catch on.

Trade associations are mostly helpful in providing lists of further contacts but have to remain impartial as far as their members are concerned. Not surprisingly, therefore, they are reluctant to offer opinions.

Corollary suppliers

A corollary supplier supplies a product or service which is related to the target's. For example, potato merchants and fish merchants are corollary suppliers to fish and chip shops. They can be an excellent bet, less for their specific comments about the target than for their industry knowledge.

Distributors

Distributors are crucial in many industries, especially in North America. Because of the way the market is structured, some companies have little direct contact with the end-users of their products. Where this is the case it is important to speak to distributors to obtain a clear view of the market's needs and opinions because they know a lot more about the target company, its strengths and weaknesses and the strengths and weaknesses of its products. Like former customers, former distributors can also be an excellent source of information, as can non-distributors. The best suppliers tend to attract the best distributors, so it pays to talk to distributors who do not handle the target's products as well as those that do.

Specifiers

In some industries, construction for example, specifiers are central to the buying decision. Their power tends to wax and wane with the business cycle, and will be more pronounced with some products than with others but the importance, for example, of architects and surveyors as specifiers of certain building products, of GPs as specifiers of pharmaceuticals and of the IT department as specifiers of computer hardware and software, should always be allowed for.

As specifiers can be responsible for preparing criteria or an overall project specification which can be more or less favourable to certain companies' skills, understanding their power relative to the ultimate buyer is important. With some products it is much easier for the actual buyer to substitute an alternative to the one specified than it is for others. An investigation into a company making a safety-critical fire-prevention product found that the company was over-priced and over-specified compared with the competition. If the due diligence team had listened only to the opinions of the actual buyers – the ductwork contractors – the conclusion would have been that this company had no future because its share would be eroded by competitors with low specification products and lower prices. However, the contractors' opinions did not count for that much in the end. Because the item was safety-critical there was little chance of the specifiers – the heating and ventilation engineers – allowing the contractors to substitute a lower specification.

Regulators

The future plans of regulators are only a factor in a minority of commercial due diligence reviews, but on occasion they can be critical. For instance many of the European health and safety laws and recycling/anti-pollution regulations can have a profound effect on entire industries. Today in the UK, old car oil is collected from garages, has sludge and other debris removed and is sold to coal-fired power stations as a means of regulating the burn-rate. True to the old saying 'Where there's muck, there's brass', collecting and reselling waste oil is a profitable business. At first sight the major question in CDD might be, 'what is the future for coal-fired power stations?' The answer is 'not bad'. The real cloud on the horizon is that in a few years' time European laws aimed at stopping the incineration of waste products will come into force, and waste oil is included in that classification.

Suppliers

Suppliers can know a lot about the market. They can also be completely useless. Some of the bigger companies, even those supplying commodities, keep a watching brief on their customers' industries. Aluminium suppliers, for example, are usually knowledgeable about the aerospace industry, where they have a big presence, and the automotive industry, where they have been trying for years to have a big presence.

Suppliers, like all information sources, can be biased. They are hardly likely to denigrate their major customers, however much they might deserve it, or to admit any lapses in their performance.

Market leavers

A company which has left a market should not be overlooked. The decision to leave a market, through the sale of a subsidiary or the closure of a business, is not easy. The strategic review and the subsequent agonizing leading up to that decision will have given management a detailed understanding of the market. The quality of their information and analysis is therefore excellent.

Pressure groups

Pressure groups such as Friends of the Earth are playing an increasing role in some markets, especially those where there are environmental or employment issues. Not all issues are pushed and pressure groups tend to be blinkered and biased so what they have to say must be treated with care and verified. Nevertheless, as some of the mightiest multinationals have found, once a pressure group latches on to to a company or an issue, the consequences can be grave.

New entrants

New entrants often get a mention as a possible source of CDD information. In theory they advertise their intention to enter a market. They will have carried out a considerable amount of independent research and will be hungry to trade information. In practice they are all but impossible to find.

Cost and duration

Apart from the breadth of the original scope, the main variables which affect the cost of a commercial due diligence programme are:

- The number of discussions which need to be held
- The type of people to be contacted
- The method of contact, that is, the way they are to be held
- The degree of access
- How willing the industry is to talk

Each of these is discussed in turn below.

HOW MANY DISCUSSIONS?

Like so much in due diligence there is no right answer as to what is the right number of discussions. The number of people to be contacted will be determined to a large extent by the complexity of the target – the number of products and number of markets, the buyer's existing knowledge and where the perceived risks lie. Deadlines will also play a part. The typical time frame of a commercial due diligence project usually does not permit an exhaustive study of every aspect of a large business so again discussions may have to be limited.

There may be a small number of sectors in certain countries which are critical to the future performance of the business. Because of this it is essential to obtain corroboration of any important findings from a number of sources. This is all the more important because a researcher can never be totally sure that some people have not been misleading during their discussions. This will not necessarily have been malicious, but for example people can get facts confused or try to hide the fact that they are not as knowledgeable as they should be.

The more important the finding is in the context of the overall project, the more corroboration is required.

You can be confident that enough research has been done only when the level of knowledge and understanding feels right. However, in practice, about 30 interviews is usually about right for a fairly straightforward review where there is, say, one product in one geographical market. Each additional market or product would add a further 20. This is a rough guide only. With particularly obscure markets or demanding information requirements, a lot more will be required.

THE TYPE OF PEOPLE TO BE CONTACTED

Getting hold of, say, a marketing director of a drugs company can take a lot longer than finding and holding a detailed phone conversation with a less pressured person in an industry less concerned about confidentiality.

METHOD OF CONTACT

For all sorts of reasons to do with non-verbal communication, personal meetings generate more and better information than telephone discussions. The problem is that CDD timescales do not permit the luxury of personal discussions. Personal meetings take up far more time than telephone calls. Time is spent in travelling and also in arranging the meeting in the first place. There is elapsed time to consider as well. It can take days or weeks to find a space in a busy person's diary.

Although all commercial due diligence practitioners will try to use a mixture of face-to-face meetings and telephone discussions, the reality is that, because of time pressure, most will end up doing mainly telephone discussions.

DEGREE OF ACCESS

A stranger calls out of the blue claiming to be a consultant researching the market. What is the typical reaction? Usually suspicion. It gets worse. The caller really wants to ask you about your biggest supplier but cannot say so openly. Calls like this tend, at best, to be circumspect, quick and fairly superficial. The researcher typically ends up doing a lot more calls and taking a lot longer to get decent information and this is on top of the extra time that must taken to find the right person to talk to. Imagine how long it takes to find the person in charge of specifying rubber door-seals in a giant automotive company. The more access a researcher can have, the better.

HOW WILLING THE INDUSTRY IS TO TALK

Some industries are extremely open. Others, such as many parts of the IT industry, are over-researched. It can, therefore, be difficult to find enough of the right type of respondent willing to talk. The automotive industry automatically assumes that anyone calling is on a spying mission from a competitor. Many automotive companies make it company policy not to talk to researchers.

Why do people talk?

There is absolutely no reason for anyone to talk to a due diligence researcher. But they do. Why? There are a number of reasons:

- Respondents go into sales mode. Stopping such respondents from talking is often more of a problem than getting them to open up.
- Good interviewers. People who carry out commercial due diligence are usually pleasant, persuasive people.
- Feeling wanted. It may be a trait of the human psyche with deep-rooted Freudian reasons, but in general people do like to help. Maybe it makes them feel wanted. Think what happens when somebody stops you in the street to ask the way. Is your instinctive reaction to say 'No, go away'? Not usually. The same generally goes for people on the receiving end of a due diligence call.
- We like talking about ourselves. Ask people to talk about their jobs and you are really asking them to talk about themselves. For most of us this is our favourite subject. Preface the questions with, 'Hello I got your name from so and so who tells me you are the world's greatest expert on tubular steel lampposts' and again the problem will be ending the conversation.
- To clarify their own thinking. Explaining something often forces you to get your own thoughts on the subject in order. In so doing you re-evaluate your notions as you go along. Very often you come up with new ways at looking at old problems.
- We might get something in return. Experienced consultants are practised at analysing an industry or a sector in a short space of time. A desk research exercise combined with introductory briefings from the client and some friendly contacts will often enable a good consultant to make some observations which even the most experienced market participant will find valuable. Good commercial due diligence exercises are a two-way street, not simply a process of sucking information from unwitting victims.

These last two are very important. Imagine carrying out due diligence into a target which makes vibration-monitoring equipment. Vibration-monitoring equipment tends to be used to protect big pieces of rotating equipment. These are found, for example, in steel and paper mills. Paper mills tend to be found in fairly remote locations where there are lots of trees. They run 24 hours a day, seven days a week. The plant is worth millions and if it ever stops, the cost is millions too. It is the job of the maintenance engineer to keep the plant running. To help, the mill has invested in vibration-monitoring equipment which is going to tell the engineer when preventive maintenance is required.

The engineer has researched the market and chosen what seems to be the best for the job. But can that engineer ever be 100 per cent certain? Someone who seems to know what they are talking about calls the engineer to discuss vibration-monitoring equipment. This person seems genuinely interested in why this mill chose the system it did. Suddenly the respondent has to articulate the reasons for buying one system rather than another. This in turn will justify the decision in the engineer's own mind, and therefore make the decision more comfortable. There is also the chance to ask what everyone else is doing and thinking and therefore learn if, for example, there are other things the engineer should be thinking about.

Planning discussions

From the above, it can be seen that a great deal of planning needs to go into preparing for the discussions. Each is a demanding exercise, because the researchers must achieve three things simultaneously:

- They must maintain the interest of the person they are speaking to. This means being polite (perhaps even charming), but more importantly it means asking intelligent, stimulating questions, and occasionally providing interesting information or ideas in return.
- They must keep the discussion directed towards the areas of interest without appearing manipulative.
- They must constantly evaluate the information they are receiving and assess it in the context of the information they already possess. The direction of the conversation may be radically affected by what is said during it.

Questions therefore need to be very carefully thought through and will need to be ordered and asked in such a way that the person contacted is not intimidated or alienated. For example, it is no good leaping in with a load of consultant speak about 'business models' and 'paradigm shifts' to a maintenance engineer in a Swedish paper mill.

RECOGNIZING THE INFORMATION GAPS

Inevitably there will be information gaps. There is no such thing as perfect market information, especially not in three weeks. For example, market sizes are often a problem as they usually have to be put together from conflicting, and less than complete, information. While quantifying the market is important, especially if the target has a large share, understanding trends and factors driving profitability within the market can be even more important. It is less important to know whether the market is worth £100m or £120m than to know that there is a new technology about to be launched which in five years time will cut market size by 50 per cent.

Reporting

COVERAGE

CDD is not an intellectual exercise. As a discipline it lies somewhere towards the centre of a continuum which stretches from pure market research at one end to high-level strategy consulting at the other. It is information-based consulting. It draws conclusions based on findings in the marketplace. It would be wrong to expect a CDD report to come up with a perfectly informed and verified analysis of a market and a target company's position within it. Although CDD professionals can cover a lot of ground in a short time it is essential to be realistic about what can be achieved in the time available. On the other hand, there must be firm, relevant conclusions based on solid information. Too often CDD reports end up as either a collection of quotes and interesting market facts, with no argument and no conclusions, or a collection of conceptual charts.

INTERIM REPORTS

It is a good idea to have some form of interim reporting, but it is best not to call for a full blown written and presented report. A quick telephone update is best although, if the due diligence programme is being managed properly, this is going to happen anyway. Commercial due diligence tends to be cumulative in its results: 40 phone calls will yield much more than double the result of 20. It is therefore difficult at the halfway stage for the CDD team to come up with much more than vague results and half-formulated theories. The team will not yet be entirely sure of its ground and will be reluctant to put forward firm conclusions in case they have to change them at the final report stage.

Naturally, also, they will not want to make the results entirely negative as this may lead to their work being ended with undesirable consequences for their fee. For this reason it is a good idea to probe for whether the work done to date has come up with unacceptably negative results. It is pointless carrying on if there is little chance of the deal going ahead. One commercial due diligence study found after one week that there was reason to doubt the integrity of the proposed buy-in candidate and the whole investigation process was therefore stopped.

OUTPUTS

The outputs of a commercial due diligence exercise fall into three parts:

• Facts and analysis
• Opinions based on the facts and analysis
• Conclusions and recommendations.

Facts and analysis

For each of the target's products and geographic markets, a due diligence report will contain some or all of the following headings:

• Size and growth rate of the market
• Segmentation: in which segments does the target operate?
• An evaluation of the strength of the target's competitive advantages
• Market price level, past and expected
• Target's comparative pricing
• A review of existing competitors and an evaluation of the potential threat to the target from each
• How often does the target lose out to competitors in open competition?
• A review of the potential threat from new entrants and/or new technology
• A review of distribution/routes to market: what are the distributors' attitudes to the product (for example, high volume, high margin and therefore emphasis on price)?
• Relative size and strength of the target's distribution system
• Customers'/distributors' attitudes to the target, levels of support, service and so on
• Customers' immediate sourcing intentions
• Management.

It may sound obvious but analysis should be logical and based on facts. Ideally, a good piece of analysis will be supported by evidence and flow in a logical sequence such that the reader comes to the same conclusions as the report before being told what those conclusions are. All too often consultants make the mistake of thinking that charts and diagrams in themselves constitute good analysis or, worse still, have standard templates which their company rules dictate must always be completed. Unfortunately, due diligence does not lend itself to this type of approach. In the words of a 3i investment adviser, 'It is a cottage industry. Each investigation is different from the last one.'

Opinions

Based on the above, a good CDD report will contain opinions on:

* the target's sales growth: market growth plus market share gains
* the target's pricing prospects.

If it is carried out by someone who really knows what they are doing and who has faith in the quality of the research, those opinions will be translated into numbers.

Conclusions

A short executive summary should contain the conclusions. The main thrust will be 'What does the future hold for this target company/as a result of doing this deal?' Ideally the conclusions will draw together the report from an investor perspective, that is, trying to understand the discounted value of the long-term cash (DCF) the business is likely to generate. This is a difficult exercise to carry out with any absolute certainty and will be riddled with subjectivity, but that does not mean that the DCF principle should not at least form a framework for the report's conclusions. If the CDD exercise has been properly carried out, subjectivity will at least be based on first-class desk research and the results of a large number of interviews with people who know what they are talking about. What is needed is something which is roughly right, based on available information.

The conclusions should also highlight any of the deal-related issues which might have a bearing on negotiations. Discussions in the marketplace, for example, might have revealed that the marketing director is incompetent and needs to be replaced or that customers are intending to take their business elsewhere.

Corporate intelligence

A close relation of commercial due diligence is corporate intelligence. Corporate intelligence really only differs in the nature of the investigative digging that is done. Whereas commercial due diligence will focus on markets and competitive position, corporate intelligence will be much more concerned with individuals. It could range from simple background checks to vetting key prospective employees for honesty, right through to the kind of dirt that is often unearthed in hostile bids. If, as a prospective buyer or JV arranger, you have any misgivings about the owners of the target or the senior management that may come with it, there are a number of companies that specialize in corporate intelligence.

Many of the information sources will be similar. The proliferation of electronic source data now means that corporate investigators spend a long time peering into their computers. In the US, for example, many court records are available online while more qualitative information is available at several specialist sites, such as *CompanySleuth*. The latter compiles information about US public companies, providing links to a general company overview and also links to very specific types of information about the company such as real-time news, rumours, insider trading information, trademark and patents owned by the company and SEC filings. Besides desk research, investigators will also talk to contacts who may be able to shed light on the individual concerned. Companies which specialize in this sort of work will always talk down the importance of the seedier types of investigation they carry out, but raking through dustbins and surveillance can also play their part.

Conclusion

Commercial due diligence is the process of investigating a company and its markets. Traditionally it has been the poor relation of legal and financial due diligence. As a discipline which, in the right hands, can provide the best available forward-looking information on a business, it is indispensable to the due diligence process. It relies heavily on primary sources to get the most up-to-date facts on markets and market participants. Ideally it should look beyond the immediate deal to the competitive future of the combined entity.

7 Human Resources due diligence

The aim of Human Resources (HR) due diligence is similar to other forms of due diligence. It is to understand the culture of the business and its employees so that the buyer can take a decision on whether to proceed with the transaction, estimate the costs and avoid the risks of proceeding, and gather the information necessary to decide how best to manage the business once the deal is done. The benefits of Human Resources due diligence are often underestimated and its findings are often not integrated with the rest of the due diligence. Do not fall into this trap.

Human Resources due diligence is often presented from a legal angle, with good reason. There is so much relevant legislation that it is advisable to check that the business:

- is complying with it all
- has made provision to comply with new requirements

Appendix B2 sets out some of the relevant legislation to look out for. From a legal angle, Human Resources in an acquisition can get complicated, and risky, if the European Acquired Rights Directive applies. The final section of this chapter covers the implications of the relevant UK Acquired Rights legislation. The rules in Europe, which are considerably more stringent than in the UK or US, can also be a major concern.

But the legal issues are by no means all that needs to be covered. Apart from the plethora of employment measures which could land the buyer in (expensive) hot water, perhaps more important to ultimate success is the human factor in acquisitions. Acquisitions bring with them a great deal of employee uncertainty. However comprehensive the financial model, however well the price was worked out, however skilfully the deal was negotiated and the contract drafted, you still need to recoup the premium paid. How likely is that with a disloyal, uncooperative and demotivated workforce? In short, get the HR bit wrong and you are quite likely to get the whole lot wrong.

According to some studies, employee problems are the cause of up to half of all acquisition failures,[1] a fact confirmed by the importance of the 'soft keys' in KPMG's study of successful acquisitions (see Figure 7.1).

Objectives

The primary objectives of HR due diligence, then, should come as no surprise. They are to:

- Identify any potential deal breakers

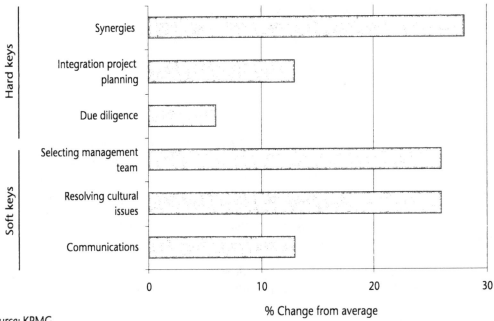

Source: KPMG

Figure 7.1   Pre-deal activities and success

- Uncover significant liabilities which can be brought to the negotiating table
- Assess the potential costs and risks (such as huge culture differences) and the strategy required to contain them
- Identify and prioritize the HR issues that need to be dealt with during integration
- Identify and prioritize the HR issues that need to be dealt with post-integration.

PLANNING

The precise form of a Human Resources due diligence investigation is going to depend on three features of the transaction in question:

- the reasons for the deal
- the type of business being acquired
- the form of the transaction, that is whether it is a share deal or an assets deal.

The reasons for the deal

First be clear what you intend to do once the transaction completes because that is going to determine where you focus your efforts. Below are a series of topics for employment due diligence and the sort of questions that might be asked under each. These are general questions. As no two deals are the same, it is as difficult to generalize here as in any area of due diligence. Like all other forms of due diligence, why you are buying will to a large extent determine what you do. In an 'overcapacity M&A' employees are a nuisance. If you are buying a competitor's factory to close it down, your concern is going to be redundancy costs.

The main concern of employment due diligence is assessing and minimizing redundancy costs. If you are buying to merge or incorporate into existing operations, then terms and conditions of employment in the target relative to those of your own staff are going to be your main focus. Other types of M&A on the other hand, the 'geographic roll up' for example or where M&A is used as R&D, would view certain employees as a major asset. The concern in such cases will be to see that Human Resources issues unlock value. Attention will focus on key employees transferring and once they have transferred that they are properly incentivized and securely locked in.

Also be on the look-out for changes that need to be made quickly post-completion. People expect change soon after a deal is done, so it makes sense to make as many changes as you can. It follows, therefore, that if you do not know what changes you want to make before you own the business, you will be floundering in the critical first 100 days after the business is yours. Not only that, at least half the money you have spent on employment due diligence will be wasted.

Do not take integration planning too far though. The law, at least in Europe, imposes certain duties on employers to consult with the workforce. Any consultations and negotiations with the workforce must be carried out in good faith, and not after irreversible decisions on, say factory closures, have been made.

The type of company

The type of business will also play a part in determining what to look for. A manufacturing company is likely to be unionized and subject to collective agreements. A purchaser will inherit both the agreements and the industrial relations, so important questions will be:

- What are the collective agreements?
- What is the strike record?
- How good (or otherwise) are management/union relations?

Manufacturing also involves machinery and often potentially hazardous working conditions.

- What is the accident record like?
- Are there potential claims floating around that could crystallize post-completion?

With people businesses, the issues tend to be more about maintaining incentives.

- Is there a scheme in place that allows employees to buy company shares at favourable rates?
- If so, does the purchaser need to maintain that particular incentive and how?
- What about share options?
- How are those to be transferred?
- What does the existing option scheme say about early leavers?

Share deal versus assets deal

Finally with Human Resources due diligence, you must be clear about the form the deal is going to take. An asset sale may well let you pick and choose assets and liabilities, but in Europe it will not let you pick and choose people. In the EC when a business is transferred, the transfer is governed by the Acquired Rights Directive – otherwise known in the UK as the Transfer of Undertakings (Protection of Employment) Regulations 1981 or TUPE. Compared with a TUPE transfer, a share sale is often a non-event from an employment law perspective as is discussed in the final section of this chapter.

Collecting information

The due diligence process will begin with an information request (see Appendix A2 for a list of possible questions) followed by management interviews. It is also worth looking for information which is in the public domain. You would be surprised how much information can be gathered:

- Often you can find standard terms and conditions/industry-wide agreements.
- Newspapers (often held online) can tell you a lot about the target and its industrial relations.
- A search of the register of employment tribunal cases can also speak volumes about the general state of industrial relations in the target. The number of tribunal claims is often symptomatic of the wider picture.
- Annual reports increasingly have to report on employees.

As ever, due diligence advisers should be encouraged to work together in collecting and analysing information. For example, the financial due diligence is going to throw up Human Resource information such as payroll costs and organization charts.

CONSTRAINTS ON INFORMATION-GATHERING – THE DATA PROTECTION ACT

It goes without saying that Human Resources due diligence involves the disclosure of employees' personal information. Personal data is regulated by the EC Data Protection Directive, which was translated into UK law as the Data Protection Act 1998. If the target has not obtained its employees' consent to the disclosure of their personal information the seller will almost certainly be breaching the Act. On the other hand, the confidentiality around M&A makes it most unlikely that a seller is going to tell employees that their personal data will be disclosed to a potential purchaser. There is no way round this and many legal advisers, when questioned, will look at their shoes and admit to ignoring the law in this area.

In the UK, for intra EEA[2] transactions there is a draft Code of Practice for guidance. This suggests that sellers:

1. As far as is possible make employee information anonymous so that individual employees cannot be directly identified. For example use numbers instead of names and/or job titles.
2. Where it is impossible to disguise the character to whom particular information relates, even after trying to anonymize it, conditions should be applied to its release. For example if it is obvious that information relates to the MD, the vendor should tell the prospective purchaser that the information should:

   - Only be used for the preparation of the bid

- Not be further disclosed beyond its advisers
- Be kept secure
- Be returned or destroyed once a bid has been submitted or there is a decision not to proceed

If data is going outside the EEA, life gets very complicated if not, theoretically, impossible. Unless the destination country has laws which ensure adequate protection of personal data, the Data Protection Directive prohibits its transfer. This is a tough test and one which most countries fail. The European Commission has only recently judged US data protection laws to be adequate.

Jurisdiction

There are huge national variations in labour law. Even in the EC, where there have been attempts at harmonization, laws and practices differ between countries. We poor toilers in the UK have to be grateful for a maximum working week of 48 hours, 8 days of public holiday and a minimum of 12 days' annual holiday. In France we would not be allowed to work more than 35 hours and in Spain our holiday entitlement would be 14 days of public holiday with another 30 days' annual holiday entitlement on top.

Custom and practice often varies as well. For example, unions in Germany are viewed very differently from the way they are in the UK or USA.

Once again, the advice with cross-border acquisitions is to engage advisers with local employment law experience in every jurisdiction where there is a sizeable number of employees.

Finally under this heading, it is also worth remembering that multi-jurisdictions can apply. An employment contract governed by a foreign jurisdiction is subject to English law if the citizen in question is working in the UK. Where there are particularly mobile executives it is worth comparing jurisdiction clauses in their contracts with where they work.

Topic headings

Generally speaking, the potential purchaser is looking not just for problem areas but also for post-deal issues. Appendix A7 contains a checklist. The sorts of concerns you are looking out for fall under six headings:

- Employee information
- Payroll information
- Staff structure
- Terms and conditions
- Industrial relations
- Relations with statutory bodies.

EMPLOYEE INFORMATION

Deal issues

- Is the business overstaffed?
- Is the business complying with legislation relating to part-time and disabled employees?
- Are there critical areas of the business in the hands of contractors? (This could for example throw up intellectual property issues. See Chapter 14.) What needs to be done to tie them in? Can they be tied in? (In certain cases, say where contractors own critical intellectual property, this can be a deal breaker.) How much will it cost? Are they in fact employees for tax purposes under IR35?[3] Are there any potential liabilities arising from this?

Integration issues

Basic employee information, dates of birth, length of service and so on will give a profile of the workforce and allow you to come to a view on issues such as:

- Possible redundancy costs. (Remember also that large-scale redundancies can take a long time to implement because of the need to consult the workforce.)
- Basic attitudes: how readily is the workforce likely to accept change? For example an old workforce with a long service record is going to have a very different attitude to relocation from a young workforce with a historically high turnover.
- Adequacy of the workforce. How skilled is it compared with what you want post-deal? Will it do or is it up to doing any extra or different types of work or ways of working that may be required post-acquisition? Are there training issues?
- To what extent is the business reliant upon contractors and fixed-term and casual employees? Is this likely to cause a problem? Do some of these need to be tied in post-deal? If so, how much will it cost?
- Fixed-term employees may have waived certain statutory rights but the waiver is only valid if their employment is ended on the due date and in any case (because of a change in the law) workers with fixed-term contracts may not now be able to waive unfair dismissal rights.
- Who is on maternity leave or secondment and how is their return going to be handled?

Finally under this heading it is also a good idea to prepare for the questions that are going to be asked once the deal is done. The human race can be strange at times. It does not like uncertainty. Bad news is therefore much better than no news at all. As there are few occasions more calculated to create uncertainty than an acquisition, it is as well to use due diligence as a means of preparing for all the employees' questions. Questions are usually along the same lines:

- Will our site close?
- Will my terms and conditions change?
- Will the bonus system change?
- Will I be made redundant? If so, what is the package like?
- Will I have to move or change jobs?

It is not only target employees that will be craving information, the buyer's own workforce will be feeling only slightly less apprehensive and will want the same sort of questions answered.

PAYROLL INFORMATION

Deal issues

- Are there any hidden liabilities? Not properly accruing for holiday pay is a classic example of a hidden liability. If you buy a business in the second half of the year when most holidays traditionally fall, you may find yourself paying for the whole of the workforce's holidays rather than just your share. Working Time Regulations dictate that workers are entitled to four weeks paid holiday per year. Has this requirement been met? Discretionary bonuses are another classic hidden liability. They are not always as 'discretionary' as a purchaser may imagine.[4]
- Is anyone paid less than the statutory minimum wage?
- Are there any discriminatory pay structures? Different pay for men and women 'doing the same job' (ask if there have been any job evaluations recently) and different pension arrangements or other benefits for full-time and part-time workers are examples to watch out for.
- Are employees paid a reasonable amount or will they need an increase to bring them up to the going rate? If so, this ought to be factored into the price you are paying. Are bonuses and incentives adequate?

Integration issues

- Are pay, terms and conditions, and perks such as the company car scheme, broadly in line or will changes in terms and conditions have to be made on integration? TUPE may play a part here as under a TUPE transfer (see below) employees cannot agree to trade benefits – even if it results in them being better off overall.
- Will any bonus or incentive schemes (for example share options) fit in on integration?

STAFF STRUCTURE

Integration issues

- Who are the key workers? This requires you talk to people to find out. There may be a high degree of dependence on a person who is not particularly high up or high profile so some probing may be called for.
- What is the relative importance and performance of acquired employees vis-à-vis any existing employees where there is an overlap? Is there potential for rationalization? This can be extremely difficult to gauge without a lot of access. Such access is rare even in agreed acquisitions.

STAFF TERMS AND CONDITIONS

Deal issues

- Are there any enhanced redundancy costs or golden parachutes? How much will these cost?
- Are there any unusual terms and conditions?
- Are there any discriminatory or illegal terms and conditions? Most companies now have a common retirement age for men and women but how many have updated contracts to take account of the Working Time Regulations? Has the target put the necessary time recording in place to prove that the business is complying with Working Time Regulations?
- Have any contractually binding promises been made about terms and conditions post-transfer? If promises have been made that are not contractually binding, the effect on morale of dishonouring them will have to be assessed.

Integration issues

- Are there any gaps or weaknesses in employment contracts? Do they need updating in the light of legislation (for example, Working Time Directive or the Employment Rights Act) or to address inconsistencies? For example if an employee has a right to permanent health insurance it is pretty difficult to justify a clause in the contract which allows the employer to dismiss an employee for long periods of sickness.
- Are there any restrictive covenants in place? Are they adequate and will they work? Can you change them anyway? (TUPE will stop you changing basic terms and conditions as Credit Suisse found out to its cost – see below.) On this point it is worth noting that it may no longer be possible to put employees on 'gardening leave' (that is to exclude them from the company's premises once notice has been given) unless there in a clause in their contract saying so.

INDUSTRIAL RELATIONS

Deal issues

- Union representation could be a deal issue or an integration issue. Look at union membership. If you have spent years repelling union representation, buying a business which brings with it strong union representation may be exactly what you do not want. A purchaser may want to withdraw recognition if its own workforce is not unionized; however, this may backfire as there is now legislation requiring compulsory union recognition. Alternatively, buying a business with union A if you have union B may spell disaster if the two unions are going to slug it out for dominance under your ownership.
- Examine the sickness and disability records very carefully – and marry these up with insurance. You are unlikely to find anything quite as horrific or expensive as asbestos-related illnesses these days, but you never know.
- What consultative bodies are in place and do they comply with legislation (for example, Works Council Directive)? Are these sufficient for any consultation that may be required as part of the deal or are there gaps which need filling?

- Are there any claims against the company (past, present or future)? Will they transfer? If so the purchaser will need indemnities. Ask about recent dismissals to evaluate whether there is a danger of claims arising. A purchaser buying shares would retain any liability. There are time limits for claiming unfair dismissal – three months in the UK – and redundancy compensation and equal pay claims – six months – but processing claims can take time so it is wise to go back beyond these limits. It is not just the cost of dealing with these claims that is an issue (currently a maximum of £60 100 for unfair dismissal, uncapped for whistle-blowing), the management time and effort involved should also be an important consideration.

Integration issues

- Redundancy agreements vary with business. What is the standard agreed procedure in the target? For example, there may be agreed ways of selecting people to be made redundant or, as mentioned above, there may be enhanced redundancy terms.
- The industrial relations history is a valuable part of piecing together a profile of the workforce. Similarly, the extent to which grievance procedures have been used will be a good indication of inherent problems in the business.
- Health and safety again features as part of building up the profile. Look at the accident book. What is the health and safety record like?

RELATIONS WITH STATUTORY BODIES

Deal issues

Health and safety is an area where legislation has pushed more responsibility on to companies. Due diligence should review the target's compliance with the legislation and if possible health and safety specialists should inspect the site. Injuries lead to claims and can also lead to the need for an expensive upgrading of worker protection. In some cases, inspectors have ordered critical equipment to be shut down with potentially very expensive consequences. But it is not only inside the factory where health and safety issues lurk. To take an extreme example, asbestos claims have had a devastating effect on many companies and it has not just been workers exposed to this terrible dust who have been successful in the courts.

Cross-border issues

EUROPEAN WORKS COUNCILS

In pan-European deals, there may be a requirement to consult with a European Works Council, under the European Works Council Directive (Directive 94/45/EC). The Directive applies to member states of the European Union and also to countries in the European Economic Area (the 'Member States').

The regulations apply to:

- community scale undertakings. These have at least 1000 employees in the Member States, including at least 150 employees in total in each of two of these states; or

- community scale groups of undertakings. These have at least 1000 employees in the Member States, including at least 150 employees in one undertaking in each of two of the Member States.

Where the transaction is not subject to EC rules, there is a *de facto* obligation to consult Works Councils where they exist. For example in France, a merger or acquisition cannot be concluded without the opinion of the works committee. The works committee's role is to represent and defend the interests of the company's employees. But although the committee has to be consulted, it can only give an opinion. It cannot veto the transaction. However, if it does not like the deal, it can make life difficult for the purchaser by being slow or simply not giving an opinion.

The obligation to consult is true for share sales as well as for asset sales. It is a common misunderstanding that the obligation does not exist for share sales. It does.

Therefore, even if a transaction does not come under European regulations, it is as well to determine early on whether the jurisdiction in which the target is situated requires an opinion, or even approval, from employee representatives. US acquirers in particular should note that Works Councils are not the same as unionization. In the UK unionization is about 34 per cent of the work force, but there are practically no Works Councils. In France, where worker protection is much higher on the agenda, unionization is about 9 per cent of the workforce, but Works Councils are present in virtually every enterprise.

REDUNDANCIES

If redundancies are planned following completion, the need to understand local law becomes even more pressing. Most European countries do not give employers the free hand to hire and fire that they have in the US and, to a lesser extent, the UK. It is also a mistake to see Europe as a homogeneous whole. The law may have a common basis, but procedures vary widely.

In some countries there is a requirement to consult on ways of minimizing the impact of redundancies on the neighbourhood and in some, even a requirement to take account of social factors, such as age and number of dependents, in deciding who to make redundant. This is if redundancies are allowed at all.

In France, for example, the law is to be tightened so that redundancies are only permissible if a firm is in serious economic difficulties which cannot be resolved by other means. Having convinced the courts of 'serious economic difficulties' there are then two rounds of consultation which are going to take six to nine months to complete. The second consultation is on a social plan to reduce the numbers of redundancies and minimize their impact, for example by outplacement. If the labour authorities or the courts do not like it they can force the employer to change the social plan. The cost of redundancies is also relatively high. The legal penalties for getting the procedure wrong can be severe, as can the damage done to the target's relationship with its remaining workforce.

Warranties and indemnities

The problem with warranties as far as Human Resources is concerned is that they usually exclude single claims below a certain threshold (*de minimus*). The effect may be to exclude most employment-related claims. As a lot of small claims could end up costing a substantial sum in aggregate the purchaser may want either to set a *de minimus* for aggregate claims or use indemnities instead.

The other advantage with indemnities is that sellers often underestimate the risk of a claim and will therefore agree a little too hastily to open-ended indemnities, especially where the indemnity may be an alternative to a price reduction.

Cultural issues

Cultural due diligence, if properly carried out, can play an important part in planning for the post-acquisition aftermath. The unfortunate fact is that due diligence is rarely conducive to it being properly carried out. Due diligence is still the preserve of lawyers and accountants with perhaps the odd operational manager helping out. Although some of the softer HR issues, like culture, may well emerge in due diligence, they are unlikely to be allowed to have much of an influence on the shape of the deal but they are just as important as the HR-related legal and financial issues, such as redundancy costs or TUPE transfers. Therefore it is also important during HR due diligence to get a handle on:

* How and when the two management teams will be brought together
* Human Resource barriers to integration such as cultural differences between the two organizations

Culture is a slippery concept. It is probably best thought of in terms of the beliefs that guide the behaviour of people in an organization. It is

The personality and character of a company, derived from generations of people and experience, and leading people inside a firm to behave in certain characteristic ways without thinking about it.[5]

To take a very simple example of a famously failed acquisition to illustrate how important culture can be, the cultures of Sony, a Japanese manufacturer, and Columbia Pictures, an American moviemaker, could scarcely have been more different when, in 1988 Sony bought Columbia Pictures for $3.4 billion. In 1994 Sony wrote down $2.7bn on the deal, and, to add insult to injury, was fined a further $1m in 1998 for delaying its disclosure of the full scale of the losses. According to John Nathan,[6] this was an acquisition motivated only by senior executives' desire to please Akio Morita, Sony's founder, and involved little consideration of cultural fit.

The problem with culture is its unpredictability. It is something which can, but might not, throw a spanner in the works of the most carefully laid plans. Gathering hard cultural evidence is also a fairly uncertain task. Nonetheless, just by getting out, kicking the tyres and talking to people it is possible to gain some pretty good impressions. For example, the physical environment and the way people behave towards you, and each other, will often give a lot away. Particular topics to watch will be:

* Attitude to risk and uncertainty
* Attitude to rules and regulations

- Speed of change
- Speed of decision making
- Focus on the big picture rather than detail, or the other way round
- Time horizons – in some sales-led organizations, for example, the long term is tomorrow afternoon.
- The importance of hierarchy, status and the maintenance of power. Is there a directors' dining room where the chips are specially cut so they have square ends? (A real example from the UK engineering industry, believe it or not.)
- Formal versus informal systems
- The degree of openness: how much information is shared?
- Individual versus collective responsibility. As perverse as it may sound, for example, many 'people' organizations operate as a collection of individuals rather than as a coherent well-oiled machine.

A more formal approach would be to use some of the models developed by academics. Academics have tried to characterize culture in a number of different ways. Miles and Snow, for example, categorized organizations into three types according to how they behave strategically. This is summarized in Table 7.1.[7] According to their classification, each is going to behave very differently from the others. For example, whereas defenders fear change, a prospector culture positively thrives on it.

Charles Handy[8] came up with another way of classifying culture, this time relating culture to hierarchy. Again the different cultures will behave very differently, as is shown in Table 7.2. Culture is very important to post-acquisition integration. Clearly, for example, a role culture is going to be very difficult to integrate with a personal culture.

But there is an extra dimension to the whole culture question which goes beyond physical integration. According to Johnson and Scoles,[9] 'matching of strategy and dominant culture is likely to become embedded in successful organisations over a period of time'. This

Table 7.1 Miles's and Snow's characterization of culture

Type of culture	Characteristics of strategic decision-making		
	Dominant objectives	Preferred strategies	Planning and control systems
Defender	Desire for a secure and stable niche in the market	Specialization; cost-efficient production; marketing emphasizes price and service to defend current business; tendency to vertical integration	Centralized, detailed control; emphasis on cost efficiency; extensive use of formal planning
Prospector	Location and exploitation of new product and market opportunities	Growth through product and market development (often in spurts); constant monitoring of environmental change; multiple technologies	Emphasis on flexibility; decentralization control; use of ad hoc measurements
Analyser	Desire to match new ventures to present shape of business	Steady growth through market penetration; exploitation of applied research, followers in the market	Very complicated; coordinating roles between functions (for example product managers); intensive planning

Table 7.2   Handy's characterization of culture

Type of culture	Characteristics	
	Modus operandi	Suited to deliver
Role culture	Structures and systems	Efficiency Repetitive tasks
Task culture	Shared values Ad hoc procedures	Projects or tasks Innovation
Power culture	Command	Rapid response
Personal culture	Personal creativity Expert power	Innovation

can have enormous implications for future strategy if the purpose of an acquisition is to change the strategy of either the target, the buyer, or both. For example, there will be some fundamental cultural mismatches if the key to success in an acquisition is shifting one, or both, organizations from pursuing, say, a strategy of innovation to commercializing a product involving mass marketing, low cost production and tight cost controls. As 'culture is likely to drive strategy'[10] culture must change pretty drastically in these circumstances for the acquisition to be successful. This needs to be picked up in due diligence and built into the post-acquisition plan.

With cross-border deals, culture becomes even less straightforward. Hampden-Turner and Trompenaars[11] have attempted to profile the determinants of national business culture. They give seven dimensions of cultural difference, many of which correspond to the rather more informal checklist given above. They are:

- Universalism v. particularism: universalism is about a single approach based on rules, regulations and codes of practice. Particularism is the opposite. It is about taking everything on its merits. America, for example, is a very universalist culture, France, is particularist.
- Analysing v. integrating: an analysing culture sees managers as being most effective when they analyse, breaking problems into discrete parts and relying on facts and numbers. An integrating culture looks at the bigger picture, and relies more on patterns and relationships. The first is of a mechanical culture whereas the second is much more intuitive and creative. The US is the most analytical culture whereas France tends towards the other end of the spectrum.
- Individualism v. communitarianism: America is the land of the individual; Japan is the land of the team.
- Inner-directed v. outer-directed: this describes the focus of guides to action. An inner-directed culture, such as the USA, leans towards the self as the most important guide to action whereas other cultures will rely more on what are perceived to be the demands of the outside.
- Time as sequence v. time as synchronization: in other words, is the dominant culture to do things quickly or to do things in a coordinated way? This manifests itself in the 'long-term view'. Japan takes a very long-term view, the UK a lot less so.

- Meritocracy v. ascribed status: again the contrast between the USA and France is quite stark here. The Americans are the meritocrats, the French have a much more feudal approach.
- Equality v. hierarchy: what counts most: freedom of the individual or is individuality subordinate to the needs of the firm and its hierarchy?

Whether culture matters in the end of course depends on what plans you have for the new acquisition. If it is going to be totally absorbed then it could be argued that cultural fit does not matter so much as the culture of the acquirer. Whatever this is, it must be an attractive alternative to those people in the target company that you want to keep. If on the other hand the plan is for integration then it helps enormously if the two cultures are similar and, if not, that the acquirer knows what to do about it. The integration of a small, lean, mean, entrepreneurial steel stockholder by a large, lumbering, bureaucratic, process-driven, unimaginative steel producer had to be handled in such a way that the complementarity of the two businesses was not lost. This meant making sure that the steel producer did not overrun the stockholder. The key was to keep them completely separate with an arm's length trading relationship which gave the steel producer first refusal on supply to the stockist but not an absolute right. This might sound perfectly obvious, but it would not have been the steel producer's preferred solution. Left to its own devices it would have tried to control all aspects of the stockholder's operations. Entrepreneurial freedom would have been ground out, market share lost and the management would have left to set up on their own. In short, ignoring cultural considerations would have meant destroying all that made this an attractive acquisition in the first place – the stockholder's ability to penetrate parts of the market that the steel producer could not service.

TUPE

TUPE contains far-reaching rules for the protection of employees' rights on the transfer of an undertaking. It decrees that all employees will transfer automatically to the buyer on the same terms and conditions of employment they had with the seller. As mentioned above, its effect is to prevent acquirers in an asset purchase from picking which employees and which employment conditions they are going to take on. They have to take the whole lot.

Earlier it was mentioned that compared with a TUPE transfer, a share sale is often a non-event. Table 7.3 highlights the differences. TUPE applies where all or part of an economic entity is transferred and where the entity retains its identity following the transfer. An economic entity means an organized grouping of resources which has the objective of pursuing an economic activity, whether or not that activity is central or ancillary. The term 'economic entity' seems key. The transfer of an activity, such as a contract, would probably not be covered by TUPE if no assets and no staff transfer because there would be no economic entity as defined above. The same goes for the sale of just assets. Again, no economic entity is being transferred.

Retained identity is also important. In one case a factory used in a business making diesel engines was sold and subsequently used in a business manufacturing turbines. Assets were sold and employees transferred but it was ruled that there was no transfer of an undertaking because the business post-sale was different to the business pre-sale.

In spite of the foregoing discussion it is worth bearing in mind always that case law is far

Table 7.3 A share sale v. a TUPE transfer

Share sale	TUPE transfer
With a share sale there is no change of employer: the company is still the employer.	With TUPE, when the seller ceases to be the employer the buyer becomes the employer.
No need to consult employees about the transaction.	There is an obligation on both seller and buyer to inform and consult employee representatives about the transaction.
No right to claim automatic unfair dismissal.	TUPE gives employees special protection against dismissals (either by buyer or seller) which are connected with a TUPE transfer. Such dismissals are automatically unfair unless they can be shown to be for an economic, technical or organizational reason entailing changes in the workforce. This is known as an ETO.
Change of contract terms fairly straightforward.	Case law has made it difficult for employers to change terms and conditions of employment in connection with a TUPE transfer – even where an employee freely consents, the employee is free to argue that that change is invalid under TUPE.

from clear and it is perfectly possible for two employment tribunals, faced with exactly the same facts, to reach opposite conclusions as to whether or not TUPE applies. Also TUPE does not apply only to the sale of businesses. It can also apply when a franchise agreement is terminated, when an operation is outsourced or an outsourced operation is brought back in-house, and to internal reorganizations where a business, or part of a business, and its employees are moved from one group company to another. (So sellers can forget about trying to get round TUPE by a hive down or hive up of assets into a different company internally before a transaction and purchasers should be aware that, even in share purchases, later restructuring may be caught by TUPE.)

The best advice to purchasers, therefore, is that if there is any doubt, assume TUPE applies.

The factors to be considered in trying to decide whether or not it does apply were set out by the European Court of Justice in *Spijkers* v *Gebroeders Benedik Abbatoir CV* (1986):

- The type of undertaking or business
- The transfer or otherwise of tangible assets such as buildings and stocks
- The value of intangible assets at the date of transfer
- Whether the majority of staff are taken over by the new employer
- The transfer or otherwise of customers
- The degree of similarity between activities before and after the transfer
- The duration of any interruption in those activities.

Sometimes, of course, it may not be clear which employees should transfer. For example, some employees may not spend all their time in the part of the business to be sold. To avoid any doubt, sellers and buyers will often agree a list of those who will transfer.

CONSEQUENCES IF TUPE APPLIES

In the old days, a seller could sell the assets of a business and make all the employees redundant. The buyer could then selectively re-hire the employees it wanted on terms and conditions that could be worse than they previously enjoyed. TUPE is designed to prevent this type of behaviour. Where an undertaking is transferred from A to B TUPE applies in the following ways.

Contracts of employment

Individuals who were employed by A immediately before the transfer automatically become employees of B from the time of the transfer, on the terms and conditions they previously held with A.

Employees get, in effect, continuity of employment. The purchaser has no power to impose terms and conditions different from those of the vendor. The transferred employee has no right to insist on any superior terms and conditions already being enjoyed by the purchaser's current staff.

What about benefits, such as share options? Case law suggests that transfers under TUPE may be limited to performing the terms of the seller's scheme rather than replicating the benefit.

An employee can choose to object to the transfer. Where an employee does object, his or her contract will automatically terminate on transfer. Alternatively the employee might resign and claim constructive dismissal in response to the buyer's anticipatory breach (see below).

As far as due diligence is concerned, the buyer will be particularly keen to confirm that key employees will transfer and not object.

Transfer of rights and liabilities

Company B inherits all A's rights and liabilities in relation to individuals transferring. In other words, the buyer inherits liability for all the seller's wrongdoings pre-transfer (except for failure to consult – see below). Furthermore, the seller is released from any obligations towards transferred employees once the deal is done.

It is clearly an important element of due diligence to make sure that the seller has not been up to anything which will rebound on the buyer once the deal is done. Personal injury claims will almost certainly transfer. Others to watch for are discrimination in all its forms, unfair dismissals and wages arrears. Due diligence and legal protection are separate weapons and it is therefore also a good idea to get something in the sale and purchase agreement saying that the seller will contribute to the costs of such pre-transfer breaches if there are any.

A curious by-product of liabilities transferring under TUPE is that not only does liability for negligence transfer but so does the right to an indemnity under the seller's employer's liability insurance. The purchaser, therefore, can claim under the seller's insurance policy for any successful claims for pre-transfer accidents. Nevertheless, it is still a good idea to get an indemnity to cover any such claims.

Collective agreements

If the entity is not merged into the purchaser's business and thereby maintains its distinct identity, collective agreements with a trade union recognized by A are inherited by B.

Union recognition   Where A recognizes a union as far as the transferring employees are concerned, and again if the entity maintains an identity of its own after transfer, B must recognize the union.

If an entity is merged, other trade union recognition provisions may come into play. If the majority of workers in a collective bargaining unit are members of a trade union requesting recognition, recognition will be compulsory. If at least 10 per cent of a unit are members of the union, the union may lodge a request for recognition. If the employer refuses, there may be a ballot. A majority in favour of at least 40 per cent of those entitled to vote will result in compulsory recognition if there are more than 20 employees.

Due diligence therefore needs to ascertain the extent of union membership and whether there is a recognition agreement in place or whether recognition has been requested.

Information   Company A must inform recognized trade unions about the consequences of the transfer, and B must provide A with sufficient information to enable this to be done.

Consultation   In certain circumstances, it may be necessary for A or B to consult with recognized trade unions or elected employee representatives about the transfer. This is dealt with below.

Dismissals

Dismissal of any employee (whether before or after the transfer) for any reason connected with the transfer is automatically unfair unless the reason is 'an economic, technical or organisational reason entailing changes in the workforce' (an 'ETO Reason') in which case the dismissal is fair if reasonable in the circumstances. The words 'entailing changes in the workforce' mean that the ETO defence is not as widespread as might be first imagined. It is only available when the employer is changing the structure of its workforce by reducing numbers or changing functions. This means that the only dismissals which in practice would be allowed as an ETO Reason would be genuine redundancies or because of major restructuring.

Any pre-transfer dismissals made in connection with the transfer are automatically unfair, and a buyer will be liable for any pre-transfer dismissals made by the seller in connection with the transfer. Buyers should look for an indemnity to guard against this.

OBLIGATIONS THAT DO NOT TRANSFER UNDER TUPE

Obligations that do not transfer are:

- Occupational pension rights – yet. This may change in the very near future. Amendments have been made to the Acquired Rights Directive which enable each Member State to decide whether pension rights should be brought into the national laws which enact the Acquired Rights Directive. As mentioned below, the UK is long overdue in implementing these changes. Leaks to the newspapers suggest that in the UK pensions will not transfer.
- Objecting employees. If employees exercise their right to object to the transfer they will usually be deemed to have resigned. It is worth mentioning again that this right should be remembered if there are key employees you are keen to keep. As mentioned above, if their objection is not to the transfer but to the buyer's plans to change working conditions, employees can resign and still claim compensation against the seller because of the buyer's anticipatory breach of contract. This liability will not transfer from seller to buyer.

- Criminal liability. Criminal liabilities remain with the seller. These might derive from breaches of health and safety or of the Working Time Regulations prior to transfer. Any civil liabilities will, however, transfer to the buyer.

HARMONIZATION

In practice the buyer of a business will often wish to harmonize the terms and conditions of employment of new employees with the terms and conditions of existing employees. Under TUPE, even if transferring employees agree to changes in their terms and conditions, it is by no means certain that any agreed variations following a TUPE transfer are valid. Credit Suisse First Boston found out to its cost when employees, who had transferred from Barclays de Zoete Wedd, agreed to be bound to new non-compete and non-solicitation clauses in exchange for significant cash bonuses. The Court of Appeal ruled that, because the agreement amounted to a waiving of rights under TUPE, and was, therefore, to the employees' detriment, the new clauses were not binding even though the employees had agreed to them.

Thus an employee could sign a written agreement consenting to a change but this would not be binding and the employee could subsequently claim to be employed under the old terms. The safer route from a legal point of view is to make the contractual changes by dismissing employees and immediately reemploying them on new terms. This might not be universally popular with those affected and would therefore have to be explained very carefully. There may, in fact, be a legal obligation to consult with trade unions or employee representatives as there is when more than 20 employees are affected by redundancies. Just to rub salt in, their dismissals would still be automatically unfair. This would give rise to an entitlement to a basic award for unfair dismissal, and a compensatory award if employees could show a continuing loss, for example by showing that they were going to be worse off than under the old terms.

Time is a great healer. The longer that harmonization can be delayed the less likely it will be considered 'in connection with' the TUPE transfer. But be warned, there is no set time. The employment tribunal will decide each case on its merits.

The real key to harmonization is to find an operational reason for changing terms and conditions which is unrelated to the original transfer. A completely new set of benefits introduced across the board for all employees might do it. Clearly, one of the consequences of TUPE can be an increase in employment costs!

COLLECTIVE CONSULTATION

There is an obligation for the seller to inform and consult either trade union representatives or employee representatives on all TUPE transfers. Representatives must be told:

- That a relevant transfer is to take place
- When it is to take place
- The reasons for it
- The legal economic and social implications of the transfer
- The measures the employer, or the buyer, is planning to take in relation to the affected employees.

If there are no plans, say so. If there are plans, the employer has an obligation to consult with representatives of the employees who are transferring. Plans could include redundancies, restructuring, contract changes and changes to working practices. Consultation must be genuine, that is undertaken with a view to reaching agreement, with the seller duty bound to consider, and respond to, any representations made. It is no good turning up to consultations with decisions clearly already made. The purchaser is required to give the seller the information it needs to discharge its consultation obligations.

There is no time period laid down for consultations – only that they must take place 'long enough before the relevant transfer' to enable consultations to take place. The regulations even set out the rules on electing employee representatives. The Collective Redundancies and Transfer of Undertakings (Protection of Employment)(Amendment) Regulations 1999 say that as far as electing employee representatives go:

- Arrangements should be made to ensure the election is fair.
- The employer must determine the number of representatives to be elected to ensure that the interests of all affected employees are represented and there is no restriction on numbers.
- The employer must decide whether to have one class of representative for everyone or different representatives for different types of employee.
- The representatives' term of office needs to be decided. Naturally it should be at least as long as the consultation period.
- Only affected employees can stand for election.
- Employees must be allowed to vote for as many candidates as there are representatives to be elected.
- Voting should be done in secret.
- The employer must make sure that votes are accurately counted.

There is no real way around consulting. Certainly the need to preserve confidentiality will not be accepted by the courts as an excuse for not consulting with the workforce. 'Special circumstances' which make it impractical to consult may be allowed, but they are few and far between. In addition, the employer must demonstrate that it has done everything it could in the circumstances to comply with its consultation obligations.

SOME PRACTICAL POINTS

As already mentioned, the obligation to consult falls on the seller. It is its employees who are transferring under TUPE. Strictly speaking, the buyer's role is confined to providing the seller with information on what measures are proposed. In practice, the buyer would be foolish not to be involved in any pre-completion consultation. Furthermore, the TUPE principles established by cases have a habit of changing. It is advisable, therefore, for a buyer to obtain an indemnity from a seller in relation to failures to consult under TUPE.

A seller may well find that TUPE puts him in an impossible position. For example, suppose a deal is signed and about to complete. Stock Exchange rules say you have to release price sensitive information to the market. On the other hand TUPE says you have to consult with the workforce before the deal is done – which means disclosing price sensitive information to the workforce ahead of the market. There is no right answer to this sort of dilemma. Which makes the seller most uncomfortable: not informing the Stock Exchange or the possibility of a protective award against him under TUPE? The latter will cost a maximum of 13 weeks pay per affected employee.

What the seller really needs, of course, is time between signing and completion. As the TUPE transfer will not take place until completion, there is then time to consult.

Again, all the procedures outlined above about electing employee representatives and consulting with them cannot, under the letter of the law, be avoided. However, in practice, a seller may be able to consult directly with individual employees, especially if there is no union representation. This will probably not be enough to satisfy the TUPE requirements but obviously if individual employees feel they have been kept informed, then they are much less likely to bring a claim that they have not been collectively consulted. If they do bring a claim, the employment tribunal would take into account the fact that some consultation had taken place before it makes an award.

AND FINALLY ON TUPE

There are two last things to remember. The first is that European Directives are implemented differently in different countries. The UK's approach to implementing European labour laws tends to be to implement the minimum it can get away with. This is not the case in many other European countries so do not automatically assume that all of Europe is the same as the UK: it is not.

The second is that the law is constantly changing. The UK, for example, is long overdue in implementing the new (June 1998) Acquired Rights Directive. Watch for changes. When TUPE is amended it is quite possible that it will include an obligation on a buyer to provide occupational pension rights.

Conclusion

Human Resources can be a source of considerable risk in a deal and the importance of the human factor in successful acquisitions should never be underestimated. Human Resources due diligence is not always easy because of the constraints imposed upon it by the data protection legislation. It is further complicated by the different rules and regulations even in jurisdictions with the same sources of employment law. But because of its importance, it needs to be done well. It needs to be done from both a deal and a post-deal perspective and it must cover both 'hard' and 'soft' issues. The Acquired Rights Directive is a particularly complex and uncertain piece of legislation which will further complicate asset deals.

8 *Management due diligence*

Management can add more value to an acquisition than almost anything. On the other hand, 'there is no prospect so good that incompetent management cannot screw it up'.[1] Most private equity investors will tell you that their decisions on whether or not to invest in a target will be driven more than anything by their views on the management. Even without dire warnings about the dangers of the wrong management, intuitively, a settled and secure top management team deliberately chosen to balance each other's strengths and weaknesses has got to be better at sorting out the aftermath of an acquisition than one which fears for its future or has been cobbled together without reference to the tasks in hand or, even worse, as a political compromise.

With somewhere between 50 and 75 per cent of key managers leaving of their own accord within two to three years of being acquired,[2] why is management due diligence so rarely carried out as a discipline in its own right? To take an extreme example, according to the DTI report into Robert Maxwell's business affairs,[3] Samuel Montagu failed to read the 1971–73 Department of Trade and Industry reports in sufficient detail. 'These set out in severe terms how unsuitable Maxwell's business methods were. Samuel Montagu, however, did not think it necessary to know in detail how Maxwell had run companies before flotation.'[4]

The reason why management due diligence is not carried out more is a mixture of the following:

- Often it is carried out informally. It tends to be something that is undertaken almost subconsciously rather than as a recognized and distinct part of the due diligence process.
- Management due diligence, as propounded by those who carry it out, comes across as such a black art that it is not widely understood.
- Another powerful reason is the old chestnut that acquirers get so wrapped up in the legals and financials that they neglect the other forms of due diligence.
- Very often a purchaser will only get proper access to management once the deal is done.
- There is often a feeling that it only needs to be done if there is going to be a merger or a reorganization of businesses.
- It is frequently half done. Purchasers will often commission management referencing, for example, by employing a headhunter to rummage through the pasts of key management.

Although management due diligence is still far from being carried out on every deal, there are a number of factors combining to make it more common:

- The need for transparency, objectivity, and fairness in appointing a new management structure
- The complexity involved in management selection

- Similar assessments are now common in many large businesses, which means it is becoming a generally more accepted practice.

Against its widespread use in M&A is the unfortunate complexity of management selection. It is difficult at the best of times to get the management structure right. In the heat of a deal, it is practically impossible without excellent planning. On the other hand, the selection process cannot be too slow. If it is, the evidence suggests that key people leave and morale drops to damaging levels. If the selection process is not managed properly, politically motivated turf wars can develop, again with detrimental consequences for the combined business.

Many acquirers continue to rely on their judgement and intuition. The argument for a rigorous process of evaluation is that it gives new insights into managers' capacity to deliver, thereby reducing some of the uncertainty, and hence risk, in a deal.

Management due diligence provides an impartial external perspective on management. It uses disciplined methods to evaluate management, both as individuals and as a team. This is a process that takes us well beyond initial impressions or self-reports by the managers themselves.

Approaches to management selection

The starting point to selecting new management is knowing how much integration there is going to be. For businesses which, for example, are bought because they are poorly managed and which are going to stand alone, the evidence suggests[5] that success rates will increase if the management is replaced. For fully integrated businesses the opposite applies and you will want to pick the best from both management teams – or at least recognize where the management needs to be strengthened. One way to do this is to pick the leader for each area then let the leader appoint the team from the overall pool. The advantage of this is that it is quick and that the leader has a vested interest in picking the best people. The drawbacks are:

- how do you select the leader?
- the leader's relative lack of knowledge of the management in the other company.

The latter problem could be overcome by appointing two leaders, one from each side, but opting for a solution that does not give clear leadership usually creates more problems than it solves.

The other way is independent management appraisal.

Management appraisals

Management appraisals seek to give an objective assessment of senior managers' capability both individually and collectively. They set out to evaluate management's ability to meet the challenges facing the business and to provide an external benchmark with which to compare more intuitive judgements. The capabilities required to succeed may vary to some degree according to the nature of the business and the market it is in. A high tech start-up is going to require different skills to a rationalization acquisition in a mature industry.

APPROACH

The appraisal approach to managerial due diligence will generally place more emphasis on structured interviews conducted by experienced assessors than on psychometric tests. This is not to say that psychometric tests do not have a role to play – they do – it is just that they are not as acceptable to senior managers, and in the right hands, a structured interview can be fairly reliable.

If interviews raise particular concerns about an individual that could be clarified in a more intensive assessment, psychometric tests may be used to give a deeper insight into that individual's predispositions, attitude, leadership style and so on. They are also particularly useful in putting together effective management teams.

Before assessors can begin they must first be clear what skills, resources and experience are needed for an acquisition to be successful. The aim is then to collect data in order to be able to judge the degree to which target managers (and maybe also managers in the buyer's company) possess the attributes needed.

Information collection

There are five main ways in which management appraisal information is collected. These are not mutually exclusive.

- Documentation analysis: reviews of CVs, job evaluations and anything else written by or about the managers being examined.
- Past-orientated interviews: fact-based, structured interviews where the interviewer will gather data on past performance. The interviewer starts at the beginning of the candidate's career and works through to the latest job. Questions for each of the different positions held will be of the type 'What would your colleagues from those days say were your strengths and weaknesses?', 'Give me an example of a conflict and how you handled it', 'Tell me about failures', 'Tell me about a project which was your responsibility'. Often there will be a 'good cop bad cop' style of interviewing. The theory is that the past is the best predictor of the future.
- References: these are discussions with people who have seen the manager in action. Current and former colleagues, 360-degree feedback sessions, analysts, investors, advisers, customers and suppliers are the most obvious sources. Information from the last two groups could very easily be gathered as part of the commercial due diligence.
- Work samples: work samples are answers to hypothetical questions. Target management is asked to answer a series of 'what-if' type questions, such as 'How would you manage the integration of these two companies?' 'In such and such a role, what would be your priorities going forward?'
- Under certain circumstances the audit can also include experienced practitioners watching the team in action and so observe the quality of their interactions and of their relationships with each other. This involves shadowing managers for a day.

Appendix B3 lists the commonly sought management competencies.

Relative effectiveness

What little research there is suggests that past-orientated interviews are the most reliable.[6] Reference-taking is useful, but only to find out about someone's track record as part of management referencing (see below) rather than management assessment. It may expose known problems although this cannot be guaranteed. References tend to be poor predictors of future performance and the reliability of the information received is often difficult to evaluate.

CARRYING OUT INTERVIEWS

Why are interviews so effective and so widely used when there is a myriad of ready-made psychological tests with prescribed methods of scoring available? The truth is that each has its proper place (which is why the topic of psychological testing is covered below). The real advantages of interviews is that they:

- Do not require specialist knowledge and equipment
- Can be tailored for the specific acquisition under review
- Give the interviewer the opportunity to explore or probe certain responses
- Can be made to take account of all sorts of situations and all sorts of people not taken into account by standardized tests.

However, to be truly useful, interviews must be properly planned and properly carried out. They are not cosy chats but controlled situations in which one person, the interviewer, is in charge and directs proceedings. As a rough guide this means the interviewee doing about 85 per cent of the talking. Of course, to direct proceedings you need to have a pretty good idea of what it is you want to achieve – which makes this form of due diligence no different from any other. Management assessment interviews typically last about two hours. This is the minimum time required to really understand what individuals' achievements have been and what their capabilities are.

Interview style
Whoever is assessing management has a choice of three interview styles:

- Dialogue. This is the style adopted mostly by headhunters and selection consultants in one-to-one interviews. They see themselves as operating as an honest broker, which, with management assessments, is exactly what any intermediary should be aiming for. The aim is to establish a genuine dialogue where both parties put themselves forward honestly but in the best light. Real opinions are expressed and if difficulties are encountered both parties will talk them through in a genuine attempt to solve them.
- Conventional interviewing. This is the interview style that will be familiar to many. The interviewer deliberately establishes and maintains distance from the interviewee. No relationship is developed and there is certainly no trading of opinions.
- Stress interviewing. This is where the interviewee is deliberately put under pressure by the type of questions and the manner in which they are asked. It is apparently popular amongst those acquirers who spent their formative years in English boarding schools, justified as a means of finding out 'what someone is made of'. What they forget is that for every insight produced under such conditions many more are lost because of defensiveness, hostility, lack of rapport or simply because the person on the receiving end can see it for what it is and plays the game accordingly.

Interview structure

As structured question-and-answer sessions, interviews have a beginning, a middle and an end. The beginning is possibly the most important, though everyone would argue it should not be. The reason is that first impressions are important. Although careful interviewers will try to avoid early judgements, voice, appearance and body language are all important influencers of the interviewer's attitude and all occur on first contact. The key is to explore favourable impressions and not be biased by unfavourable ones.

The early stages are also where interviewer and respondent develop rapport. 'Rapport' is a difficult term to define but is important because it is what creates the comfortable, cooperative relationship necessary for best results. Rapport is developed by a combination of factors:

- Opening niceties. Most people do not want confrontation. They want their dealings with others to be pleasant, and they want to be liked and seen as likeable. Empathy and normal standards of politeness will help develop rapport.
- Scene setting. The respondent needs to be told what the interview is to be about, the credentials of the interviewer, what is going to be done with the information, whether the interview is confidential, and, if so, how that confidentiality is going to be guaranteed.
- Removing anxiety. Anxiety manifests itself in many ways: hostility, forgetfulness, incomplete responses, responses aimed at pleasing the interviewer. Careful scene-setting, beginning with the least threatening questions, calm and time all help remove irrelevant sources of anxiety.

Having established rapport, the relationship has to be maintained as the interview proceeds. Things to watch for[7] are:

- The effect of the content of the questions
- The order in which they are presented
- Bias
- Emotional and other threats to good relations

QUESTIONS

Asking effective questions is not easy. Questions can perform five functions:

1. Collection. This is to fill in blanks in the CV. They will usually be of the straightforward closed or yes/no type.
2. Exploration. This aims to gain an understanding of what lies behind the words on a CV. This is perhaps the most common form of questioning in managerial assessments. Questions will most likely be open-ended. This is the most common format because it allows the respondent complete freedom to reply without suggesting what the answer should be.

Questions, of course, can vary from the extremely general to the very specific. A combination of the two usually works quite well with very general open-ended questions used as openers to a topic, with specific issues followed up when the interviewee responds. For example, the questioning might begin with a very general exploration of the CV, for example, 'What were your responsibilities at Global Industries?' to be followed later by very specific exploration of what the candidate was actually doing, thinking and feeling at the time, 'In what ways did this job broaden your experience?'.

3. Search. Here we are no longer trawling to see what comes up but instead are on the trail of something we know exists but which may not come to the surface unless we dive in and get it. Search is very important in management assessments because it should allow us to get to what really makes the managers tick. Questions can relate to any part of the CV, past or present, and are probably best illustrated with examples:

- How do you handle conflict? Tell me about the worst disagreement you have experienced during your career and what came of it
- How do you get ideas accepted?
- Tell me about your relationship with your boss
- What do you feel was your most worthwhile achievement?
- What problems do you find when dealing with subordinates? How do you handle them?
- What has been the most satisfying achievement in your career to date?
- What are the three most important skills that you have developed in your career so far?

Search will also relate to the future:

- Why do you think you can be effective after the acquisition? What do you think you can offer that the new organization needs going forward?
- Which of your qualifications and experience do you feel are most relevant?
- What do you *not* have that you think will be needed going forward?

4. Probe. Probe is used to dig deeper, when the interviewer is not sure that what has been heard is correct or complete. Probe is also used to counter evasion – not uncommon in management assessments and given the levels of experience of the average interviewee this should not be surprising. Questions might include:

- Can we just go over that once again?
- I am sorry, but I must be clear on this one. Why exactly did you do that?
- We seem to have wandered off the subject . . .

Effective probing can also be silent or near silent. A nod of the head or an 'I see' or 'Go on' to give encouragement or a slightly raised eyebrow to indicate surprise may be all that is needed to dig deeper.

5. Check. A check aims to do just that: to check that the interviewer has understood correctly. The most effective means of checking is to paraphrase what the interviewee has just said. Another is to ask the same question some time later.

BODY LANGUAGE

Answers to questions do not tell everything. Body language can often tell a lot more and, because it is hard to disguise, it can often be nearer the truth. For these reasons it is important to be on the look-out for subtle, spontaneous reactions. Few interviewees at this level will blush, but many will look away or at their shoes when not wholly convinced by the answer they have just given.

Similarly, the assessors must ensure their body language and verbal messages do not say different things or their body language does not reveal what they really think of the manager or the answers given. On the other hand, body language can be a great help in encouraging the interviewee to talk.

THE CONCLUSION

It is important that the interview ends with both sides feeling it has been a worthwhile exercise. In particular interviewees should not be left feeling that there has not been a proper opportunity to say everything that they feel needs saying or that they have been denied the opportunity of really selling themselves. The interviewer, as controller of the process, can avoid a sense of dissatisfaction by winding down the interview in a slow premeditated way. Save some of the easier questions for winding down, signal clearly that the end is in sight, ask if there is anything else the respondent wants to cover, and if there is, keep listening and keep making notes – unless the interviewee is particularly anxious, in which case it might be wise to lay down tools and give the interviewee the chance to open up. Many do when the pressure is off.

Psychometric tests

Something like 70 per cent of companies will use some kind of psychometric testing at some stage on their workforce. Psychometric tests quantify personality. Personality, like ability, is a key influence on performance. It is also the key to building a balanced team.

Psychometric tests are usually self-reporting questionnaires which are used to uncover aspects of personality. They ask about preferred ways of behaving and of relating to other people. Carrying out psychometric tests properly and professionally means either consulting a chartered occupational psychologist or going on, and passing, a prescribed training course. Reputable publishers will not supply tests unless the person carrying them out is suitably qualified.

Although there are many different forms of personality questionnaire – there some 1200 on the UK market alone – they all tend to fall in to one of two psychological camps:

- Type. These assign the respondent to a specific personality type.
- Trait. These categorize according to personality trait, where a trait is an aspect of personality which the respondent possesses to a greater or lesser extent.

We will look at testing personality types first, explore how different personality types influence team behaviour and then discuss the assessment of personality traits.

PERSONALITY TYPE

By far the most widely used type of questionnaire is the *Myers-Briggs Type Indicator®* (MBTI®). This is explained in more detail in Appendix B4. Type questionnaires owe their structure to the work of Swiss psychologist, Carl Jung. At their most basic they categorize human behaviour into four base types, hence the term 'four quadrant behaviour' (4QB), although many of the commercially available tests go well beyond this, breaking the basic four types into many more sub-types.

Jung's work, published in the 1920s, developed a theory to describe the predictable differences between the ways in which people behave in different situations. His theory basically says that variations in behaviour are caused by the way we *prefer* to use our minds. The word 'prefer' is key because Jungian theory is very much based on an 'either/or' view of personality.

Jung starts with the proposition that there are two ways in which our mind reacts to information:

- We receive it (perceiving). Or
- We process it (judging).

There are, according to Jung, only two ways of perceiving:

- Sensing
- Intuition

And two ways of judging:

- Thinking
- Feeling

Thus, there are four key processes which we use to understand the world around us. These are shown in Figure 8.1.

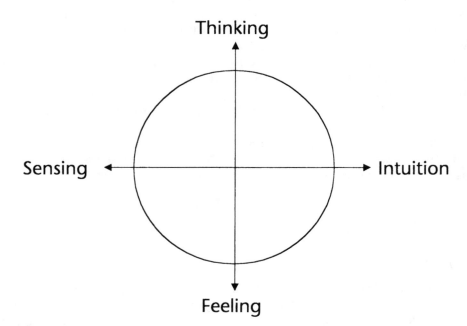

Figure 8.1   Jung's personality types

Thinking–Feeling

Thinkers take a detached and logical approach but may overlook the human side of things. Feelers are the exact opposite. They base their decisions on their likely impact on other people. At work this translates into a desire to please.

Sensing–Intuition

Sensors are usually practical and take things one step at a time. These are the people who prefer dealing with facts and detail. The intuitive types prefer the big picture. They tend to follow their noses rather than rely on their senses. They work in short inspirational bursts rather than make steady progress.

Jung overlaid two further divisions, extravert and introvert.

These days, Jung's basic ideas are still used although the descriptions to identify the four main quadrants seem to have moved to DISC:

- **D**ominant or Driving
- **I**nspiring or Influencing
- **S**upporting or Steadfast
- **C**oordinating or Compliant

Under normal circumstances, type questionnaires are best used for development and training purposes, although they can be used to select people for jobs if the questionnaires are designed to capture the amounts of a particular characteristic a respondent possesses so that comparisons can be made between candidates. As far as management assessments are concerned they can be very valuable because of the insights they can give in team building. Type tests can help show the sort of environments in which people prefer to work, the way in which they are likely to go about their work, and the ideal personality of any colleagues with whom they would work best.

TEAMS

John Adair, a management guru, argues that any corporate or organizational dynamic has three parts to it:

- the team
- the task
- the individual.

He likened them to three interactive and overlapping circles, as shown in Figure 8.2. Each circle has an influence on the others, but should never overwhelm them. Each has a set of needs which need to be met for the team as a whole to be successful. Any imbalance will mean failure:

- Individuals all have their own social, personal, professional needs. If one or more individuals selfishly assert their needs to the detriment of others, the team is divided and the task is unlikely to be accomplished.
- Task must be clear and completed but must not overwhelm the individual or the team. Many organizations are task-driven and there is nothing wrong with that. The problems come when teams and individuals feel undervalued. The result is high staff turnover, with

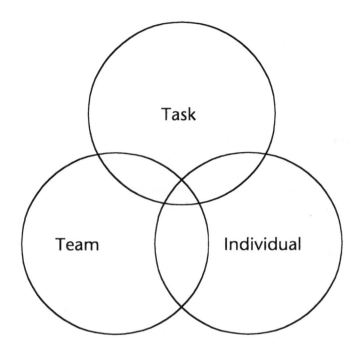

Figure 8.2   Team dynamics

the consequent cost of recruiting and training, and only shallow experience resulting in bad decisions and lower standards.
- Team must be coordinated and operate efficiently but, like the task, must not overwhelm the individual.

Although focused teams are invaluable in certain circumstances, the more common is the balanced team. A task-driven organization will probably naturally tend to recruit dominant **D** types. The problem with **D**s, and for all the other types, is that for every strength there is a weakness. Assertive, decisive, direct high **D** types are also aggressive, impatient and insensitive. Two or three high-**C**s running a business would result in immaculate sets of accounts, a first-class reporting system and brilliant sales literature. On the other hand, the sales effort would be laughable.

Questionnaires like the *MBTI*® and Belbin's Team Role Inventory can provide considerable insight into the way a person interrelates with others, their preferred role in group situations and their favoured work environment. This can help understand the strengths and weaknesses of a team.

Belbin suggests that there are eight primary roles which people adopt in teams:

- Shaper: the driver, the agenda setter.
- Chairman: the team's controller. This is the person which makes the team cohere and shapes how it moves towards group objectives.
- Monitor-Evaluator: this is the analytical, tenacious type whose role is to evaluate ideas and suggestions.
- Plant: an unorthodox, imaginative ideas generator.

- Team worker: a sympathetic diplomat who supports team members and builds team spirit.
- Company worker: a stable, cautious organizer who translates ideas into action.
- Completer-Finisher: this is the person whose role is to get the job done. Tends to be disciplined and conscientious.
- Resource investigator: this is the communicator with the outside world. The extravert, enthusiastic, 'life and soul of the party' type.

PERSONALITY TRAITS

Trait questionnaires measure the different amounts of personality characteristics which we all possess. The theory is that the traits are predictive of behaviour. Questionnaires set out to measure between 3 and 30 of the 20 000 or so personality traits that are said to exist. For example, two of the most commonly used psychological tests in the UK are 16PF (Sixteen Personality Factor Questionnaire), which, as the name suggests, measures 16 personality traits, and the Occupational Personality Questionnaire® (OPQ®) which measures 30 traits. In other words, not all tests set out to measure all traits. This does not matter too much since there are probably only five that really count. There is a huge body of research which suggests that personality can be broken down into five dimensions or domains. There is another body which asserts that in fact three dimensions underpin all observable behaviour. The real argument amongst psychologists, therefore, tends not to be whether we should attempt to get closer to measuring 20 000 variables, but whether in fact we should use three rather than five personality dimensions.

The five dimensions of personality, often referred to as the 'Big Five', are as follows.

Action

This dimension is all about an individual's attitude towards others. At one end are the type **D**, tough minded, do it and do it now, individuals who are results-orientated, who have little time or patience for those needing support and who tend to work best with other **D** types. At the other end of the dimension are the warmer, people-focused individuals. They have a genuine concern for other people and achieve results by listening and through consensus.

Thinking

This dimension is really about structure. The high-structure person is tidy, systematic and leaves nothing to chance. The low-structure person does not worry too much about formal structures or schedules, as long as things get done. They have a much greater preference for the big picture rather than the detail.

Relating

This dimension refers to how a person relates to other people. The extravert hogs the limelight, is sociable and outgoing – and impulsive. The introverted person has a tendency to take a more cautious and restrained approach and does not relish open competition with other people.

Feeling

Feeling is about self-assurance. The high self-confidence individual is relaxed and optimistic, calm under pressure, enjoys responsibility and being put to the test. Low-confidence individuals are more pessimistic, cannot take pressure well, question their abilities, and prefer predictability to challenges.

Conformity

Conformity is about the way in which an individual responds to change. The conformist is happiest operating within the status quo, solves problems by applying well-tried methods and is better at implementing plans than creating them. The non-conformist is much more change-orientated, innovative and concerned with individual expression to the point, sometimes, of resenting structure and order.

Management referencing

Even if they do not feel the need for full-blown management appraisals, many acquirers want to satisfy themselves on the background and integrity of management teams, especially if management are expected not only to stay but also to be central to the success of the acquisition. In these circumstances they are likely to require some management referencing. The process is as follows.

First of all a CV will provide the basic background information for the individual(s) concerned. The next phase seeks to expand and verify the information contained in the CV. This is done through a mixture of desk research and primary information sources. Typical questions would include:

- Are the qualifications and job/education history accurate?
- How has the person performed in the past? Is this as claimed?
- How honest are they? What is their reputation as far as integrity is concerned?
- What is central to their motivation? What makes them perform?
- Where do they want to go?

Typically due diligence investigations will cover:

- Address: confirmation that the manager lives at the address claimed; brief assessment of the residence.
- Credit: any county court judgements or other bad credit associated with either the person or the address?
- Media checks: are there any past articles which may cause concern?
- Past experience check: interviews with previous employers to confirm information on the CV (dates, remuneration, responsibilities and so on), reasons for leaving, and any information on past performance and character.
- Verification of professional memberships.
- Industry enquiries: to try to establish whether there is anything in the manager's background which might cause concern. Is the individual seen as competent, honest and respected? Ex-colleagues make particularly revealing sources.
- A list of current directorships and shareholdings.

Reporting

Reports should give an insight into individual managers and into the capabilities of the senior management team as a team.

For individuals, there should be an executive summary on each of the key managers assessed, which:

- Profiles their capabilities against a broad range of general management competencies
- Matches these against the managerial challenges that will need to be addressed over the next few years
- Highlights their strengths and weaknesses
- Benchmarks them against senior managers in other organizations
- Indicates what areas of development or support would compensate for the weaknesses
- Provides the behavioural evidence to back up these conclusions

For the team, or proposed team, the report should contain a profile of the senior management team which:

- Maps out the overall strengths and weaknesses of the management team as a whole
- Identifies where individuals' strengths complement each other
- Exposes any specific experience or capability that may be lacking in the team

Reporting will probably be against some or all of the following nine attributes, although more detail may be sought depending on the nature of the acquisition and its integration. For a more detailed checklist of management competencies see Appendix B3.

- Strategic vision: here the measure is the degree to which the candidate is able to formulate and articulate a vision of the business several years down the road. To do this requires the candidate to show an entrepreneurial streak coupled with a realistic understanding of the environment in which the business operates. In turn this requires more of an external than an internal focus.
- Leadership/communication. Interviews would point to a candidate who has confidence and conviction, who can build and motivate teams, who sets goals and objectives, guides staff towards them and who is quick to confront any performance problems.
- Customer and market orientation. Investigations demonstrate empathy with customers and the needs of the marketplace. Candidates will be able to respond to and anticipate change and be able to build the same customer/market dedication in the staff.
- Teamwork
- Performance orientation. Evidence of delivering, for example, profit or sales growth (or both) and a personality which sets and communicates firm business goals and tracks performance against them.
- Functional capability. This usually boils down to technical – if the candidate is a professional such as a production or finance director – or industry knowledge, if knowledge of an industry is more important than technical skills.
- Change orientation
- Energy and resilience. Evidence of drive, stamina, hard work and resilience is key.
- Ability to deal with pressure. Candidates can control responses in times of stress and are not uncomfortable with ambiguity and complexity.

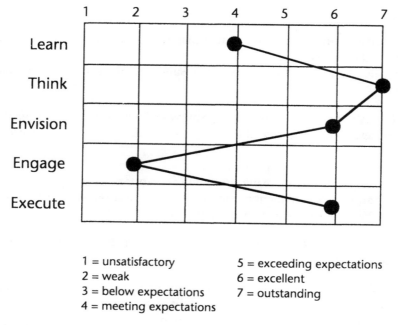

1 = unsatisfactory
2 = weak
3 = below expectations
4 = meeting expectations

5 = exceeding expectations
6 = excellent
7 = outstanding

Figure 8.3   Competency profile

Each member of the management team is plotted on the following matrix:

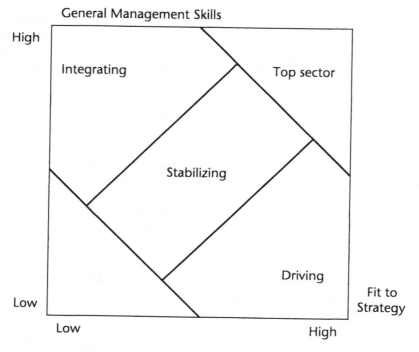

Figure 8.4   Assessment of the management team

Often the above topics are rolled into broader headings as is shown in Figure 8.3, which is a good example of the type of summary produced by a typical executive search consultant.

Typically, the consultant will report on each individual and the team as a whole, drawing always on external benchmarks of ability. Figure 8.4 shows how the combined abilities might be summarized in diagrammatic form. Each member of the management team would be plotted on the chart and an assessment made of the team's overall balance. As well as the diagrammatic representation there will be a commentary of the manager's rating against each attribute and an assessment of the strengths and weaknesses of each.

The point to remember is that management assessments are just that: assessments. Even with the help of psychometric testing, this is not an exact science which is why it is so important that the consultant has wide-ranging Human Resources experience.

Management assessment reports may reinforce opinions already held or expose specific risks to be plugged. On the other hand, their conclusions might come as a complete surprise. There may then be a case for revisiting the data and checking things out in more detail.

Appendix A8 provides a short checklist for management due diligence reporting.

Communication with management

Inevitably, management will be nervous about management assessments. All that can really be done about this is to tell the truth. The script might go something like this:

- A management audit has been commissioned as part of the commercial due diligence.
- This is our normal practice with all acquisitions. The aim is to give reassurance that there will be a balanced team in place which can deliver results in spite of the challenges.
- Everyone has their relative strengths and weaknesses but in a balanced team these are compensated for.
- This process is a rigorous, disciplined and independent way of establishing what these are and identifying where, if at all, some development or support is needed.
- It is an opportunity for management to demonstrate their capabilities.

Reports are confidential but feedback to managers can usually be arranged. Feedback will normally consist of a run through the main conclusions of the assessment, exploring the implications of these to individuals and/or for the team as a whole.

Who should carry out the assessments?

As mentioned above, someone with experience of recruiting and interviewing at a senior level should carry out the assessments. Normally it is the province of headhunters and other similar specialists such as firms of business psychologists. The main reason for this is the ability to benchmark what they find against their experience in the wider world. The last people to carry out management assessments should be general consultants who tend to assess against their own views of the world and their own prejudices. Usually sadly lacking in real world experience, they have no external frame of reference.

Post-acquisition planning

It is one thing to decide which managers or groups of employees are key. It is quite another to retain them once the deal is done. Before negotiations have even finished, employees will start to become anxious. Ideally, therefore, key employees should learn of their fate well before due diligence ends. Understanding their motives and getting the culture right is a start, as is understanding what you want from them.

However, very often there is no substitute for cash, not just to retain employees, but also to ensure their performance through the uncertainty of the negotiation period. The reason for considering this as a due diligence topic is that, according to findings from McKinsey and Watson Wyatt,[8] 'generally, retention incentives add 5 to 10 per cent to the total cost of a deal – enough to wreck it – and it is therefore vital to anticipate them.' Once quantified, the cost of retention incentives can be fed into the valuation model just like all the other due diligence findings.

Conclusion

The right management is critical to the success of a deal. It must make sense, therefore, to include management appraisals in the due diligence programme. The objective is to assess management's capability, both as individuals and as a team, in the context of what needs to be achieved post-acquisition. The approach places most weight on past-orientated interviews but supplements these with other types of interview and possibly also psychometric tests. A Human Resources professional should be able to benchmark the target management against managers in similar positions, with similar challenges, in other organizations.

Assessment will not tell everything there is to know about individuals – no method of assessing people is either foolproof or completely reliable – but a structured, disciplined approach probably provides the best balance between reliable insights on the one hand and time, resources and disruption on the other. Managerial insights add an important extra dimension to the other elements of due diligence and therefore to the understanding of the target and its integration. It will also allow the identification of employees who are key to the business going forward which in turn means that the costs of retaining key employees can be anticipated while the deal is still being negotiated.

9 *Pensions due diligence*

The pension scheme could quite easily be worth more than the company being bought. Under normal circumstances, it is easy for the buyer to miss potential liabilities and just as easy for the seller to give too much away. Given the sheer size of the numbers involved here the consequences of doing either are potentially huge. Pension obligations can continue for many years after the employees have stopped working. Therefore, until there is evidence to the contrary, assume pension issues are going to lead you into some material black hole. This is especially true in these days of low inflation, relatively low equity returns and, in the UK, a change to more prescriptive accounting rules requiring extensive disclosures.

Detailed due diligence will be required if the purchaser is acquiring the pension scheme(s) as part of the transaction. Purchasers will not want to have to make large, one-off contributions to the scheme(s). The biggest concern, therefore, will be funding deficits. Other issues will include:

- Are there major claims against the scheme(s)?
- Is the buyer inheriting pension promises outside the terms of the approved company scheme? For example, highly paid employees often have a contractual promise that they will be paid a pension based on their full salary with any excess over the Inland Revenue pensions earning cap paid by the employing company.
- Is the acquired scheme to be merged with existing schemes? If not, does the buyer wish to 'red circle' the acquired schemes so that no new employees join them?
- Is the purchaser happy to continue providing defined benefits (for example where pension is linked to number of years in the scheme and final salary) or is there a wish to move to money purchase schemes?
- Is the purchaser happy to provide a company pension at all or will they want to move to personal pension schemes?
- If the inherited scheme is non-contributory (that is where only the employer contributes) does the buyer want to introduce employee contributions?

Types of scheme

In the UK, company pension schemes are very common. The system is described in more detail below. In most European countries, there are two types of scheme: a mandatory state-provided scheme which will provide base benefits, and private company pension schemes, usually guaranteed by an insurance policy, which give additional pension benefits.

THE UK PENSION SYSTEM

Apart from the state national insurance system, there are two main types of pension scheme which may be encountered in due diligence:

- Personal, where the individual saves for retirement
- Occupational, where the pension is organized through an employer, which sponsors the plan

Occupational pensions can either be defined benefits schemes or money purchase, or even a mix of the two. Personal pensions can only be money purchase. Defined benefits schemes, as the name suggests, provide benefits which are defined in advance, usually as a proportion of the individual's final salary, that is the salary at, or near, retirement, and a multiple of the number of years in the scheme.

Money purchase schemes (otherwise known as defined contribution schemes) are really just savings pots. The money contributed is invested and on retirement is used to buy an annuity or some similar approved benefit.

Personal pensions can only be provided by a provider (a financial institution such as a bank or unit trust). Occupational schemes are governed by trustees and can be insured or self-administered. For a number of reasons, as schemes get larger they tend to become self-administered, if they were not self-administered from the start. Reasons include the relatively high cost of insurance-based schemes, the fact that direct investment can often yield much better returns than an insurance contract and companies becoming more experienced with time. Insured schemes can also be inflexible.

In the UK, there is a salary cap on pension schemes. This means that earnings above the cap are not pensionable in an approved scheme. For this reason, a third type of scheme may well be encountered. This is the unapproved scheme. Unapproved schemes cater for the pension arrangements of those earning more than the cap.

DEFINED BENEFITS SCHEMES

Defined benefits schemes are the most problematical as far as due diligence is concerned, because the ultimate cost of final salary schemes is a big unknown. This is the crucial issue for due diligence. It depends on a whole host of factors outside a firm's control, such as investment returns, the length of time employees stay in the scheme and the length of time pensioners live after retirement. It was not long ago that employers found they could suspend their pension contributions because of the high number of early leavers from their schemes following restructuring exercises, and relatively high investment returns. That position has reversed dramatically in recent years.

Because the ultimate cost of defined benefits schemes is unknown, actuarial valuations will normally be carried out on a regular basis, probably every three years. Actuarial valuation tries to assess the value of the pension scheme's assets and the present value of future pension payments. The difference between the two determines the scheme's solvency and the level of future contributions needed. The rub, of course, is that there is no one right way to determine a scheme's solvency and so there is considerable scope for disagreement between buyer and seller. FRS17, a relatively new U.K. pensions accounting standard, may help, but in all but the simplest deals early actuarial advice is a must.

Type of transaction

The nature of the transaction is going to have a bearing on the treatment of pensions. Basically there are three different types of transaction to think about:

- Purchase of an entire company
- Purchase of a company which is part of a larger group and participates in a group pension scheme
- Purchase of assets

Any joint ventures bought along with the acquired company may bring further complications.

PURCHASE OF AN ENTIRE COMPANY

When buying a UK company in its entirety, the chances are that the workforce will come with their own pension scheme. The purchaser therefore needs to determine whether the scheme:

- Is adequately funded? Adequate funding may not simply be a case of meeting actuarial liabilities; there may be hidden nasties such as no provision for sex equality or for 5 per cent increases.
- Meets the expectations of the workforce? As a minimum, expectations will be set out in employment contracts.
- Contains any 'hidden' costs? Hidden costs can arise for a number of reasons. If, for example, the buyer's intention is to wind up the existing scheme and bring the acquired workforce into an existing scheme there may be 'switching costs' where insured schemes are concerned.

In theory, the funding position of UK company defined benefit pension schemes will be much more transparent following the introduction of FRS17 from early 2002 onwards. Whereas the old standard, SSAP 24, encouraged smoothing and allowed considerable actuarial judgement, FRS17 is much more prescriptive regarding actuarial assumptions and methodology. It calls for assets and liabilities to be valued at each period end and requires more extensive disclosures.

The new standard starts from the assumption that the assets and liabilities of a pension plan are essentially assets and liabilities of the employer and should therefore be recognized at fair value on the company balance sheet. Operating costs of providing benefits are recognized in the period in which employees earn them and finance costs and other changes in the value of assets and liabilities are recognized in the period in which they arise. FRS17 should be a considerable aid to understanding pension costs and liabilities and comparing them between companies.

PURCHASE OF A SUBSIDIARY/ASSETS

If a buyer is inviting the acquired employees to join an existing scheme, or is setting up a new one on their behalf, it is common for actuaries acting for each side to agree to a bulk transfer of funds and to the amount to be transferred. They will usually agree on one of three bases:

- Cash equivalent amount.
- Past service reserve (which takes into account future salary increases).
- Share of the fund. Where a company is being transferred out of a group the rules may allow a share of the group fund to be transferred, rather than just a package of transfer values (the rules are unlikely to allow it for an asset deal). This may be a much more attractive option, and certainly one to try as a negotiating tactic, although it is best first to check that the fund is not in deficit before opening negotiations.

Transferring employees may well have to remain in the seller's scheme while the new arrangements are sorted out.

Negotiations between buyer and seller will not involve the pensions scheme trustees. The assumption will be that the pension fund trustees will cooperate, which they probably will, but from the purchaser's point of view it is probably a good idea to understand what the purchasing company's own scheme's rules are on transfer payments and what sort of flexibility the trustees have. As the trustees of the vendor's scheme have to be satisfied that the amount agreed is reasonable and that they can pay it under the Trust Deed and Rules, the rules of the vendor's scheme also need to be understood before negotiations get too far.

TUPE

As already mentioned, in the UK, no rights relating to an occupational pension scheme will transfer to the buyer under regulation 7 of TUPE. Sellers will often seek to secure a deal so that pension rights will continue, and buyers will often provide pension rights for industrial relations reasons, but as yet no occupational pension rights will automatically transfer under TUPE. The same goes for life insurance and health insurance if these are provided through occupational pension schemes. This is not the case in every European country.

The situation with personal pensions is different. If an employee has the right to an employer contribution to a personal pension scheme, this obligation will transfer to the buyer.

The actuary

The buyer will normally use an actuary to carry out due diligence on pension arrangements and to advise on negotiations. What precisely the actuary will do depends on the nature of the transaction.

WHOLE SCHEME

If the deal involves taking over an entire pension scheme, the actuary will:

- Value the scheme, that is assess the scheme's ability to meet expected liabilities. Actual valuation is not the straightforward scientific exercise some might think. It involves a myriad of assumptions, and the buyer certainly cannot rely on the seller's assessment of future liabilities
- Ensure statutory requirements, such as equal pay, have been provided for.
- Advise on any unfunded promises
- Advise on any creative accounting involving pensions.

BULK TRANSFER

If the deal involves taking a transfer from the seller's scheme the actuary will:

- Negotiate the size of the transfer and its terms and conditions
- Advise on the cost implications of an inadequate transfer
- Advise on any creative accounting (as above).

Information

In order to get going, the actuary needs to know:

- The size of the deal
- Initially, the number of employees transferring and their average pay and length of service.

These will allow the actuary to gauge the level of input required from him.

Early on the actuary will need:

1. A full list of those transferring along with details of age, pay, length of service and contracts of employment, including details of employees earning more than the pensions cap. There is an obvious overlap with Human Resources due diligence here and the two sets of advisers must talk to each other
2. For each scheme from which employees are transferring:

   - The Trust Deed and Rules
   - Member's handbook
   - Announcements made since both of the above were last updated
   - Confirmation that equal pay and increases are provided for
   - Latest actuarial report/review.

3. Information on any unfunded pension commitments, both approved and unapproved
4. Verification that Revenue Contributions Agency (CA)[1] approval and so on has been obtained
5. Whether there is any Occupational Pensions Regulatory Authority (OPRA) interest.

Obviously an essential part of the due diligence will be to obtain an accurate list of the employees transferring. This may sound fairly straightforward but, as mentioned under employment due diligence, such lists can often be inaccurate because they omit the names of individuals who are part of the deal but may not actually work for the company being bought. Such people are easy to miss. If they are missed they themselves may miss out as they will be entitled only to the benefits they would get if they had left the vendor's scheme and joined the purchaser's. This can be embarrassing to say the least.

WARRANTIES AND INDEMNITIES

There is one subtlety as far as pension warranties and indemnities are concerned and that is that, in the UK at any rate, trustees run occupational pension schemes and trustees are not bound by any action that is in breach of trust. To be worth anything, indemnities must, therefore, be given by the vendor and not by the trustees of the vendor's scheme. Particular issues to watch out for include the following:

- If buying a family firm watch out for pension promises which are unfunded. Once a sale is contemplated, it is quite common for the family to give employees valuable, but unfunded and undisclosed, pension rights. Therefore, a warranty to deal with unfunded liabilities is always advisable, however small the deal.
- Where buying a company with an insured style occupational pension scheme and if valuation is to be carried out post-completion, the purchaser can *try* to obtain an indemnity from the vendor to cover the possibility that the insurance policy backing the scheme is enough to meet the liabilities. This, however, is unlikely to be given and in any case opens the seller to the risk that the vendor will want a similar *quid pro quo* if there proves to be a surplus.
- A purchaser needs to be certain that if a vendor's scheme cannot pay the agreed transfer amount, then the vendor will make up the shortfall.

Dealing with a surplus

Until recently it was common for occupational schemes to be over-funded. Where a company is being bought on a multiple of profits, there is no justification for paying extra for the surplus in an over-funded scheme, since accounting standards will have already made sure that profits have been adjusted upwards to reflect lower company contributions. Even if the value of the surplus is not reflected in the purchase price, it is rarely worth much to the purchaser:

- After a number of public battles over surpluses, members are now expecting surpluses to be used for their benefit rather than being stripped out of the scheme.
- The law requires surpluses to be used to fund a 5 per cent escalation to pensions in payment.
- Following the Barber case,[2] the cost of equal provision may eat up any theoretical surplus.
- Recent (1995) regulations have made it more difficult to return surpluses, while minimum funding requirements (also introduced in 1995) make surpluses rarer.

Conclusion

The importance, and nature, of pensions due diligence depends partly on the target's existing pension arrangements and partly on what the purchaser is intending post-transaction. If the target has a defined benefits occupational pension scheme, then the sheer size of the monetary risk makes close scrutiny of the funding of future pensions liabilities a must. This is a complex, highly technical, area which can be further complicated by the type of transaction, whether or not the target's employees are coming out of a larger scheme and the attitude of pension fund trustees, so it pays to use a good actuary with whom you can work. The actuary can also advise on post-acquisition planning. If, on the other hand, the target company runs a defined contribution scheme, or employees are contributing to personal pensions, funding is less of an issue, but there may be industrial relations issues which have to be addressed.

10 *Tax due diligence*

This is a complex and highly technical area, which cannot be done full justice here. Nonetheless, it is possible to give a broad understanding of the issues and processes involved so that as a buyer you can be more effective in managing taxation due diligence. It is about both risk and opportunity. Done well it can be very beneficial for the transaction. The management challenge is to keep tax advisers focused on the job in hand. For the buyer, it is important not just to understand what the tax risks and opportunities are, but also their likely impact.

Anglo-Saxon practice is for there to be a tax indemnity, often referred to as the tax deed. This means, in theory at least, that the seller will pay any pre-deal tax which falls due after the deal is done. In practice, indemnities are not quite as fail-safe as that (see Chapter 1) and therefore buyers carry out tax due diligence so that, at the very least, they know what they might be taking on. Tax due diligence can also be a very important topic in deal and post-deal structuring.

Because the tax objectives of buyers and sellers are often miles apart, tax can be one of the meatiest negotiating issues. That said, many misunderstandings arise because of the different approaches taken on domestic transactions. Recognize, therefore, that practice varies enormously around the world and just because you do things one way at home does not mean that that is the way everyone else does it. For example tax deeds are long in the UK and some other jurisdictions such as Australia. The North Americans have short, general indemnities. The Europeans tend to leave tax to the warranties. Once again, then, it should be stressed that where an acquisition has an international dimension it is important to take local advice.

Here also, perhaps more than anywhere else, the importance of getting due diligence advisers to work together needs to be emphasized. Tax overlaps with both legal and financial, which means that whoever is working on tax must liaise closely with the financial and legal advisers to ensure that information is properly shared, that nothing falls between the cracks and that there is no duplication of effort.

Finally, although corporate taxes are the ones that grab all the attention, the other taxes are likely to be the most troublesome for the following reasons:

- The need for filings and audits means that corporate taxes tend to better organized.
- Other taxes tend to fall below the radar of senior management and it is often difficult to find someone who knows the full picture.

Objectives

The objectives of tax due diligence are fourfold and will not come as any surprise. They can be divided into two groups:

1. Transaction related:

   - To find and protect against tax exposures which are not reflected in the purchase price. Protection could be through a reduction in, or retention from, the price, appropriate warranties and indemnities or by excluding, or rejecting, certain disclosures
   - To plan for tax issues which will arise as a result of the deal
   - To structure the deal in the most tax efficient manner.

2. Post-completion related. Integrating the acquisition in the most tax-efficient manner subject to commercial objectives.

Tax due diligence is therefore fairly straightforward and obvious. It aims to:

1. Identify and evaluate tax liabilities

   - For which there are no provisions
   - Which will be triggered as a result of the transaction.

2. Assist in structuring the deal.
3. Assist in planning for the future, for example how to minimize tax costs going forward.

Transaction-related tax due diligence

Sellers give tax indemnities. These guarantee that if any tax relating to the seller's period of ownership falls due, which has not been provided for in the accounts, the seller will compensate the buyer for any loss. With such a cast-iron guarantee against unforeseen loss, why bother with any transaction-related due diligence at all? The answer is that the tax deed should be seen only as a backstop and not as a prime means of avoiding risk.

1. As has been pointed out in Chapter 2, an indemnity is only as good as the person giving it.
2. There will be time limits on indemnities. There always are.
3. There are probably going to be *de minimus* provisions too.
4. Some extra protection, over and above the tax deed, may be called for and hence a need to negotiate warranties. This is impossible without knowing where the tax risks lie.
5. Past liabilities are only part of the story. For example, the transaction itself might trigger liabilities.

The principal taxes to be considered are:

- Corporate taxes
- VAT/sales taxes
- Employment taxes such as income tax – known as Pay As You Earn (PAYE) in the UK – national insurance/health care taxes (NHI in the UK), payroll taxes and deductions
- Employee benefit reporting
- Stamp duties, transfer duties and capital duties on the acquisition

Personal taxes of the target's shareholders may also be of interest, especially those such as inheritance taxes, estate duties and gift taxes which may be charged to the target company.

TRANSACTION STRUCTURE

The structure of the transaction is going to have a bearing on the tax due diligence exercise. If the acquisition is of assets, the only two taxes which will be relevant are Stamp Duty and VAT. As these are both levied on the transaction itself, they are easily identified. The major issue for the buyer is which assets to cherry-pick. The more assets it takes, the higher the transaction value and therefore the higher the Stamp Duty. For this reason, as well as the wish to avoid arguments over which debts are collectable, it is fairly common for the buyer of assets not to take over debtors.

A company, on the other hand, comes with the baggage of its previous tax affairs as these remain with the company. If a company is being acquired, tax due diligence is normally much more wide-ranging with investigations covering most of the taxes mentioned above.

ACTIVITIES

The main activities involved can be summarized as follows:

- Review of corporate tax returns and computations
- Review of correspondence with tax authorities and the status of agreements on outstanding computations
- Understand the details of any inland revenue investigations and of tax audits by foreign tax authorities
- Analysis of corporate tax and deferred tax provisions in financial statements
- Review of quarterly payment procedures

Inevitably the investigating accountant is going to take a different, probably much less aggressive view (from a tax-saving perspective), than whoever first did the returns and computations. The important point is not who is right or wrong, but the size of the potential exposure and whether or not it is material.

BRIEFING ADVISERS

In addition to the general advisers' briefing and the headings for terms of reference outlined in Chapter 3, it is advisable to discuss, agree in advance and document the specifics of the tax investigation. These will include:

- Materiality levels. The final report should focus on the important issues. The last thing a buyer wants is a report which contains every little detail. The level at which tax issues are to be reported should, therefore, be agreed in advance.
- The companies to be investigated. This will really only be an issue where the acquisition is being made from a group of companies. It may sound a little odd at first to suggest that the tax advisers should be instructed to investigate companies other than the target. The reason is that some tax authorities, and the Inland Revenue in the UK is one of them, have the power in certain circumstances to collect tax from a company which has been in the same group as a defaulting company – even if it is not still in the same group.

- The time period to be covered. In the UK there is a statutory limitation period of six years for non-fraud cases. In other words, in the UK, any tax returns more than six years old cannot be reopened and reinvestigated. Given this, playing safe would mean looking back six years. The more usual, though, is to review the previous three years and then, depending on the findings, take a view on going back further. Time, cost, access and availability of records will also play a part in deciding on the time period to be covered. Buyers should also bear in mind that the chances of an unexpected tax liability suddenly appearing from six years ago are considerably less than from two or three years ago. For non-UK jurisdictions the same factors will play a part, so the starting point for making a decision on timing will be to ascertain the statutory limitation periods.
- Taxes to be covered. As well as the usual suspects listed above, there may be specialist taxes, depending on the industry.
- Areas of risk specific to the transaction. If, for example, the target has aggressively managed tax in the past, for example by inflating stock costs (such tax avoidance ruses are a national pastime in France), what are the chances of the purchaser becoming liable?

Do not let your tax advisers dive straight into the detail. Make sure they get an overall feel for the company, its history, and why it is being sold. Let the tax experts work out whether there are any specific tax risks associated with this type of business and, above all, make sure they fully understand the issues which are important to the would-be buyer. Even better, make sure they contribute their knowledge and experience to the written terms of reference.

The buyer's advisers should understand the seller's, as well as the buyer's, tax situation. It is frequently possible to structure the deal to minimize overall tax liabilities. Saving tax for the seller ought to be tradable, either directly as money off the purchase price or in exchange for some other contentious issue which comes up in negotiations.

INFORMATION SOURCES

Data rooms

Data rooms often contain vast amounts of data, but as far as tax is concerned they are unlikely to give more than a rough outline of the target's tax history. Sometimes there are a lot of detailed calculations but no explanation, at other times the tax levied will be split by business but there will be no geographical split. Furthermore, although it may be possible to identify and quantify specific exposures, it is often difficult to see whether a provision has been made for them in the accounts.

It is, though, worth the tax adviser visiting the data room, not only to review the documents on tax but also to have a look at the basic company documents.

- What shares have been issued and what rights attach to them?
- Are they ordinary shares?
- Who are the registered shareholders (and therefore who will be giving warranty and indemnity protection)?
- Have there been any repayments of capital which the Revenue could count as a distribution?
- Is there anything, such as owners being resident abroad, which suggests extra protection might be needed in the event of a breach of warranty?

- Are there any shareholder agreements, especially ones which govern control of the target?
- If so, do these have a bearing on group structure?
- What is the group structure – and, just as important, is this the structure that the seller's tax advisers or tax department is working to?

It sounds obvious but it is well worth the tax advisers drawing up their understanding of the group structure and confirming it with the seller. It is surprising just how often the seller's company secretary, tax and treasury departments all work to different group structures. It is also not unknown for local movements not to have been recorded centrally.

This is a particular danger where foreign subsidiaries are involved, but is by no means confined to overseas movement. As mentioned in Chapter 5, there have been occasions when it was discovered during due diligence that the target's intermediate holding company had been sold in a previous transaction without anyone on the seller's side noticing.

Risk profile

At an early stage in the diligence exercise, a useful piece of analysis is to build up a profile of the target's risk as far as tax is concerned. Table 10.1 highlights the sources of tax risk in a target company as an aid to building up such a profile.

Table 10.1   Profiling the tax risk in target companies

	Low tax risk	Medium tax risk	High tax risk
Deal structure	Assets-based	Share-based	Share-based
Company type	Single company	Multi-company	Multi-company
Company business	Simple	Complex	Specialist sector
Span of operations	Wholly domestic	Some overseas operations	Substantial overseas operations
Tax rate	Losses (which are not being paid for)/tax rate close to standard	Tax rate below what it should be	Low effective tax rate
Tax planning	None	Some evidence of tax planning	Evidence of aggressive tax planning
Compliance	No issues	Moderate compliance arrears	Heavy compliance arrears
Tax audits	Recent clean tax audits	Recent tax audits	No recent tax audits
Disputes with the Revenue	No items under dispute	Few items under dispute	Many items under dispute
Transfer pricing	Not an issue	Policy in place	No documentation
Length of time in business	Recent start up	Long trading history	Long trading history

Direct questions

As with most other forms of due diligence, the next step is a list of questions for the vendor. With tax, these questions very often take the form of warranties for the seller to disclose against (see Appendix A10). Ideally this will be followed by face-to-face meetings with the seller's tax manager and/or advisers.

Tax warranties

The principal role of tax warranties is to find things out rather than put the seller on the hook. With tax, the seller is put on the hook with a tax indemnity.

There are two ways in which to use tax warranties in due diligence:

- As the starting point of the process
- Later on, to confirm what the tax adviser has found out through direct questioning

Tax due diligence questions are therefore answered, or confirmed, by disclosure against tax warranties. This being the case, it is very important to make sure answers are not vague and incomplete. Oral disclosures should be resisted, as should general statements. The tax adviser will want to know not just that certain transactions took place, but will need all the details of those transactions and any supporting documentation (like any legal opinion on whether tax avoidance manoeuvres were likely to succeed). The adviser should also cross-check disclosures against information obtained in due diligence.

In all cases additional warranties will be drawn up at the end of the process to elicit information on any areas of uncertainty or where the position needs clarifying.

Non-disclosure   On the face of it, there is no real incentive for the seller to disclose anything on the tax front which might cause problems in the negotiations. After all, there is going to be a tax deed which puts the seller on the hook with the buyer for any tax liabilities arising, for which it is responsible, once the deal is done. In the UK, at any rate, a seller should think long and hard before not disclosing, as Section 397 of the Financial Services and Markets Act 2000 (see Chapter 2) will apply.

Another oft-cited reason for not disclosing against certain warranties is that the Inland Revenue might want to see disclosure letters. The seller will argue that disclosing against, say, tax avoidance will only give the Revenue notice of transactions which the seller is concerned might not work. The answer is twofold:

1. The Revenue may very well want to see disclosures but there are question marks over whether it can in fact, legally, demand to see them. They may even be protected by legal privilege.
2. The buyer's and the Revenue's interests are likely to coincide. From the buyer's perspective, the greater the likelihood of Revenue interest in certain disclosures, the more the purchaser wants them to be made. Revenue interest means that the Revenue consider there might be something for them to get their teeth into. In turn this means potentially unprovided tax liabilities either because of 'difficult' tax avoidance schemes or inaccuracies in past file returns.

So although some sellers may be reluctant to disclose against warranties, they have no excuse not to.

AREAS OF INTEREST

The risk profile should give the tax adviser a pretty reliable feel for the priorities and therefore prevent getting into too much unnecessary detail. Depending on the exact nature of the transaction, there are a number of areas for each type of tax which are likely to be of most concern. These are covered in the following sections, starting with corporate taxes.

Corporate taxes

Compliance record   A company reaps what it sows. The tax adviser will get a good feel for the future from the target's compliance record. Usually, a company's compliance record is a pretty good guide to how it will be treated by the tax authorities. A poor record and you can almost guarantee that the authorities will look very carefully at everything a company submits to them.

In the UK, self-assessment was introduced for accounts ending on or after July 1 1999. This means that a company is now required to:

- Calculate its own liability for corporation tax
- File a return with the Revenue by the filing date (12 months after the year end)
- Pay the tax it has calculated as due
- Keep records for six years

The Revenue:

- Has up to 12 months from filing to launch an inquiry into a return
- Will issue a closure notice once an inquiry has been resolved

Checking whether or not self-assessment returns have been correctly submitted will be an important element of tax due diligence on UK companies.

Past transactions   The tax adviser will look at past transactions. It will come as no surprise that the adviser will be particularly interested in anything which might be a potential exposure but which has not been provided for in the accounts. If possible, these should be quantified. Tax avoidance transactions would be a good example. Companies and individuals only engage in tax avoidance schemes if they are worth the bother. They are also risky. By definition, then, some of the biggest potential exposures lie with tax avoidance schemes and especially ones which have yet to be examined by the tax authorities. Indeed a very good question always to ask is, 'has the target provided the Revenue with full information?'

The other element to this topic is past M&A transactions where the target may have given or received tax warranties and indemnities. These should also be reviewed and the risk of crystallization assessed.

The status of current tax negotiations   Once the deal is done, the purchaser will be responsible for tax compliance. The purchaser wants to ensure:

1. A smooth transition. The purchaser will need to find out where tax negotiations with the authorities have got to, and which matters will have to be taken up once the target is

under new ownership. As well as noting major issues with the tax authorities, the purchaser should also find out whether they are isolated issues or likely to re-occur.

2. That there are no significant disputes with the tax authorities on computational matters. The most common areas are:

   • Capital allowance claims and bad debt provisions
   • Un-agreed valuations (which could have an impact on capital gains liabilities)
   • Outstanding transfer pricing disputes. Transfer pricing is an increasingly important area of scrutiny for tax authorities, so there could well be disputes between the target and the tax authorities.

3. That claims and elections are made within statutory time limits. If there are deadlines for making claims, when do they expire? Have claims been made? Time limits could easily expire while the deal is being negotiated.
4. That, if consent has been given for a joint claim or election, this cannot be withdrawn.

Often special agreements are made with the tax authorities and it is important to understand what these are and whether they will continue.

Any group transactions   If the target is a member of a group there may be some particular risks which need to be covered:

• There may have been inter-group transfers which give rise to de-grouping charges on capital gains once the deal is done. Under certain circumstances assets can be transferred between group companies as a way of minimizing or deferring capital gains. If a company leaves the group within six years, any such capital gains liabilities will be triggered.
• There may be a similar issue with intra-group Stamp Duty relief.
• The buyer may need to understand the system for group and consortium relief surrenders and whether any payments are outstanding. Individual companies which are part of a group often do not bother to pay each other.
• Whether the target is liable for any taxes of the group companies not acquired. Apart from the case mentioned above, where an ex-group company defaults, there are other dangers with group companies. For example transfer prices could be judged not to be have been at arm's length with the result that the target should have paid more tax than it has.

The availability of tax losses   Tax losses can be extremely important to the viability of a transaction and are often important in justifying the deal internally. The reality is that they can easily be lost. Try to make them contingent. Avoid paying for tax losses, if at all possible, unless and until you use them.

If you are paying for tax losses, whether it is up front or on a contingent basis, they should be investigated and:

• They should be paid for only once they have been agreed.
• The seller should warrant their availability.
• Nothing should be done which will cause them to be disallowed.

If you are not paying for them, then they are a bonus. There is no need to investigate them and no need to have the seller warrant their availability. It is probably not a bad idea, though, to make sure that nothing is done that could cause them to be disallowed – subject to the overriding principle that commercial considerations should always prevail. There are two types of tax losses: trading and capital.

TRADING LOSSES

In the UK, trading losses can be carried forward indefinitely and be set against the profits of the same trade. The losses are disallowed if, in the three years either side of a change in ownership of the target, there is a major change of the target's trade. This is to stop the buying and selling of tax losses. In other jurisdictions expiry times can sometimes be quite short. For this reason, expiry times need to be carefully investigated as they may prevent tax losses being useable.

CAPITAL LOSSES

In the UK, pre-entry rules can restrict the use of capital losses.[1] They can only be used in the group in which they are incurred. Capital losses which have arisen as a result of connected party transactions can only be set off against gains with the same connected party. Both of these could have an effect on the gains and losses of the target.

Capital assets   If the target has 'chargeable assets' such as properties and goodwill, the buyer should endeavour to get historical information from the seller on costs, values and such like. This will allow the buyer to calculate potential liability on any later sales, whether or not asset sales are planned as part of post-acquisition integration. The seller should also be asked if the assets have been subject to any rollover relief in the past which would affect tax computations in the future. This occurs where assets have been sold and any capital gains made at the time have been rolled over into other assets of the target. This has the effect of reducing the base cost of the assets concerned and producing a higher capital gain when those assets are sold.

Records   The state of the target's records is important under 'pay and file' so that the buyer is satisfied that returns have been properly submitted and that the target can prove this to the Revenue. In certain other cases (such as with VAT, see below) there is a statutory duty to keep certain records for a certain time.

Cross-border acquisitions

Transfer pricing   Transfer pricing is a mechanism which was, and still is, widely used as a means of reducing tax. Not surprisingly, then, transfer prices are something which tend to excite the tax authorities, especially those in the higher tax regimes. At the same time transfer prices are almost impossible to get right. In theory a transfer price policy based on arm's length relationships using market prices will satisfy the tax man. In practice 'market prices' are notoriously difficult to define. What happens with industrial intermediates where there is no significant free market? What about price reductions for packaging or administrative savings for sales to group companies? And it is one thing having a policy, but to what extent is policy followed? Because of all these difficulties, transfer pricing is an area of significant risk in cross-border acquisitions. Due diligence should determine the target's exposure to transfer pricing adjustments and any likely tax liabilities. This will include an examination of the transfer pricing policy of the group of which the target is a member and an assessment of how that policy has been implemented across the group.

Overseas reviews   If the acquisition operates overseas, due diligence will need to establish whether there are any outstanding issues with the relevant tax authorities. Local advice will be needed. This inevitably involves more time, more cost and significantly more project management to make sure that the right quality of information is received at the right time. In some jurisdictions there may also be an issue around controlled foreign companies.[2]

Tax clearances required for the transaction   Certain clearances may be needed for the transaction to go ahead. The purchaser should make sure they:

- Have been applied for
- Have been properly drafted
- Are submitted in good time

VAT/sales taxes and customs duties

Is the target VAT-registered?   The first, and crucial, VAT question is whether the target is registered for VAT.

- If it is not, should it be? Have the registration thresholds been exceeded during the previous 12 months? Are they likely to be exceeded in the next 30 days?[3]
- Are there likely to be any penalties for late registration?
- Have any measures been taken to rectify the lack of registration?

Areas of concern   Assuming the target is VAT-registered, the tax adviser will examine VAT returns for the past two years to make sure VAT has been properly accounted for. The following issues should be checked, and reported on:

- Have returns been correctly filed within the correct time limits? (Particular problems are reclaiming VAT on excluded expenditure and not charging VAT on inter-group charges where there is no group VAT registration.)
- Has tax been paid on time and, if not, has interest, or any other penalty, been adequately provided for?
- Are the accounting systems adequate to produce monthly returns? As well as the adviser's own assessment, the outcome of the last control visit will provide useful information here.
- Are disputes likely with Customs and Excise?
- Is the target a member of a VAT group?[4] If so will it be jointly and severally liable for the liabilities of other group members? The buyer needs contractual protection against any such outstanding VAT liabilities in the sale and purchase agreement.

The VAT treatment of the actual acquisition also needs careful consideration. Any mistake here and one party or the other might find itself liable for VAT on the entire consideration.

Customs duties
Customs duties should not be forgotten. The tax due diligence needs to confirm that:

- Customs duties have been correctly calculated.
- There are no outstanding issues from any customs audits and that any previous issues will not re-occur.
- All duties have been properly paid on imports and, if not, that any outstanding duties and any interest or other penalties have been correctly provided for.
- Any issues identified with customs duties will not recur.

Employment taxes
The principles that apply to employment taxes are similar to those that apply to VAT:

1. Have the relevant taxes been correctly deducted and paid over on time? This may sound fairly obvious but in some areas in some businesses, for example, there may be a fairly large number of contractors who, because they are not on the staff, are paid on invoice with no deductions for Income Tax and National Insurance. Is this permissible under Inland Revenue definitions of self-employment (IR35) or will the purchaser subsequently become liable for taxes which the seller should have deducted?
2. Have year-end returns been correctly filed? In the UK these would be forms P9D, P11D, P14 and P35. Benefits in kind in general, and Directors' P11Ds in particular, are always an area of concern, usually rightly. Have all the benefits been properly accounted for? (If not, tax will not have been correctly calculated either and the buyer may find itself liable for the shortfall.)
3. What dispensations have been agreed with the Revenue? Have any special arrangements been made? Will they survive the transaction?
4. Have there been any enquiries by any of the relevant authorities? If so, what was their outcome? Are they finished? Are the same issues likely to arise in the future?
5. Are there any share schemes or profit related pay schemes? If so:

    - What are the rules?
    - Has the Revenue approved them?
    - How will they be affected by the transaction?

Stamp, Transfer and Capital Duties
Stamp Duty in the UK has been steadily increased over the past few years. It is now at the point where it can amount to a substantial amount of money. This is another tax that should not be passed over. The tax adviser should naturally review any outstanding liabilities and any impact the transaction might have on the buyer's Stamp Duty position. In the UK, the main effort, though, is likely to go into minimizing stamp duty on the transaction itself.

With asset acquisitions there are a number of planning opportunities which the tax adviser should be asked to explore. For example, for assets that do not have to be registered (like goodwill), it may be possible to execute the purchase agreement outside the UK.

THE REPORT

The due diligence report should include the issues set out above. Below are listed the general headings the report should cover. The report should give you the facts and it should also allow you to build up a good picture of the target company as far as tax is concerned. Typically it will contain the following:

1. Executive summary with key recommendations
2. Scope of the review and any limitations on the investigation
3. Current status of negotiations with the tax authorities:

   - Years closed, years open
   - What issues are still being discussed

4. Compliance history:

   - Previous audits and investigations and their outcome
   - Details of past penalties or interest

5. Current liabilities and provisions:

   - Factual details of current tax liabilities and provisions made to cover them
   - Ditto, as far as is possible, for future liabilities
   - Any liabilities which have not been provided for
   - Details and assessment of potential exposures and areas of risk
   - Effective tax rate, how it is calculated, assessment of whether it is likely to worsen

6. The effect of the transaction:

   - The risk of liabilities crystallizing as a result of the sale
   - Any tax liabilities that could be triggered on post acquisition reorganization
   - An evaluation of any pre-sale tax planning undertaken by the seller

7. Planning opportunities. Usually these will be the more obvious opportunities based on the due diligence findings and what the adviser knows about the purchaser's plans. However, there is nothing to stop the buyer asking for a fuller analysis of any tax planning opportunities that might be available.
8. Conclusions. Is the tax provision adequate? Problems which will need to be addressed, tax profile, recommendations for both the transaction (extra protection and so on) and for future planning.

The other important thing to remember is that you do not want advisers simply to cover the ground. You also want specific recommendations, so press for these. Ask for a presentation of the report and do not be afraid to ask direct, commercial questions like, 'If you were buying this company, what would you do? 'or 'What do you think are the chances of this potential liability crystallizing?' and make sure you get direct, commercial answers. Do not be satisfied with highly technical references to obscure paragraphs of various pieces of tax legislation.

TAX INDEMNITIES

The Tax Deed of Indemnity is given by the seller. It is a safety net which allows the purchaser to recover any losses from the seller if a tax liability arises which is not provided for in the accounts. In it, taxation needs to be defined in a way that covers all types of liability in all jurisdictions. For example, not all countries have VAT as such, but most have sales taxes. There should also be a procedure for pre- and post-completion tax filings and, as with indemnities in general, a claims procedure should be set out which protects the interests of both parties. Again, as with indemnities in general, the buyer needs to be aware of exclusions and time limits.

Transaction-related tax planning

As a very minimum the buyer needs:

- Access to any records, correspondence *and people* who may be needed in post-acquisition negotiations with the tax authorities
- To agree who should be responsible for resolving outstanding issues with the tax authorities. This needs careful thought because if the (tax-indemnified) buyer is in charge, will it settle too easily? On the other hand, if the seller is to agree outstanding issues how hard will it fight if it thinks the tax will be picked up by buyer?

Also under this heading comes all those things which happened before the sale but which could resurface once the deal is done. The most obvious is the availability of tax losses, discussed above. If the target has unused trading losses, the position might change with a change of ownership. The same applies to other reliefs. Are they going to be available to carry forward?

On a more exotic level there are circumstances where tax liabilities can be triggered when acquired companies' share structures are reorganized, for example with a bonus issue of shares or a repayment of share capital, because of something the acquired company has done pre-acquisition.

Integration-related tax planning

Inevitably during due diligence the tax adviser is going to build up a comprehensive profile of the target's approach to taxation. This will be an enormous aid in integrating the target's tax affairs into those of the acquirer. How well, or otherwise, has the target handled its tax affairs? Does it have its own tax department? Does that department handle everything or does it leave the really complex stuff to outside advisers? To what extent does it rely on the expertise and, more importantly, the connections of advisers and tax managers in overseas jurisdictions? Can the buyer keep these connections?

It is frequently the case that the target must be merged with existing operations. For example, where the acquirer has operations in the same territory there are generally tax benefits to be had from creating a single tax grouping of companies in that territory. The restructuring necessary to achieve this may give rise to capital gains problems.

The target will also need to be integrated into the target group in the most tax-efficient way. It may be that some of the target's assets are going to be sold. The investigation should aim to identify how best the target can be integrated, for example which company in the acquiring group should buy it and whether any liabilities are going to be triggered by reorganizations.

STRUCTURING

Such post-acquisition planning becomes even more important with international acquisitions as some form of post-acquisition holding company restructuring may be called for to minimize tax. It pays to acquire foreign companies with the right place. You do not want to be moving them around once they have been acquired. This in turn may require the cooperation of the seller who may not be too keen to reorganize at the same time as trying to get the deal done.

Wherever possible, acquisition tax structuring is seeking to obtain a tax deduction for funding costs. This includes not just loan capital but also the costs of raising finance, which can be huge, and any transaction costs, such as stamp duties, related to doing the deal. In addition, the buyer will want to provide for the repatriation of funds from acquisitions made in other countries. For all buyers the most important structuring objectives are therefore likely to be:

- Avoiding double taxation
- Maximizing relief for interest on borrowed funds
- Minimizing withholding taxes
- Obtaining a step-up of assets for depreciation purposes
- Obtaining relief for acquisition costs.

This means that it is difficult to separate the tax aspects of the transaction itself from the longer-term post-completion tax planning. Each of the above points is dealt with in turn below.

Double taxation

A company resident in the UK will generally be liable for UK corporation tax on its income from all sources worldwide. It may also be liable for overseas tax on income which falls within the tax net of other countries. Also, dividends and interest paid by overseas companies to UK shareholders may have suffered withholding tax in the country of origin and then be taxable again in the UK.

Double Tax Relief (DTR) exists to reduce that rather heavy tax burden. In essence, it ensures that the taxpayer pays no more than the higher of the two rates involved. DTR is given according to the terms of double tax agreements which the UK has entered into with most countries in the world. A UK business buying a non-resident company needs to make sure that it does not pay tax on the same profits in more than one country without at least offsetting the tax paid at the lower rate against any tax due at the higher rate.

Maximizing interest relief

The starting point for tax structuring is an idea of the tax rates that apply in those countries where the target operates. The single most important reason why tax advisers need to be involved with structuring the transaction is because most acquisitions will be financed at least partly by debt and the financial success of the deal will be profoundly influenced by how much tax relief can be claimed for the interest on that debt. As interest is tax deductible in all the main trading nations, the trick is to ensure that interest is borne in the optimum location. Much of the tax planning for multinational operations is concerned with where best to locate the group debt in order to ensure the maximum relief for deductions and the minimum tax cost on the receipt of interest. A multinational company may have a choice as to where it locates the debt to fund M&A activity. It will obviously make sense to locate the debt, and therefore the interest payments, in a jurisdiction where profits are being taxed at a high effective rate. Locating debt in those countries where there are taxable profits against which it can be offset is called 'debt pushdown'.

The effectiveness of debt pushdown will depend on four things:

1. Vendor structure. For reasons which should become obvious in the next few pages it is going to be much easier to push debt down if the vendor is selling lots of separate companies.
2. Geographical split of historical earnings. The past may not always be a reliable guide to the future but in this case it is probably not a bad starting point. Clearly, you do not want to push debt down to countries where there are no profits and in the absence of other data, the historical earnings split is a good guide to where they might be made in the future.
3. Allocation of purchase price. The amount of the purchase price allocated to a country is going to determine how much debt can be pushed down to that country. Be warned though, the vendor is going to have ideas on this too.
4. Limitations imposed by tax rules in each of the relevant counties:

   • The ability to offset interest against trading profits
   • Limitations on the amount of intra-group debt (or thin capitalization, see below)
   • Withholding taxes on interest payments

The mechanics of debt pushdown are simple. A Newco in a country acquires the target in the same country. The idea is that the interest Newco has to pay on the loans needed to buy the target can be offset against the profits which the target makes. Most countries' tax rules allow this – although in some jurisdictions some form of post-acquisition merger may be required to make it work.

Thin capitalization   In order to prevent taxable profits being eliminated by the use of acquisition debt, most countries have rules which restrict to some degree the amount of related party debt which can be used in a company's capital structure. The rules vary enormously from country to country and detailed research is needed in each situation to avoid breaking the rules. Also thin capitalization, as it is called, is often negotiated with the tax authorities on a case-by-case basis. In the UK, the Inland Revenue's guidelines are debt/equity of 1:1 and profit before interest and tax (PBIT) of at least three times interest where debt is intra-group or guaranteed by a parent. If you exceed these limits with intra-group debt you will probably be OK, if you can demonstrate an arm's length relationship on transfer pricing. The US bases its rules on what it thinks third parties would lend. Germany has quite prescriptive rules.

Withholding taxes on interest   Most tax treaties between the main industrial nations reduce any domestic withholding tax rates on interest to zero. However, with publicly issued debt there may be an issue in some countries about verifying the residence of all beneficial owners and hence a need to route funds through a finance company in the Netherlands or Luxembourg where there is no withholding tax on interest as a matter of domestic law.

Withholding taxes on dividends

Withholding taxes on dividends can be a significant levy on the repatriation of profits. These withholding taxes are reduced under double tax relief and have largely been eliminated on dividend payments between parent and subsidary companies within the EU. Any withholding taxes which continue to be suffered may be creditable against taxable income in the recipient's jurisdiction.

Dividends are not the only way to repatriate funds back to the parent. Apart from royalties, most of these alternative repayment methods are free of withholding tax although this should be checked on a case-by-case, country-by-country basis. Transfer pricing is one way but, as already mentioned, this is coming under increasing scrutiny from the tax authorities.

Step-ups

If assets can be stepped up to their market values for tax purposes, then there will be a tax saving. The good news is that most countries grant a step-up where assets are acquired and most (the UK is an exception) will allow depreciation of intangibles as well as tangibles. There are also a limited number of countries where a step-up is available for tax depreciable assets where the shares of the target are acquired.

Obtaining relief for acquisition costs

We are now in the realm of quite specialized tax planning techniques which are beyond the scope of a book on due diligence. At this level of specialization, money spent on a good tax adviser is money well spent. Here it is necessary only to be aware that there are a number of ways of getting relief for acquisition costs. One, for example, is to split intangible assets from the acquired company then lease them back to the new acquisition, sheltering the resulting lease charges in a low tax regime. In this way the purchaser can get a deduction against highly taxed profits and receipts in a low tax jurisdiction. Tax advisers should be encouraged to report on the options and the practicality of using such techniques.

Conclusion

Although in Anglo-Saxon jurisdictions sellers will give a tax indemnity, the principle of *caveat emptor* makes it advisable for buyers to make their own enquiries into the tax risks of a transaction. But tax due diligence should not be restricted to the transaction. It can also play a valuable role in post-acquisition structuring.

Corporate taxes are the usual focus for most people, with an emphasis on any tax planning on the part of the target, but the biggest risk can often lie with the other corporate taxes. These should not be neglected. Data rooms and disclosures against tax warranties are valuable information sources but, as with other forms of due diligence, there is no substitute for direct access. Cross-border acquisitions introduce an extra layer of complexity, both for the transaction and for tax planning. Local advice should be taken on transaction related tax issues and advisers should be encouraged to report on any tax planning opportunities with cross-border acquisitions.

Taxation is a highly technical, complex and ever-changing discipline. To be done properly, it needs to be carried out by experts. However, the potential size of liabilities which could be acquired, or of the savings which are available if the deal is most effectively structured, make this a rewarding area if it is carried out properly. The issue for most purchasers who are not tax experts will be understanding the results and their commercial consequences.

11 *Environmental due diligence*

Environmental due diligence is often the first concern of many US buyers schooled by their own very stringent domestic regulations. They will carry out environmental due diligence first and, if the target company does not emerge relatively cleanly (no pun intended), they will call off the deal. Although environmental laws have been around for a long time,[1] in many jurisdictions they are now much stricter and more rigorously enforced. In the UK, there could even be personal liabilities. No wonder environmental audit is becoming a much more accepted part of the due diligence process.

Objectives

Mention environmental problems and the picture which comes to the fore in most people's mind is of contaminated land and chimneys belching out acrid smoke. A prospective buyer should not be lulled into assuming that such obvious examples of environmental risk are the only concerns. There may be other, seemingly less obvious matters we would like to know about and which come under the heading 'environmental due diligence'. Asbestos surveys, for example, would be one, as would the assessment of fire risk. There could also be environmental-related commercial concerns to think about. Barrie Pearson,[2] for example, discusses the case of an electroplating company with scope for considerably increased business but which had almost reached effluent limits set by the local authority and where negotiations to increase the limit had failed. Other commentators, quite rightly, stress the need to understand the threat of broader ethical and social risks an acquisition may bring. For example, at the time of writing it would be difficult to find an acquirer for a company such as Huntingdon Life Sciences.[3]

Just as important as soil contamination in an industrial site are the operational liabilities. If a target business is not complying with the relevant legislation, or will find it difficult to do so in the future, the buyer could find itself landed with a substantial capital programme to upgrade facilities, with substantial costs to match. As capital expenditure to comply with environmental regulations tends to have no financial payback, prospective acquirers need to know how much could be necessary in the future.

We should not, therefore, think of environmental liability just in terms of nasty chemicals or dirty chimneys. In assessing the potential liabilities arising from the target, environmental due diligence has two strands. The following require identifying and quantifying:

- Environmental risks which would be inherited. A potential liability for cleaning up contaminated land would be a good example.
- The costs of meeting any continuing obligations, for example upgrading equipment and procedures. This could be a big item where there has been significant non-compliance with environmental regulations.

Timing

Environmental due diligence can have the longest lead time in the entire transaction. If Phase 2 investigations (see below) are required, the process is going to take a long time indeed. Phase 2 involves soil and water sampling and digging holes. Not surprisingly a lot of negotiation is needed just to get access to carry out Phase 2. It stands to reason, therefore, that if environmental due diligence is required, it should be kicked off sooner rather than later. Furthermore, the environmental state of play may be a deciding factor in the structure of the deal. The possibility of inheriting the environmental nasties with a share purchase could be an important factor in going for an asset deal.[4] The sooner the buyer has the information to be able to come to this conclusion, the better. What usually happens, of course, is that this decision is taken well before the environmental consultants have even pulled on their wellies.

Why do I have to do it?

Again, just like any other form of due diligence, the starting question is do I have to carry out environmental due diligence at all? If so, how much? As always, the trick is to do as much inquiry as is reasonable and appropriate under the circumstances. Enquiries can therefore range from a few questions to a full-blown study with samples, drilling and all the rest. Whatever the effort, the end result should be a quantified understanding of the implications of a deal together with appropriate corrective actions.

In defining the size of the environmental due diligence, there are the usual due diligence concerns:

- Size of deal
- The worry of relying solely on warranties and indemnities
- The financial status of the parties involved
- The level of risk acceptance or risk aversion
- The benefits (not to mention the great feeling of self satisfaction) of being able to negotiate from a position of knowledge
- The cost of the inquiry.

And there are some questions which are special to environmental due diligence:

- The nature of the business to be acquired and previous uses of the site(s). I was once involved in buying a steel stockholding business in the Birmingham area. Steel stockholding is a fairly innocuous business as far as contaminating land is concerned. However, Birmingham is an area of the UK where manufacturing activity can be traced back many hundreds of years. Not surprisingly, therefore, the stockholding site had had a score of different uses over the years. These ranged from oil blending to rubber processing – so many in fact that we wondered which was the most valuable asset: the site or its mineral rights. Had the business been located in a brand new warehouse constructed on agricultural land we probably would not have bothered with a site investigation. This does not mean that if the firm being bought is a modern 'clean' business located in a new industrial park there are automatically no environmental problems. How do you know that industrial park was not built on an old rubbish dump which is still producing industrial strength methane in serious quantities? In many ways this type of scenario is worse than some obviously polluted industrial site. If environmental problems were not expected, they are likely to be much more significant, and much more problematic to deal with in negotiations, because they will not have been factored into the transaction.

- Number of sites
- Legislation/penalties. The law varies enormously throughout the world, both in terms of who is liable and what is considered as 'contaminated' and therefore what needs cleaning up. In the UK the law will force a clean-up of contaminated land only where there is a pressing need.[5] In contrast, the US Superfund model adopts a system whereby if a substance is located in the ground above a certain threshold level, clean-up is automatically triggered.
- Future legislation. Keeping up with rising standards can be expensive, and most environmental authorizations will contain upgrading conditions which will vary as new standards emerge
- What you want the site for. Under UK law, there will be a big difference in the value of contaminated land if current use is to be continued (in which case the contaminated land provisions apply) than if the plan is for redevelopment (where the planning system could force a clean-up). Clearly if the development potential of surplus land is built into the deal price, price is going to be much more severely affected by contamination than if the price is based solely on the earnings potential of the target as a going concern.
- Local authorities may require a clean-up. In the U.K., under the Environmental Act, there is a duty on local authorities to inspect land that is of environmental concern. Although it will take some time to get round to inspecting all the worrying sites on their patch, an acquisition could prompt a local authority to inspect a site and it may require some remediation if in its view there is 'significant likelihood of significant harm'.

Process

Step 1, just as with any other form of due diligence, is to decide what work needs doing and who is going to do it. The answer may be that not much work does need doing at all – the seller may have told you everything you need to know. In the old days, *caveat emptor* meant that there was no real incentive for sellers to volunteer information about contamination. New contaminated land provisions may change all that. The more information the seller gives the buyer, the more likely the seller can now escape liability. When it comes to contaminated land, if the seller tells the buyer everything the buyer, is 'buying with knowledge' and any liability is transferred. As far as the buyer is concerned, this means treating the results of environmental due diligence extremely carefully. It could very easily result in liabilities transferring to the buyer which might otherwise have remained with the seller. To make matters worse, there is a suggestion[6] that in transactions since 1990 between large commercial organizations, buyers will be assumed to have the necessary information where they have been permitted to carry out their own surveys.

On top of the perils of 'buying with knowledge' environmental due diligence can be something of a double-edged sword for both sides. Before a seller, or a buyer, commissions a written report, it is worth thinking through what the consequences might be.

The legal position in the UK for contaminated land is set out in the Environment Act 1995. It is basically as follows:

- The regulators can impose clean-up orders on 'appropriate persons'.
- Top of the list of 'appropriate persons' is any person who 'caused or knowingly permitted' the polluting substances on to the land in the first place.
- If it proves impossible to find someone who has 'caused or knowingly permitted' contamination, the regulators may turn to the owner and occupier of the land.

Written environmental reports may therefore provide evidence for regulatory clean-up actions, civil actions or, even worse, criminal prosecutions. Imagine what would happen if the report is disclosed in any subsequent legal proceedings where:

- The deal has not gone ahead and the seller knows of the contents of the report but has done nothing to clean up the contamination
- The deal has gone ahead but the buyer has failed, without good reason, to implement the most important recommendations

Neither is going to have much of a defence and as the report was not produced because of impending litigation, it is unlikely to be legally privileged.

The situation with water pollution in the UK leaves absolutely no room for doubt as to what should be done. The Water Resources Act 1991 takes the view that any pollution in water is harmful and must be cleaned up. Just for good measure, Section 85 makes it a criminal offence to pollute the sea, rivers, lakes or groundwaters.

The same thought needs to go into considering what might be the consequences for insurance policies. It is not unknown for there to be clauses covering material non-disclosure. Environmental due diligence might conceivably highlight matters which require a seller or a buyer to notify insurers of liabilities to which policies attach.

ADVISERS

Assuming, though, that a buyer does require some due diligence, the question is who to commission to carry it out. Unlike solicitors and accountants there is no governing body for environmental consultancies. References and recommendations are, therefore, doubly essential. Most big law firms now have environmental practices. Environmental lawyers will have a pretty good insight into the who's who of environmental consultants.

Once a suitable consultancy has been selected, watch out for the consultant's standard terms of appointment. These are usually drafted to minimize their financial exposure to negligence. Check insurance cover as well. Very few consultancies seem to carry levels of insurance worth having. This is very important where there is likely to be Phase 2 enquiries because Phase 2 work could involve disturbing a site to such an extent that it actually causes damage.

CROSS-BORDER CONSIDERATIONS

Every jurisdiction is different. Clearly each site in each jurisdiction must be treated on its own merits, and the findings viewed against local legislation. However, it is also important for the overall investigation that risk is assessed in a consistent manner. What is needed is local investigation and local interpretation but a central risk assessment methodology.

The need to use local advice is reinforced by the fact that in most countries the only way to get access to public registers is to visit the offices of the relevant authorities.

Legislation is not only different around the world, but it is enforced in a different manner by different bodies. The UK has a nationwide Environment Agency, in Holland local councils have responsibility for matters environmental – except where the provincial authority or one of the ministries is responsible. In the US both federal and state regulations and procedures may have to be taken into account. Some states require a change of company ownership to be notified. Notification will then trigger an environmental investigation and possibly, as an outcome, an order for remediation. Europe, in contrast, tends to operate on a risk assessment basis. This in turn means that the same circumstances in different European countries could quite conceivably result in quite different outcomes. It is even possible that the same circumstances on different sites within the same country could lead to totally different consequences. In Spain national law can be supplemented by local laws; in Germany federal regulations are administered by a number of different agencies at state level.[7]

Of course there are a number of regions in the world where environmental regulation is not taken as seriously as it is in Europe or the USA. On the face of it, operating in these areas could give a competitive advantage. In practice any such advantage may be illusory or relatively short-lived. Not only does environmental legislation have a habit of changing, or its enforcement taking on a new lease of life, but how many European or American companies would really apply grossly inferior environmental standards overseas than they are used to at home? Some years ago the UK friction products company Ferodo set up a joint venture operation in India to produce brake pads. Having been badly bitten by asbestos litigation in the UK and USA, the last thing that T&N, the parent, would condone was the use of asbestos in India. Asbestos is a near perfect binding medium in brake pads and was therefore used extensively by the indigenous competition, despite the danger it posed to the workforce and customers alike. The result was that Ferodo suffered a competitive disadvantage in India precisely because it was not prepared to take advantage of the looser environmental controls.

BRIEFING ADVISERS

Having decided how much environmental due diligence to do and having selected an adviser, the buyer has to communicate clear and concise reasons for carrying out the work. However much advisers and others involved in a deal might pretend that due diligence findings can be summarized in a set of numbers or 'hard' facts, nothing in fact could be further from the truth. This is the case even with a topic seemingly so 'scientific' as environmental due diligence. Even here, interpretation can be everything. It is vitally important, therefore, that whoever carries out the work is briefed on the following points:

- The type of business being acquired
- The reason for the transaction. This is a heading which crops up whichever adviser is being briefed. Environmental due diligence is a good example of why advisers should understand their client's reasons for doing the deal. (And if there is no good reason or one which the client cannot articulate, maybe they should not be doing it.) As discussed above, the environmental concerns are going to be very different if one of the attractions of the

target business is its surplus property than if it is being acquired for its manufacturing output. In the first case, the bulk of the environmental risk is likely to come from potential clean-up costs. In the second case, where existing activities are going to be continued, the main environmental risks are going to be operating permits and any expenditure which might be required to comply with environmental standards. In the first case the environmental auditors will be fretting about previous uses of the site, looking for any polluting operations on site, poring over maps and worrying about geology. In the second, their concerns are going to be effluent discharges and what is coming out of the chimneys

- The nature of the transaction. As discussed already, an asset purchase will raise different issues to a share purchase
- The rationale for the work. For example, if its purpose is to satisfy lenders, the consultants need to know this. Lenders will typically take a much more conservative line than a purchaser. Insurance companies will want yet more detail
- Existing knowledge and major concerns.

The better this is done the better the consultant will be able know where to focus the inquiries.

Scope also needs to be clearly communicated. What is to be included?

- An assessment of land contamination?
- Should everything be covered that might have an impact or should the work focus on specific issues likely to have the biggest environmental impact?

The focus will probably be on some or all of the following four areas:

- The nature and extent of any land contamination
- The presence of substances which may cause contamination in future
- The degree of compliance with environmental regulation
- Environmental management

Appendix A11 gives a basis for scoping an environmental due diligence study. In addition to the scope of the work to be carried out, terms of reference should also include the usual contractual items mentioned in Chapter 3.

Land contamination

Land contamination and clean-up costs will be a concern in many deals. Traditionally, this is a two-stage process:

- Phase 1 review, which is a review of existing knowledge, public data and other information on the target to identify any areas of concern
- Phase 2 review, the intrusive enquiries required to monitor, sample and fully analyse any concerns raised in Phase 1

Self-evidently, each site is unique so the work will be site specific.

INFORMATION SOURCES

Desk research

The first step in the actual work is usually a desktop study. This stage begins with the consultants trawling through relevant information sources listed in Appendix B5 to weigh up the chances of the land or surrounding area being contaminated. At the same time they would examine:

- The physical characteristics of the area, the hydrology and geology for example
- The economic context, for example land use
- Records of statutory bodies to identify anything which could be on the receiving end of pollution such as boreholes and rivers. One of the important things to bear in mind is that pollution can travel. Environmental consultants should always to be thinking not just in terms of what contaminants might be present, but also the likelihood of them travelling and having an impact on a wider area.

This assessment will in all probability set the scene for any subsequent Phase 2 work.

Data rooms

If there is a data room involved in a transaction a lot of this information should be in there. Data rooms will usually contain some or all of the following:

- Environmental consultants' reports
- Environmental policies
- Lists of any hazardous materials kept on site
- Details of accidents and spillages
- Details of breaches of consents
- Enforcement notices (following environmental damage or breach of compliance).

Management information

No system is perfect, but if a target is employing a formal system for environmental management, such as one based on ISO 14001, it does at least prove an awareness of the risks its operations pose to the environment and that controls are in place to manage that risk.

When reviewing management information, it is worth bearing in mind what is in place now and what the position will be once the deal is done. If the target is part of a bigger company which has been able to rely on corporate resources, there may be a cost to be factored into the deal which reflects the cost of not being able to draw on the parent's corporate environmental organization.

Regulatory authorities

There should be a fair amount of information in the public domain. For example, in the UK, regulatory authorities, such as the Environment Agency and the relevant local authority, will be able to provide authorizations, permits and licences, and also details of any enforcements. The local water company will have details of consents to carry out any trade effluent discharges.

Depending on how sensitive the transaction is, a Phase 1 study can obtain a considerable amount of useful information from talking to the regulatory authorities about any concerns they may have. As is the case with tax, past relationships with the authorities can be a good indication of how they are likely to treat a site or company in the future. Past problems are likely to be watched and a change of ownership may be viewed as an opportunity to get better environmental behaviour.

Site visits

Following the initial desk research comes the site visit(s). It may not be necessary to audit every site owned or occupied by the target. The idea is to identify those sites where material issues are likely to be identified. For those sites where a visit is justified, the objective is not to carry out detailed drilling or sampling, but to see the site and see how operations are carried out. The environmental auditor will aim to:

- Further assess the nature and extent of any contamination
- Audit the presence of substances which may cause contamination in future
- Understand the degree of compliance with environmental regulations
- Audit environmental management

Further assessing the nature and extent of any contamination   The aim here is to build a detailed picture of the site and surrounding area and to retrieve all relevant information. This might include:

- Interviews with all relevant site personnel. (This is a potentially tricky area given that environmental issues can be very sensitive and disclosure of past accidents/practices may well involve site personnel having to admit breaches of environmental regulations.)
- Obtaining details of company/site management structure
- Gaining an understanding of the site's history – especially details of processes that have been undertaken on the site
- Reviewing any site studies. The seller or the target's management should be asked to provide any documents that could identify past or present environmental problems. Examples of these are listed in Appendix A2, but would include, for example, contamination studies, geotechnical reports or any other details of current environmental conditions.
- Details of any chemical accidents/spills.

Audit the presence of substances which may cause contamination in future   The environmental consultants will be keen to review and document the following:

- The presence of restricted substances
- The layout of site services
- Packaging, handling, distribution and containment of hazardous materials

Understanding the degree of compliance with environmental regulations

Under this heading comes a whole host of rules and regulations with which the target business may have to comply. The environmental consultant will want to gather details on:

- Environmental permits
- Discharges to the environment (that is to air, water and ground). Where there are discharges to the environment, the buyer needs comfort that they are fully authorized.

Depending on the circumstances they may be controlled either by the environment agency or the local authority in the UK

- Waste disposal. The management of waste, as well as its disposal, could be licensed. Even if it is not, its disposal needs to be done in accordance with the law.

Environmental management   This heading will include:

- Existing policies, standards and practices
- Current environmental monitoring programmes
- Outstanding regulatory or civil action or nuisance complaints from neighbours
- Methods of addressing environmental liabilities

Phase 1 conclusions

Now it should be possible to review the target site and, more importantly, come to a view on whether there are any environmental issues which will have an impact on the deal. These will normally be set out in a report at this stage. If there are potentially serious issues which require further investigation, you might have to commission a Phase 2 investigation.

PHASE 2 INVESTIGATIONS

Phase 2 relates to soil and groundwater contamination. The objective is to quantify the risks from contamination generated within the site or which has come from adjoining sites.

The work will probably involve sampling the soil and groundwater and analysing the samples in a laboratory. It may be done in stages. It is something best left to experts adept at identifying hot spots of contamination on a site and skilled at not unduly disturbing contamination during their enquiries. The last thing you want is for the enquiries themselves to give rise to liabilities. Because of this very risk, sellers sometimes resist Phase 2 audits. Often only the negotiation of extensive indemnities against damage caused by the investigation is sufficient for sellers to grant access. As mentioned above, the risks inherent in Phase 2 audits explain why insurance cover is something to consider when selecting environmental consultants.

Phase 2 work can be not only costly and risky, in the sense that the investigations themselves can make contamination problems worse, but it can also take a long, long time.

Reporting

The report should permit the purchaser to evaluate the environmental risk. This is not just a question of dealing with the problems identified, but also the costs and other mechanisms needed to deal with compliance in the future. One thing is absolutely certain: the regulatory regime is not going to get any softer.

The final report should contain the following headings:

1. A description of the issues identified, for example:

- Legal and/or policy requirements
- Areas of significantly bad environmental performance

2. An assessment of how management has dealt with them. This could, for example, be an assessment of their environmental performance against statutory and/or corporate standards (if available).
3. Inefficiencies in current practices
4. Non-compliance issues
5. Steps required to rectify any concerns, non-compliances and so on
6. Priorities for environmental improvements
7. Current and future requirements and an assessment of upgrade requirements
8. Possible means of achieving these improvements, together with costs and timescales
9. A review of whether any of the above costs have already been accounted for, for example, through provisions or insurance
10. Indemnities needed
11. Any other potential risks and the chances of them crystallizing

At this point the purchaser has to decide what to do next. It may well be that the potential exposure is a function of the following:

1. The legal framework – depending on the jurisdiction, liability may be more or less than at home.
2. Legislative changes – it pays to check out what legislation is in the pipeline and how it may affect you.
3. The structure of the transaction – As discussed above, an asset sale will avoid the buyer inheriting current and contingent historical liabilities incurred by the seller. A share sale means the legal entity remains intact which in turn will mean inheriting all the liabilities such as:

   • Liability for past acts or omissions
   • Liabilities attaching to assets previously owned by the company (for example a polluted site which has been sold but for which it retains contingent liability in respect of clean-up)
   • Liability under environmental warranties and indemnities previously given by the company (for example on any assets previously disposed of).

4. Insurance cover – with a share sale, the target will also inherit all historic insurance policies. If it was the member of a group it will keep group cover even after it has left the group. Chapter 16 covers insurance due diligence in more detail, but basically you will have to inspect the insurance documents, both yours and the sellers, to assess what environmental risks are already covered and to make sure that you are going to comply with the insurer's conditions. Sellers may qualify warranties and indemnities to exclude items that would be covered by insurance.

Legal protection

Having reviewed potential liabilities the purchaser will need to consider how best to protect itself. It may use one or more of the mechanisms available, namely:

- Price adjustment
- Insurance
- Asset sale rather than a share sale
- Exclusion of certain assets
- Warranties and indemnities
- Rectification of any problems at the seller's costs.

PRICE ADJUSTMENT

As well as 'selling with knowledge', any polluter or landowner may be able to transfer any liability when land is sold by reducing the purchase price and making it explicit that the reduction is to reflect remediation costs. But even when all risk is passed to the purchaser the seller may still be liable in the eyes of some third parties.[8] Where there is a price reduction for environmental reasons the seller will therefore want the comfort of an indemnity which allows him to recover any costs from the purchaser. He may also want to consider combining the indemnity with an obligation for the buyer to clean up.

INSURANCE

Insurance can be taken out for a number of environmental risks. The insurers will probably want to assess the risks for themselves and will definitely want to see the results of any environmental audits. Environmental insurance cover is becoming increasingly restricted, often to identifiable incidents. Policies covering the clean-up of land are available but often the amount of cover is capped.

ASSET SALE RATHER THAN A SHARE SALE

As already mentioned, an assets sale will break the link with a target's historical liabilities. It will, however, require the transfer of environmental consents and an assignment of insurance policies, if there are any. It will not do away completely with the need for warranties and indemnities from the seller either. The buyer should seek some protection from pollution which occurs after it has become the owner or occupier of a site but which is the result of acts or omissions of the seller before the deal was done.

EXCLUSION OF CERTAIN ASSETS

Excluding certain assets could be the most effective way of excluding potential liabilities from the acquisition. For example, it is quite common to find that before environmental awareness was anywhere near as high as it is now, and that was not all that long ago, companies used a far corner of the site to dump old machinery, scrap products or even spent chemicals. There is unlikely to be any good reason why a buyer should include these, often PCB- or arsenic-infested, grassy knolls in the deal.

WARRANTIES AND INDEMNITIES

Environmental due diligence has come a long way in the last decade but, like just about every other due diligence discipline, it suffers from one weakness. It cannot be relied upon to discover and quantify every risk that there might be inside a target during the typical due diligence time frame. This means that the buyer must use warranties and indemnities, as well as due diligence and the other forms of protection, in its battle against unwanted liabilities.

Indemnities give the buyer the best protection. Ideally the environmental indemnity will provide that the seller will meet the costs incurred by the purchaser in any claim arising from any of the risks previously identified and disclosed. As it is often in a seller's interest to give a full environmental disclosure in order to 'transfer with knowledge', the purchaser may end up seeking specific indemnities. Any indemnity will usually be for a specified time, it may not cover all losses and there will be *de minimus* provisions and caps. Trigger provisions should also be negotiated. The indemnity should not just be triggered in the event of a formal order by the authorities. The need to keep in with the regulators often means that work is carried out before they have to resort to formal proceedings. Finally, it is advisable to commission a survey to establish a benchmark of contamination at or near completion so that there are no arguments later about how much pollution was caused since completion by the buyer's activities on the site and how much is genuinely down to the seller's pre-deal activities.

If an indemnity is not negotiated, there may be a warranty about compliance with the environmental laws and the obtaining of all necessary permits. The seller will be asked to warrant that it has:

- Complied with all applicable laws
- All the permits it needs to carry out the business
- Not been party to any environmental litigation
- Not caused any toxic or hazardous release into the environment
- No obligations to remedy soil at any site.

Warranties may be perfectly adequate where environmental problems are limited. As with all warranties, there may be difficulties in relying on them in practice in the event of a breach. Also, just because there has been compliance with laws and licences does not mean that no liability can arise. There may still be contamination on the property, the liability for which could pass to the buyer. The seller should also be asked to warrant any documentation provided. As mentioned above, sellers may qualify warranties and indemnities to exclude items that would be covered by insurance.

Because of the time it can take for environmental problems to manifest themselves, the time periods for warranties and indemnities in the environmental field need to be considerably longer than in most other fields. Five to seven years is typical, but much longer periods are not unknown.

Given the potential size of claims in this area, sellers can be expected to defend themselves with vigour against any claims, so warranties and indemnities need careful drafting. This is another reason for commissioning environmental due diligence as early as possible, to give the lawyers plenty of time to study the results and draft the necessary protection.

RECTIFICATION OF ANY PROBLEMS AT THE SELLER'S COST

This last remedy is often best for the buyer but it often leads to lengthy debates over the extent of rectification. There is a big difference sometimes between compliance and best practice. Here, the wise seller will require a covenant from the buyer that the work will be completed within a given time after completion.

In addition, sellers may try to limit liability by excluding responsibility for any contamination which was there before they bought the site. Whether or not contamination arose before a seller's occupation can be extremely difficult to prove. Some mechanism may have to be found to get round this. Sometimes liability is apportioned according to type of substance, alternatively it might be agreed to split any post-completion clean-up costs. Often this is done on a sliding scale arrangement where the seller initially takes the bulk of the liability with the buyer's proportion of the liability increasing with time.

CONCLUSION

Environmental due diligence is becoming an increasingly important pre-acquisition investigation. Although it will usually focus on contaminated land and discharges to air and water, there are a number of other topics which might be considered, such as ethical risks (and the consequent possibility of attracting direct action from protest groups). It can take a long time to complete so it needs to be thought about at a very early stage. Also, as it can be a double-edged sword, the decision whether or not to commission environmental due diligence needs to be carefully considered.

It is normally structured into two phases, although Phase 2 is by no means always carried out. The first phase will comprise desk research and site visits. The second phase, involving intrusive investigations, will not always be necessary. Advisers need to be chosen with care and not just for their technical expertise. Their terms of engagement and levels of insurance cover can be just as important. There are a number of standard remedies available to cater for any unexpected risks. Which are used very much depends on the deal and the negotiating strength of the parties involved.

12 *IT & production technology due diligence*

IT is integral to the running and efficiency of all companies. For many it is an integral part of the product or service too. It is central to profitability. Understanding the target, protecting the potential investment in it, negotiating the deal and understanding how to extract value from it are all going to demand some form of IT due diligence.

The usual concern with IT due diligence is the holy grail of integrating information systems. Buyers with this mentality are missing out. An acquisition is a prime opportunity to make the changes necessary to elevate IT to where it belongs, as a strategic tool for creating competitive advantage. Besides, integrating legacy systems is often a waste of time and an awful lot of money.

IT due diligence potentially comes in two forms:

- Information technology (IT), that is the systems, processes and hardware used to run the business
- Production technology (PT), that is the processes, equipment and know-how used to make the products or deliver the service

The topics for both type of investigation overlap. They will therefore be considered together.

How much to do

Clearly the answer to the perennial question of how much investigation to do in this area is going to be a function of what the intentions are post-acquisition and the importance of information and production technology. If the business is going to be merged with existing facilities then investigations will probably be limited to checking that data in legacy systems can be migrated and that the system will work adequately in the interim.

The costs of merging IT systems can be colossal and the cost savings from consolidation are usually over-estimated. Not surprisingly, therefore, there is a school of thought which contends that acquirers are a little too keen to integrate systems. There is some merit in this. Unless the target's systems are woefully out of date, it should be possible to get adequate management information out of them. Most systems these days will work alongside each other reasonably well. Merging systems, the argument goes, will give you economies of scale, but at what price? What frequently happens is that a political decision, unrelated to the relative merits of the systems, is taken to use one system rather than another. Even where full integration is planned, it might be better to concentrate on compatibility between the systems rather than proceeding from the assumption that there will be a full merger of IT. While integrating hardware is relatively easy, integrating applications software is not.

If, on the other hand, this is going to be a stand-alone business where information technology is a fundamental element of competitive advantage, then clearly due diligence is going to assume a different importance than if IT is merely there to run the payroll.

Information gathering

For IT and PT due diligence, the most common research techniques are:

- Management and staff interviews
- A review of documentation relating to PT and IT practices

Levels of investigation

Acquisition due diligence should be seen as more than an opportunity to kick the tyres. An acquisition provides an opportunity to create an organization which uses IT and PT as strategic tools for the future. It presents the ideal opportunity to reinvent what has gone before and so leapfrog existing strategies.

Investigations should take place on three levels:

- The audit level. What equipment and software is there? Is it secure, does it work, who owns it, what are the outstanding commitments?
- The management level. How well does IT and technology support the business?
- The strategic level. Is the technology and organization sufficient for the future?

THE AUDIT LEVEL

Investigation at the audit level is just that. It will do little more than investigate the risks. These are fairly generic and are set out in Figure 12.1.

Vulnerability
Vulnerability is obviously a function of how many users there are on the system, and the access controls. There are two ways of accessing a system: physically and electronically. An audit will test the controls around both. If the system is connected to a public network, then the risk of unauthorized access goes up quite considerably.

Trust
Trust is fairly self-explanatory. The level of trust is defined by two factors:

- The level of confidence one can have in the employees because they have been through some sort of vetting procedure
- The trust management have in the system based on their experience of security failures in the past.

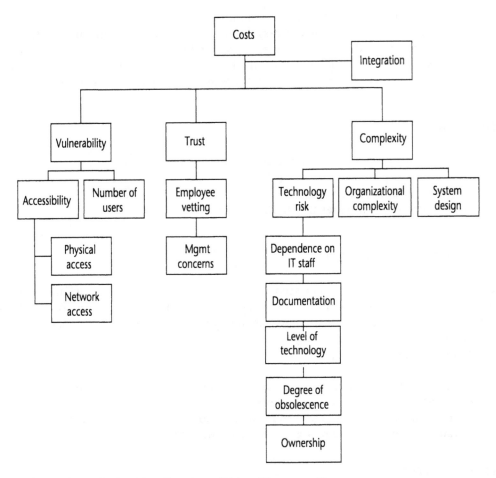

Figure 12.1   Typical subject headings for an IT due diligence audit

Complexity

As can be seen from Figure 12.1, complexity has three elements to it.

The risk from technology   The risk from technology is possibly the most pertinent to the due diligence investigation. It covers a number of areas:

- The degree of dependence on a small number of key people
- The quality of system documentation
- The level of technology
- The degree of equipment obsolescence
- Ownership, particularly of software: is it inside or outside the company?

DEPENDENCE ON A FEW KEY IT STAFF

Dependence on a few key IT staff is a critical issue. Acquisitions create uncertainty amongst employees. As a result they tend to start sending out CVs. IT skills are usually eminently transferable and often in short supply. If the target's system is dependent on a few key individuals there will be considerable risk. This will multiply if those key people happen to be contractors rather than employees.

Dependency risk will be compounded by any negative feelings they may have towards the buyer or their new roles. The acquirer should always assume that there will be major integration issues to do with people. If nothing else you can bet that one company will use different versions of Windows and business processes will be different. Minor differences such as these will grow into major turf wars if not managed properly. More serious are the cases where employees from one company are so unhappy about the imposition of the other side's systems that they sabotage the integration process by deleting data and withholding key information.[1] If there is even the merest hint of a suggestion that the target's IT staff will not be allowed to do the interesting development work under the new regime, the best of them will go. This could be either because they know or fear that they will become subservient to the purchaser's IT department or the future as they see it is going to be solely concerned with cobbling two systems together. If on the other hand they believe the future is about rewriting the IT strategy to align with the business strategy, they are likely to stay. People issues can be as important as the technical issues.

DOCUMENTATION

Clearly risk will multiply if documentation is sparse or non-existent, especially if it is in the heads of people who fear for their future.

THE LEVEL OF TECHNOLOGY/DEGREE OF EQUIPMENT OBSOLESCENCE

Level of technology and obsolescence are related. On the one hand, up to a point, the longer the technology has been in place, the lower the technology risk. Above a certain time, though, the greater the risk that it will have to be replaced shortly after acquisition, with all the cost and uncertainty that that entails.

The warning signs on computer hardware are:

- proprietary systems
- and/or more than four years old.

The problem with relatively old, proprietary systems is that the software tends not to be very sophisticated and the hardware is high maintenance which may have to be replaced shortly at the new owner's expense. As we saw in Chapter 4 the age of computer hardware may also have a direct impact on profitability. If it is old and fully written off, recent depreciation charges will have been low. Low depreciation is obviously unsustainable if the equipment is going to be replaced soon.

With software, the most critical issue is whether the software being used is customized for the target company. Standardized packages from software companies that are financially stable and have large installed bases are the safest option. This way there is much more likelihood of continuous technical support and regular product enhancements. At the other end of the risk spectrum is the target company using a package that was developed by a very small firm or worse, by one person. This creates a situation where not only is the software very expensive to maintain and enhance, but the target also remains vulnerable to the firm going out of business or of something happening to the developer.

OWNERSHIP OF ASSETS

Does the company actually own the IT assets it operates? Is the target company the licensor? If, for example, another group company actually holds the licence, some sort of sub-licensing arrangement may be necessary. Other questions to ask would be:

1. How long a duration do the licences have:

   a) Limited? (If so when do they finish?)
   b) Perpetual?

2. Are there any limitations on licensed software:

   a) Equipment on which it can be used?
   b) Locations at which it can be used?
   c) Number of users?
   d) If existing limitations are not sufficient, can they be extended and, if so, how much will it cost?
   e) Is the licence for source code or object code?
   f) If it is for object code, what guarantees are in place?

   - Will the licensor maintain the software and provide support within acceptable time limits?
   - Does the licensee get access to source code if the licensor goes out of business?

3. If the licence is for source code, does the target have an obligation to maintain the software itself or can this be outsourced?
4. Will restrictions in the software licences prevent the target outsourcing its IT function?

It is useful to see copies of all software licences and other agreements for the use and maintenance of computer systems and computer software.

Organizational complexity   If the system is totally integrated so that each function is dependent on several other parts of the same system, then the risk is that much higher. If one function fails, the whole system goes down. Single function systems obviously carry the least risk of system failure as far as the organization as a whole is concerned.

System design   The higher the number of departments which rely on a system, the higher the risk, for the same reasons as above. The highest risk systems are those where all departments are reliant on the one system: if the system goes down, the whole company goes down.

MANAGEMENT LEVEL

Due diligence should also recognize that the target's IT is not just a collection of hardware and software. The real value of technology is the value it adds to the target. Increasingly the use of information technology is critical to the operations of most businesses. Unfortunately, many managements have yet to recognize this and see expenditure on IT as an expense that must be minimized instead of an asset purchase that will improve profitability. The result is usually obsolete, and therefore inefficient, information systems.

A good starting point for this element of the investigation, therefore, is the company-wide attitude to IT. Is it seen as a strong differentiator, an important element of competitive advantage, a necessary evil or a positive hindrance to progress? How interlinked is IT with the wider business? For example, is IT treated like any other piece of capital expenditure or business development with the expected costs and benefits of a project outlined before the project is approved and results monitored afterwards? Is the target's aim to use technology to create demonstrable competitive advantage or does the process end with the delivery of ad hoc pieces of automation?

Next is going to be an assessment of the IT team, its focus and capabilities. Is the IT organization and its business processes equal to what might be expected of it? The team's focus should be at the business level rather than the product/customer level and it should be business-driven rather than technology-driven. All the evidence suggests that companies waste at least 20 per cent of IT budgets, most commonly by over-specifying hardware and network infrastructure, unnecessary customization of software packages and poor control of software licensing. Is there evidence of this in the target? Are, for example, desktop systems sized to the highest common denominator? Not everyone will need access to fast machines with a lot of memory and software, but the tendency often is to simplify system management by giving everyone the same. Has the enterprise resource planning system been unnecessarily customized? Is there a good team spirit and good, visionary leadership? The attitude of the IT team will reveal a lot and so will the decision-making routes. At what level in the pecking order are the technical/IT departments represented? In many cases these days it should be at board level.

User interviews will shed more light. Does the present system support departmental and company objectives? What do the business units and functional heads say about the IT department? Do they see it as a skilled resource that is responsive to requests?

The reason for carrying out investigations at this level is to decide whether a major overhaul of the IT systems and personnel, including perhaps significant expenditure on hardware and software, is going to be needed to maintain competitiveness.

STRATEGIC LEVEL

The strategic level is about the contribution of technology to the future. This is a mixture of two things. It is partly about using technology to create competitive advantage and partly about recognizing that IT will be an essential component of any company of the future. Due diligence questions will be along the following lines:

- How closely is the IT plan aligned with the overall corporate plan?
- What is the timescale? (Benefits from IT projects should be delivered in months not years.)
- How is IT helping to give the target the ability to respond to rapidly changing circumstances?
- How is IT giving customers added value?

This is not an easy subject area, even without the pressures of an acquisition. For example, PA Consulting, in a study called 'Increasing business value with Information Technology', found that only 40 per cent of executives polled in Europe, the US and Asia-Pacific had confidence in the business cases used to justify their companies' IT investments. Other sources[2] calculate that many companies devote nearly 75 per cent of their IT budgets to maintaining systems and infrastructures. Of the remaining 25 per cent only about a third actually delivers value.

However, if used properly, information technology can change the basis of competition in an industry quite considerably, especially where there is high information intensity in the company or the product. High information intensity is characterized by:[3]

1. A large number of suppliers or customers
2. A complex product sell requiring a large amount of information
3. A wide product range
4. A product with
   • Many parts
   • A complex, multi-stage manufacturing process
   • A long cycle time
   • A requirement for large amounts of information
   • Especially high costs for buyer training
   • Many alternative uses.

According to strategy guru Michael Porter, information technology can change each of the five competitive forces[4] which shape industry attractiveness. An acquisition gives managers the perfect opportunity for reviewing the likely impact of IT on their industry and organizing IT in the merged entity in such as a way as to steal a march on the competition. According to Porter, 'Many companies are partly in control of the nature and pace of change in the industry structure.'[5] The challenge is to determine how information technology might create competitive advantage by lowering costs, increasing differentiation or giving access to new markets.

The starting point will be a thorough analysis of the value chain with a special examination of activities that make up a large proportion of cost or are critical to differentiation. Porter recommends the following questions be asked to determine whether IT can help gain access to new market areas.

Can information technology help the company serve new segments? Will the flexibility of information technology allow broad line competitors to invade areas that were once the province of niche competitors? Will information technology provide the leverage to expand the business globally? Can managers harness information technology to exploit interrelationships with other industries? Or, can the technology help a company create competitive advantage by narrowing its scope?[6]

Capturing the benefits of IT at the strategic level of course calls for a plan. This cannot be formulated solely in the IT or technical department, nor in splendid isolation in the boardroom. At this level, technology is not about mechanizing activities previously carried out manually. It is about making sure technology creates lasting competitive advantage, which, in Porter's words, demands 'a sophisticated understanding of the requirements for competitive advantage'.[7]

Conclusion

IT due diligence is not just about the functionality of the target's systems, or about how best to manage information systems in the combined entity. IT due diligence can take place on three levels. At the audit level, a would-be buyer is concerned with checking that the system is secure, that it works and that it will continue to be secure and work after the deal is done. At the management level, due diligence seeks to unearth some of the cultural issues that may have to be tackled post-acquisition to improve short-term business performance. The strategic level investigation starts with the recognition that an acquisition, as was mentioned in Chapter 1 and again in Chapter 6, is a strategic tool for creating and maintaining competitive advantage. These days, IT is a major component of competitive advantage. An acquisition should be used as a means of ensuring IT makes its full contribution. At all three levels, IT due diligence will be as much about people as about technology and systems.

13 *Technology due diligence*

This chapter is concerned with product technology, the technology associated with the product itself. For example, with a piece of software, technology is the product. Due diligence here becomes a mixture of investigation and technical assessment. The technology has to work, but to understand its true worth due diligence needs to look beyond its specification to its worth in the marketplace, both now and in the future. Future worth depends on continued development based on understanding and responding to market needs. Harnessing the creativity of people will ultimately bring the market rewards. Therefore the human factor is just as important as the technical and market issues.

How much to do

Fast-moving markets require fast-paced decision-making. In such circumstances, due diligence can be a real burden, but incomplete due diligence can be a bigger burden long term. The *Harvard Business Review* contains the cautionary tale of AT&T's acquisition of NCR.[1] AT&T was desperate for a new growth opportunity. It fell for the notion of 3Cs, the idea that computers, communications and consumer electronics were converging to form a new industry. AT&T needed a PC capability and came upon NCR as a promising candidate. NCR made a profit on PCs and with AT&T's resources behind it, it would do even better. AT&T launched a hostile bid which, after spending $7.5 billion, it won. A thorough examination of the technical issues would have revealed some serious concerns. After the deal was done, AT&T's engineers assessed NCR's technology and found 'substantial differences between AT&T's switching abilities and basic PC technology' and also that 'NCR's PC group had no real competence in personal computing – it was a me-too assembler that supported the company's forte in mainframes.'

It is important to do enough investigation to get comfortable with the target's products, capabilities and real expertise.

Areas to cover

Appendix A13 contains a work programme for the technical due diligence typical when acquiring a software company. The remainder of this section sets out a more general approach. It is difficult to generalize on what a product technology review will involve. It will depend on the type and maturity of the technology in question. However, a detailed technical assessment is likely to cover of one or more of the areas following.

PRODUCT ARCHITECTURE

- Design. A good starting point is asking management to describe, in non-technical terms, what the technology does, how it works and how it is put together. It is surprising how often they cannot. This may not say much about the technology, but it will speak volumes about management's ability to understand and anticipate customer requirements.
- Does the technology deliver the required performance? This is closely allied with the next point.
- Is there a fit with the business plan? Does the technology perform to the standards required by the business plan, for example can the architecture support the business requirement for a fail-safe, ultra-secure, 24/7 operating environment?
- Scalability. Is the product capable of going from test-bed type applications to full-scale commercial use?
- Robustness. Will the technology and architecture cope with the demands of live commercial operations?

UNDERLYING TECHNOLOGY

- Stage of development. Where is the underlying technology in life-cycle terms? Is the technology widely developed? Who else uses it and what for? Has it been patented in other countries or by competitors?
- Is the technology indispensable or are there potential substitutes?
- Is it appropriate to the application or is it a technophile's solution?
- Can the target deploy the chosen technology?
- How appropriate is the underlying technology for the future, for example could it turn out to be a constraint to growth?

INTELLECTUAL PROPERTY

For coverage of this topic, see Chapter 14.

COMMERCIALIZATION

- Estimates of commercialization costs
- Complexity of commercialization
- Are the appropriate skills and systems in place for commercialization? Do the plans for commercialization agree with the business plan? (They are frequently miles apart.)
- Are the skills and systems required for market support in place?

ANALYSIS OF DOCUMENTATION

- Overall structure. Assessment of overall quality, including consistency and process by which business objectives are translated into design goals
- Core components. Conceptualization of product positioning and key intellectual property elements
- Environmental requirements
- Operational documentation.

CODE REVIEW

If this is necessary, it should include:

- technology assessment
- core components
- environmental connectivity.

MARKET INVESTIGATIONS

As already mentioned, technical due diligence is a mixture of technical appraisal and investigation. Technical appraisal does require the close attention of some highly qualified people with the requisite product experience. But this needs to be supplemented by enquiries in the marketplace and some Human Resources detective work.

Some pretty fundamental questions can be answered by fairly simple investigations. Questions like 'Does the product actually work?', 'How does it rate against competing products?' can be answered by asking users and potential users. These will supplement the technical assessments. Talking to existing customers, lost customers and potential customers about their experience with the products and how they rate could even be included with commercial due diligence. The trick is to get a good cross section so go for long-time users as well as people who bought the product recently. Select them at random from invoices.

Talking to users can yield some very important insights. Some time ago a large UK company had the opportunity to buy a US company that made the same products. The products in question were aircraft engine rings, basically the structural outside of an aircraft engine. These were made by a process which is best described as a sort of blacksmithing. The metal was heated, bent into a circle and the two ends welded together. This circle of metal then underwent very long and complex machining. As management saw it, the acquisition would open up the huge US market. The deal was done quickly, with only cursory due diligence. After completion the holding company called for a five-year plan from the now enlarged subsidiary. A member of the holding company's internal consultancy team was assigned to the job. He made an early visit to Pratt & Whitney, a large American aircraft engine builder and a big customer of the new acquisition. It is never a good idea to carry out due diligence post-acquisition as he found out.

His first question was about the future of engine rings made by the blacksmithing technique. The Pratt & Whitney engineer was happy to oblige with a conclusive answer. He first showed the consultant the engineering drawings for the current range of engines. The blacksmithed engine rings were shown in green and sure enough the drawings were liberally sprinkled with green patches. The engineer then produced the drawings for the next generation of engines, engines which would be flying in five years' time. Again the blacksmithed engine rings were in green but this time there were other rings on the drawings that were made using a casting technology that produced a ring which was much nearer the final shape and therefore did away with a lot of machining. These were marked in purple. This time the drawing was liberally littered with purple patches with only specks of green here and there. The technology of both the acquirer and the acquired company was about to be superseded.

A happier tale along the same lines was the case of the target company making the electro-chemical components used in products such as gas analysers. The target was not performing as well as it had over the last few years. The question was why? Clearly the product worked so a strictly technical assessment would have been a waste of time. However, technically there was every reason to suspect that electro-chemical technology was being replaced by solid-state technology. An extensive programme of interviews with instrument manufacturers revealed this not to be the case in the segment in which the target operated, although it was true in the higher-volume sectors of the analyser market.

As with commercial due diligence, getting an understanding of competitive position may also be important. A leading instruments company once had the opportunity to acquire another, very specialist, instruments producer. Technically the product range was good and up to date, but discussions with research labs around the world revealed that another company was number one by a long way due to first mover advantage. The would-be acquisition was too far behind to ever catch up and therefore would only ever pick up whatever crumbs the leader left over.

Technical support can also be critical to product performance and this will often need checking out in much the same way. Talk to customers who have used technical support and also discuss it with those that have not. What is the response like? What response does the customer want? Is it easy to get to the right person, or indeed get a right answer?

Understanding buyer behaviour and customer relationships can be extremely important. The reason the instrument company mentioned above had lost out was that the first mover company had been able to capture the most important reference sites when it was unopposed in the market. These tended to be the places, such as universities and labs in blue-chip companies, where instrument buyers had done their training. Similarly, a company may well have superb technology, but if it does not have a good relationship with its customers, it is vulnerable especially in industries, such as aerospace, where supplier rationalization is taking place.

NEW PRODUCT DEVELOPMENT

Fixing problems and keeping ahead with new releases is another important feature of product technology, although there is a fine line to be drawn in both cases. Due diligence should also, therefore, look at the decision-making behind new product releases. How often is the product updated and why? Is new product release market-driven or engineering-driven? What is the decision-making process behind development priorities? Again, is it market-driven or engineering-driven?

PEOPLE

We have already seen the need to go beyond the technical. Above all in acquisitions where there is a high level of importance attached to technology the orientation needs to be as much around people as products. As John Chambers of Cisco says, 'In this business, if you are acquiring technology, you are acquiring people ... And if you don't keep those people, you have made a terrible, terrible investment.'[2] On a less philosophical note, according to the experts, '90 per cent of software projects fail for non-technology reasons'.[3]

Just who is critical to the future and why have to be two important questions. How to tie them in might be a third. Most high-tech companies give stock options as a matter of routine. If these options are vested, employees might just be tempted to take the money and run. To prevent this the new compensation package may have to include a high percentage of unvested options.

Documentation is always an issue, and it will be a major topic for technical assessment but a related concern will be to find out who is walking round with critical knowledge in their heads. How can this be best extracted? Who on the 'critical people' list and the 'undocumented critical knowledge' list is going to be dissatisfied by the deal or going to become very rich because of the deal?

The other people issue is the level of staffing in the areas vital for the technology's future performance. Are the development, testing and technical support teams adequately staffed? 'Adequate' includes both number and quality. During a due diligence project some time ago on a market-leading instrumentation company the customers unanimously agreed that the company had the best products in its market. This was thanks to a first-class R&D department. Speaking to the R&D department of one of the main competitors, it turned out that it had recently recruited a number of R&D staff from the target company. Further investigation revealed that the target company's management had drastically slimmed down its R&D department to improve results in a disappointing year. Long term the company would suffer from a lack of new products in a market where new products were a critical success factor.

Other questions for the development and technical staff are:

- Do they have enough of the right equipment? Ask them. Of course they will always say they need more, better equipment so a truth filter will have to be applied.
- How good is the communication between the three groups – development, test and technical support? Do technical support talk to development so that problems in the field are dealt with effectively? Do they perhaps share a common database of logged faults so that they are all singing from the same spreadsheet? Is technical support fully aware of planned new features and other developments?
- Does the company have full rights to all the technology it uses? If any technology or design feature was originated by non-employees, who has the rights? (See the next chapter on intellectual property due diligence for further details.)
- Are current non-disclosure agreements in place for employees and contractors?

Conclusion

In technology due diligence, there are, of course, a myriad of technical questions to be answered. Does the product actually work? Will it work outside the lab in a commercial environment? Are there the personnel and systems in place to support it and to keep it up to date? But technology due diligence is not just about assessing purely technical issues. Just as important are the people and the market issues. It is no good having the best mousetrap if the market for mousetraps is already saturated or if potential customers do not know of its existence or if they are not really bothered about upgrading. Similarly, a winning design now will soon be overwhelmed if the key technicians all leave – especially if they end up in competition with their old company. Due diligence should cover the customers and the personnel issues as well as examining the technical merits of the product.

14 *Intellectual property due diligence*

Intellectual property is about patents, trademarks and other rights to designs and inventions. It sounds like one of those areas in which due diligence can give a fair degree of certainty. After all, many types in intellectual property are registered so as to give unequivocal rights. Is it not just a question of checking that rights are properly recorded, that the target owns them and that they are transferred on completion? The answer is 'no'.

You are about to buy a business which claims to have a unique process for cleaning difficult stains out of delicate materials at a low temperature. The process is based on a secret formula. As a business it has grown impressively in the UK over the past three years when it was set up by a young chemist with a pressing need to get oil stains out of his father's expensive yachting waterproofs after a heavy night out in Cowes.

Your plan is to buy the company and roll the process out on a worldwide basis. You have the resources – the salesforce, the reputation, the logistics infrastructure, the equipment, the capability and the finances to be able to do this. If the process is half as successful in the rest of the world as it has been in the UK, your shareholders will be carrying you shoulder-high through the City in a few years' time. What can go wrong? Or, perhaps just as important, what else needs to be in place for the plan to work?

Central to your plan is your ability to exploit the process using the secret formula. Quite clearly, if you buy the business you must have the rights – all of the rights – to both the process and the formula, now and in the future. Those rights must be yours and yours alone and they should not be open to challenge. They should also be sufficient for you to achieve your objectives. In this particular case this would mean that they could be applied throughout the world and that they were the key to a process that produces a superior, possibly unique, result. In order to gauge the sufficiency of the intellectual property being acquired it would be very useful to know whether somebody was already achieving the same result using a different process and/or formula.

This is intellectual property due diligence. It has four strands:

- Identification of the intellectual property rights (IPRs) in a business
- Ownership of those rights. As the IPRs necessary to carry on the business have to be transferred when the target is sold, a central concern of intellectual property due diligence is to establish that the seller does own the rights being sold
- Validity. Once transferred, are those IPRs sufficient to protect the acquired company from claims that its activities are infringing the intellectual property rights of others?
- Uniqueness/sufficiency. Alongside the three more legal investigations outlined above, commercially you would be wise to satisfy yourself that the intellectual property you are

buying is in fact the world-beater you think it is. In other words, are those IPRs sufficient to give a competitive edge?

A useful checklist of actions you ought to prepare for and expect your advisers to undertake would combine and include the following:

- Questions to the seller
- Questions to the seller's advisers – in this case lawyers and patent and trademark agents
- Searches in official registers, basically to verify answers to the above sets of questions
- Questions in and around the target company's industry
- A review of all relevant licences, agreements and other documentation
- A review of patent agents' correspondence and reports.

How much to do

The first thing to note is that intellectual property rights vary by territory. This means everything to do with intellectual property tends to be territorial, including:

- The rights which are actually recognized
- How much, and what sort of, protection IPRs give
- How they are acquired and registered
- How, and for how long, they are maintained
- What constitutes an infringement
- Remedies available for infringements.

Intellectual property due diligence therefore needs to take account of the laws in each jurisdiction. Buyers also need to recognize that it is impossible for an investigation to cover all territories. Consequently local advice needs to be taken in those jurisdictions where:

- Sales are significant
- Significant assets are located
- The purchaser intends to develop the business in a big way.

The nature of the target company has a bearing too on how much intellectual property due diligence to do. Where IP is relatively unimportant to the target's profitability, it might be enough merely to confirm that the IP rights are registered in the target's name and appear to be in good standing. At the other extreme, where the main asset is intellectual property, quite extensive enquiries might be required. These will go beyond the merely routine searches of registries, which aim only to verify that the target company owns the intellectual property rights it says it owns, and to searches for potential infringement of third parties' intellectual property rights. If more extensive enquiries are needed, they may extend to trying to gauge the worth of patents and other IPRs. This in turn may involve a close study of prior patents, of others' patents and interviews with technical and other people to determine how easy it might be to engineer around patents, and the likely development and subsequent product costs of so doing. Where intellectual property is central to future sales and profits it also pays to check that there are no emerging technologies that might supplant the patents in major markets.

A good example of this type of investigation was the case of a company that manufactured a patented baby product. The buyer's plan was to launch an aggressive international sales campaign. As part of the due diligence it was important to know how safe the product was against copycat products. Patents had been applied for in most major markets but there was a concern that somebody could replicate the product without infringing these patents. It was the Japanese agent which eventually gave the team the comfort needed. A very large and powerful manufacturer and distributor of baby products, it said it had only decided to take on the agency in Japan after spending three months trying to reverse-engineer the product without infringing the patent. The acquirer accepted that if a large Japanese company could not get round the patents it was unlikely anyone else could.

The type of transaction will also have a bearing on how detailed the due diligence exercise needs to be. An asset sale will require the buyer to collect all the information about the IPRs. With a share sale the IPRs are usually acquired but so are liabilities.

From the above it can be seen that there is no definitive answer to the question 'How much IP investigation should be done?' The best answer is given by the answer to one or more of several questions:

- How much risk is the prospective buyer willing to tolerate?
- How much time and money is available for IPR investigations?
- How much IP is involved?
- Is this an asset deal or a share deal?

Setting up the work

It is so easy to fall in love with the technology. Whoever carries out the IP due diligence must maintain a healthy cynicism. It is also very easy to see an exercise like this as purely a legal investigation. It is not. The IP advisers who confine the investigation to technical legal issues cannot form a good independent commercial view on the deal. They will miss important risks in the wider business arena. IPR investigation involves a fair amount of subjectivity. There is rarely the time or budget to run every unknown down to the nth degree. For example, in trying to come to a view about the validity of a patent, how does the investigator gauge the obviousness of the invention? There is no right answer and it is quite possible for two experts to come to opposite conclusions. Therefore, whoever carries out IP work should understand enough about the technical subject matter, the reasons for the deal, the importance of the deal, the market, the competition and all other relevant business and legal issues associated with the deal so that they can place the inevitable residual risks in their proper context and can explain them to the buyer in a relevant and understandable way. In turn, it is up to the buyer to make sure the IP team is thoroughly briefed.

Timing

IP due diligence often takes a lot longer than originally anticipated. Simple searches may take a couple of weeks. More complex investigations will take two months or more. Searches by themselves are often not enough. Patents have to be read and understood and often there is a need to discuss them with technical experts to get the right feel for the importance of the patents in the context of the target's competitive position.

Information sources

The starting point will be the seller. The seller should be asked to provide lists of all intellectual property rights owned by the target. Intellectual property can be defined as 'a term which describes the intangible assets owned by an individual or an organisation that are protectable as proprietary.'[1] It will include IPRs which are:

1. Registered:

   - Patents
   - Copyrights
   - Design rights
   - Registered designs
   - Registered trademarks.

2. Not registered but are nonetheless protected by virtue of unregistered rights:

   - Unregistered trademarks

3. Capable of registration, but have not been registered to maximize their protection

Appendix B6 looks at these different types in more detail.

There may also be industry-specific rights and you will probably want to include other important items which are not intellectual property rights as such, but are nonetheless important for the business going forward. These would include:

- Rights to use domain names
- Know-how/trade secrets. (This is the category into which our hypothetical formula above would fall.)

Establishing ownership

IPRs normally fall into one or more of the following categories:

- Company-owned. These are IPRs which have either been developed internally or where ownership has been transferred from third parties.
- Third-party-owned. These are IPRs which are owned by third parties. Their use is licensed to the company.
- Shared IPRs. These are IPRs developed jointly, for example through a joint venture or cooperation agreement.

Whichever category an IPR falls into, it is important first of all to ensure that the seller has the proper title. Most companies keep lists of works in which copyright or other intellectual property rights subsist but there can be all sorts of reasons why a company might not have proper title:

1. Company employees' rights. In the UK, but not in all jurisdictions, if employees invent something during the normal course of their work, the rights to the invention are owned by their employer (unless their contracts of employment state otherwise). It may sound fairly obvious but this means contracts of employment should be checked. Although it is rare to find a contract where IPRs created during the course of employment are conferred on the employee, it is certainly not rare, especially in young start-ups, to find inventors who everyone assumes are employees to be in fact freelance outside contractors. It is also possible that contracts of employment give employees some sort of compensation for the use of those rights (see below).
2. Other individual's rights. It is quite common to find that company founders have developed a product, or at least certain parts of it, prior to the target company being formed. For reasons set out in the next paragraph, if these have not been assigned to the target company, the target does not own them. Shareware also often comes with a host of restrictions on its use in other products.
3. Outside contractors' rights. Outside contractors may have been involved in the development of a product or in one of the central building blocks or early versions. In UK law, rights in works created by independent contractors vary depending on the type of work:

   • Inventions and copyrights: rights belong to their creator, regardless of whether he or she has been commissioned and paid to do the work which led to the rights in the first place.
   • Designs: rights belong to the commissioning party.

   Therefore, where a consultant develops something for a company, the consultant may own the IPRs in the developed work unless they have been transferred to the company or the terms of engagement state otherwise.
4. Company policy. In group companies there are often inconsistencies in policy and therefore no consistency as to which group company applies for intellectual property rights. It is not uncommon even for several companies in the group to exploit the same rights. In other companies the parent may apply for IPRs which are then used in subsidiary companies. Yet others have a policy of holding IPRs in a special purpose company – usually one which is ultimately controlled from a tax haven. Therefore with group companies, bear in mind that it is not uncommon for several companies to use rights which are owned and registered by only one of them. Intellectual property may have to be assigned or licensed as part of the deal if the target company is being sold out of a group.
5. Third party agreements. Title may also be affected by the terms on which technology has been licensed from third parties. In particular, the future of the target may be seriously undermined by:

   • Conditions limiting the right of the target to modify or adapt any licensed technology
   • Change of control clauses in the licensing agreement

It is therefore important to verify that all-important rights are registered in the name of the target company or in the name of the company contracting to sell them. The way to do this is to ensure that the IPRs which the target company thinks it owns can be traced back to the original development. The would-be purchaser needs to inspect all assignments and any other transfer documents from the original registration or grant of the rights through to the target company or seller of the rights. The way to deal with any doubts as to ownership is with retrospective agreements, tax implications permitting. Where the target is being sold out of a larger group and IPRs are still going to be used by other parts of that group, as already mentioned, licensing may be the answer.

The extent to which the verification exercise has to go will be a function of the risk/reward trade-offs mentioned in Chapter 2. If the ability to exploit a revolutionary product or process is central to the value of the target company, then check all rights in that product belong to the target. Software is an area of particular vulnerability because of the heavy use of contractors and freelance programmers in the computer industry. Many projects are carried out by prime contractors who in turn use freelance programmers. If the target has lots of bespoke software which is critical to the future of the business, check that both the prime contractor and any freelancers have agreed that the target owns the rights.

It is possible that the seller may have encumbered the rights and this also needs to be checked out. With registered rights the process is straightforward – at least in the UK. The law needs to be checked for each right in each jurisdiction. Encumbrances should be registered. If they are not, a purchaser buys the rights free of encumbrances. With unregistered IPRs the opposite applies. The buyer will acquire encumbered assets, whether or not it knew of the encumbrances. It would be unwise, therefore, to rely exclusively on searches and a purchaser should negotiate warranties to confirm that the target's intellectual property rights are free from charges and other encumbrances.

The seller should also warrant the extent to which any employees have any rights for compensation related to the seller's IPRs. Although the employer will normally have the rights to inventions and discoveries made by employees in the normal course of their work, it is not unusual to find that employees are compensated in some way for the use of those rights. As already mentioned, compensation can be contractual but it can also be statutory. (In the UK, see for example Section 40 of the Patents Act 1977.)

Establishing validity

There are seven 'validity' questions:

- Are all patents owned by the target active?
- Are other rights registered?
- Do third parties have any rights in any jurisdictions in which you want to extend the target's operations?
- Can rights be registered in other jurisdictions?
- For both existing patents and patents pending, is the idea genuinely novel or is it likely to be challenged in the future?
- Have all maintenance fees been paid? If not, patents the target thought it had may have lapsed.

- Are all the important licences to which the target is party adequate? This question can apply to licences granted and to licences given. Appendix A14 sets out the principal areas to investigate.

If a company has been operating for some time it may already have received infringement claims from third parties. The seller should be asked to provide details of any such claims or of any proceedings.

The effects of losing intellectual property litigation can be terminal. An injunction restraining the sale of a patented product can put a company out of business immediately if it is the only product it has. Therefore it goes without saying that a very careful assessment needs to be made of any challenges to a company's intellectual property. Where there are infringement proceedings pending, an indemnity from the seller may not be sufficient protection. If the other side wins the target will not be able to sell its product in the territories where the action succeeds and is quite likely to suffer everywhere else too. In other words, a legal solution may not be good enough. What is needed is a commercial solution, if there is one.

Whether, in the absence of claims, a buyer can assume that all is OK is very much a matter of judgement. Usually the most security a buyer will get is by making sure that core rights are registered in core jurisdictions. A seller would be very foolish indeed to warrant that registered intellectual property rights are valid. No examination of a patent's validity when it is registered can be foolproof and, given that (in the UK anyway) patents can be challenged until they expire, a claim could pop up at any time. With trademarks there is very often no detailed examination, so again revocation proceedings could appear out of the blue.

Licences

Where the target is a licensee of intellectual property, there is a whole host of further questions, most of which are self-evident only once they are pointed out.

There are three types of licence:

- Non-exclusive: this gives the licensee no protection from competition.
- Sole: this protects the licensee from other licensees but not from competition from the licensor itself.
- Exclusive: if competition laws allow a licensee to get away with it, an exclusive licence protects the licensee from all competition.

The buyer needs to assess whether licences are adequate, bearing in mind that the buyer of a business may want the target and/or its technology to do new things and go to new places. Questions will include:

- Do the licences cover the right territories?
- Are rights sufficiently protected in those territories?
- Do the licences cover everything needed? It is not unusual for rights to be confined to a particular field of application.
- Are there unacceptable restrictions? A perfectly acceptable licence agreement entered into by the target may not be acceptable to a purchaser. The most obvious would be restriction

on the sale of competing products. The target may not have had competing products when entering the agreement, but the buyer might.

- Do you understand and are you happy with the calculation of royalty payments (especially if there is a minimum)? Are you satisfied that royalty calculations cannot be manipulated? Do the royalty payments give/allow the target to make a reasonable return?
- What is the duration of the licences? Do they last long enough?
- Are there any conditions which would end the licence or its exclusivity (minimum sales targets for example)?
- Is the licensor infringing third party rights? As it will probably be impossible to verify that the licensor owns all the rights, an indemnity to cover third-party infringement claims may be required.
- Are there change of control clauses? If a licence is critical to a company's business and if the licensor has the right to terminate the agreement on change of control, the buyer of the company will want the licensor's agreement to change of control before the deal is completed. If buying assets, then any licences would have to be assigned and again there may be clauses which restrict assignment. Consent to assign will probably be needed before completion.
- Are there likely to be any competition issues?

Competition deserves some explanation. An exclusive licence can have the effect of carving up a territory and usually the competition authorities do not approve of that sort of thing. For example, Article 81(1) of the Treaty of Rome prohibits agreements which prevent, restrict or distort competition. There are, however, a number of block exemptions. The Technology Transfer Block Exemption will, for example, exempt most patent and know-how licences from Article 81(1). Similarly, the European Union takes a dim view of licence agreements which oblige a licensee to give the licensor exclusive rights to any improvements the licensee might make. The effect of intellectual property licences needs to be reviewed in the light of the competition laws in the territories in which they are implemented.

Establishing uniqueness/sufficiency

The ownership and validity of IPRs is the nearest thing there is to a lawyers' paradise. For this reason, IP due diligence can tend to be focused on the narrow legal technicalities. What matters to the buyer, though, is the commercial benefit which IPRs confer. The importance of the uniqueness/sufficiency issue cannot be overstressed. Its essence is whether intellectual property brings lasting competitive advantage. This has two main strands:

1. The extent of the competitive advantage brought by IPRs
2. Whether this is likely to last:

   - Is anyone else achieving the same end without infringing the target's protected rights?
   - Can the protection be got round, say by reverse engineering?

A competitive edge may derive from uniqueness, but uniqueness in itself may not be enough. For example, Japanese car companies tend to patent hundreds of discoveries every year. Unique as, by definition, these must be, rights to any one of them would not necessarily be sufficient to give a competitive advantage. Similarly, registered rights, such as a patent, might protect a unique product or process but if the competition can find a way of achieving the same ends without infringing the patent then again intellectual property rights will not be sufficient to give an advantage. In other words, a different way of achieving the same ends or reverse engineering to get round protected rights could undermine their competitive worth. Sometimes the patent rights themselves are so narrowly defined that it does not take much of a change to get round them.

This whole area should not be seen as one which can be covered by technical assessments alone. It could also be something to be considered under commercial due diligence. For example, the commercial due diligence for a revolutionary cleaning process could look at how potential customers clean their garments now. This might flush out a competitor who has either got around any legal protection or indeed come up with something which achieves the same result but in a different way.

The other side of the coin is what do you do if the unique idea or product you are buying has not been protected? The answer is don't panic but rather try to assess how long it would take for a reasonably competent competitor to replicate it and then decide what to do as far as the deal is concerned.

KNOW-HOW

Know-how presents special problems as far as uniqueness is concerned. Know-how can only be transferred by communication. Communication informs the buyer, but it does not 'disinform' the seller. It still 'knows how'. There has to be a non-compete covenant and the purchaser has to ensure that it will have access to all employees with know-how after the transaction is completed.

Taxation

Finally, to underline both the need to get advisers working together and to use due diligence as a tool for planning post-deal management, it is worth remembering that the way companies use intellectual property can affect their tax position. The UK government, for example, has announced its intention to introduce major changes to the way R&D and intellectual property are treated for tax purposes. This new regime will put buyers of intellectual property in a better tax position. Tax relief should be available on purchased intangible assets which are amortized.

Conclusion

Intellectual property such as patents, know-how, trademarks and copyright is becoming increasingly important as companies, especially in developed economies, seek to differentiate themselves through innovation and brand development. As a result, the proportion of companies' value made up of intellectual property can be huge. Buyers use intellectual property due diligence to ensure that the intellectual property which they think they are buying exists, can be fully exploited and is going to give the competitive advantages that have been assumed. This in turn means using due diligence to identify the Intellectual property rights in a target, confirming their ownership and validity and last, but certainly not least, confirming their sufficiency. The scope of investigation is going to vary enormously depending on the nature of the target. Although this can be a highly technical and complex legal area, there are two things to bear in mind:

- First, one hundred per cent certainty can usually not be achieved. A buyer must decide early on the trade-off between risk and investigation costs.
- Second, this is not just a legal investigation. The potential of the IPRs in the marketplace are important too.

15 *Antitrust due diligence*

The European Commission is today expected to impose record fines totalling €850m on Roche of Switzerland, BASF of Germany and several other companies for a nine year conspiracy to control the vitamins market.[1]

Fines for antitrust violations can be huge, up to 10 per cent of global turnover. Getting antitrust due diligence wrong by buying into a price-fixing arrangement can be very expensive. It can also delay the deal if merger filings are not properly filed and subsequently cause problems for a company looking to enforce contracts.

There are three areas on which to focus here:

- Merger control filing requirements and likelihood of clearance
- Antitrust risks posed by the target's activities, that is the risk of buying into an infringement
- The enforceability of the target's contracts from the standpoint of antitrust law

Merger control filings

Pre- or post-merger filings are now mandatory in many jurisdictions. The rules normally contain very strict time limits and fines for being late. In addition, sanctions for ignoring the rules by implementing before clearance can be very severe indeed. Excluding the US and EU there are 73 states with some form of pre-merger review. For an acquisition, a filing may be required in all countries where the target has assets or sales. Space does not permit an examination of them all. The counsel, once again, has to be to use local advice to help navigate the complexities of national pre-merger filing regulations. The sections below cover the salient points, from a due diligence perspective, of EC, US and UK merger control. Systems in other jurisdictions tend to be based on the US or European systems, but there remains a vast number of subtle variations.

Before turning to the details, it is worth bearing in mind that merger control can have important implications for both negotiating the deal and for post-deal integration planning. In very many acquisitions, the parties are competitors. Until the deal completes, the parties remain competitors. As we will see in a moment, the competition authorities abhor competitors exchanging information or discussing how they might behave in the future. This makes it a potential infringement of antitrust rules to exchange sensitive documents, such as market or customer information or to discuss likely future behaviour. In general, the rules will allow only an exchange of documents for deal price evaluation, and then only on a strictly necessary and need to know basis.

EC MERGER CONTROL

In the EC, all 'concentrations' which have a 'Community dimension' must be notified to the European Commission within one week or the earlier of:

- the conclusion of an agreement
- the announcement of a public bid
- the acquisition of control

Failure to comply can result in fine of up to € 50 000.

A 'concentration' occurs where one or more undertakings merge or acquire control of one or more undertakings. A 'Community dimension' is where:

a) The combined total worldwide turnover of all the undertakings concerned is more than € 2.5billion.
b) The combined aggregate turnover of all the undertakings is more than € 100 million in each of at least three member states.
c) The aggregate turnover of each of at least two of the undertakings concerned is more than € 25 million in each of the three member states included in b) above.
d) And the aggregate Community-wide turnover of each of at least two of the undertakings concerned is more than € 100 million.

'Control' is defined as the possibility of exercising decisive influence on an undertaking. With this definition even the purchase of a minority stake could be construed as control.

According to EC Merger Regulation, the 'concentration' may not be put into effect until the Commission clears the transaction. Failure to comply with this requirement can lead to fines of up to 10 per cent of the worldwide group turnover in all products and services of the corporate group involved. It is worth just reading that sentence again.

The EC has introduced a one-stop shop approach for merger notification. This means that concentrations with a Community dimension must be notified only to the European Commission, and not to the national authorities of EC member countries.

Concentrations that do not have a Community dimension might have to be notified to national authorities of the EC member countries depending on the filing requirements and standards of each of those countries. The Commission can decide to refer concentrations with a Community dimension notified to it to national authorities under certain circumstances (Article 9). Similarly under circumstances specified in Article 22, national authorities can ask the Commission to review concentrations which do not have a Community dimension.

The model for EC competition law is American competition law. American competition law is aimed at creating and maintaining free inter-state trade by prohibiting anti-competitive agreements. For example, Article 3 (f) of the EEC treaty envisages 'the institution of a system ensuring that competition in the common market is not distorted' and following on from this, the EC's Merger Regulation prohibits concentrations that create or strengthen a dominant position as a result of which competition would be substantially impeded in a substantial part of the common market. A dominant position is the ability to act in the market without effective competitive restraints from competitors, customers or suppliers. In reality it is rare for a merger to achieve this 'in a substantial part of the common market', although it is by no means clear what a 'substantial part' is. Some commentators say that from case law, a 'substantial part' of the common market might be defined as narrowly as a small member state. National merger control often imposes tougher tests. The result is that it can sometimes be better for a deal to come within EC merger control than national merger control because it is more likely to be cleared. The drawback is the huge amount of paperwork required under EC Merger Regulation.

Getting clearance

Whether or not a transaction is likely to be cleared is not an exact science. Defining the market is clearly crucial. The European Commission explains how it defines markets on its web site. Markets are looked at geographically and from a product/market viewpoint. As mentioned above, the geographical dimensions of a market are not well defined. Article 82 (formerly Article 86) of the EEC Treaty, which regulates abuse of a dominant position, bites if the dominant position is held 'within the common market or a substantial part of it', a precise definition of the latter being hard to come by.

Definition of a product market is even less certain. The crucial test appears to be whether or not there are readily available and acceptable substitutes for the product in question. If a product is substitutable (as far as both consumers and producers are concerned) it cannot form its own product market.

Combined market shares can be a good guide, but here again there are important exceptions. In the EC, the market-share threshold which usually generates closer Commission scrutiny is around 40 per cent. At one end of the spectrum, a combined buyer/target market share of 25 per cent or less raises a fairly strong presumption of no dominance. At the other end, a combined buyer/target market share of 50 per cent or more does raise a presumption of dominance. A market share of 70 per cent or higher can constitute evidence in itself of dominance within the meaning of Article 82.

However, there are no hard and fast rules. It is a firm's *ability* to abuse a dominant position which really counts. For example, even a market share of around 83 per cent in Alcatel/Telettra did not raise concerns. In that case the sole customer in the market had strong buying power and adopted a multiple sourcing policy. A lower market share may also give rise to concern. 'Collective' dominance is something else the Commission may look at. For example in a mature market for an homogenous product, a small number of producers who collectively hold a market share in the range of 60 to 70 per cent or more may collectively dominate even though their individual shares are well below any of the normal thresholds. Collective dominance occurs when suppliers in a particular market do not compete with each other because each knows it is in its interest to follow the behaviour of the market leader. This is likely to be the case if their market shares are roughly the same, their costs are similar, prices are transparent and there are high entry barriers.

Whether or not a given transaction will attract the attention of the authorities is, therefore, highly dependent on the facts of the case.

It is not only acquisitions that can come under Commission scrutiny. A joint venture (JV) may also cause the authorities concern if they think that the parent companies will collude with each other in markets in which they continue to be active after formation of the JV. The Commission applies a collusion test where two or more parent companies remain active either in the JV's market or in markets that are upstream or downstream of, or contiguous to, the JV's market.

Information requirements

For a transaction directly involving one or more countries in the European Union, legal advisers will need, as a minimum, the following information. (The list is not exhaustive.)

1. The turnover (net sales revenues) of each group in the following geographical areas:

   • Worldwide
   • EU
   • EEA
   • National in each EU and EEA country
   • National in each other European country where either of the groups involved has operations

2. Information to determine the 'relevant' markets, and for each relevant market:

   • The parties' estimates of market size
   • The revenues of each of the parties' groups in each market
   • Estimates of competitors' market shares in each market

3. Overlapping or vertically related products/services of the parties
4. Identification of demand and supply substitutes for each such product/service

Advisers will focus not only on those markets where both parties are active or where one party is active upstream and the other downstream, but also on whether there are risks under Article 82 of the EC Treaty (dominant position) and equivalent national provisions. If the target is dominant in a certain market, those conducting the due diligence should check to make sure that the commercial relationships of the target are compatible with Article 82.

It is also important for purposes of Article 81, and equivalent national law provisions, to identify markets in which the target alone or the target and the buyer together hold substantial market power. Later on we will see how Article 81 prohibits restrictive agreements but that nonetheless some such agreements may be given an exemption. In some cases, the availability of an exemption may be jeopardized if the target, or the target and buyer together, have too much market power.

US ANTITRUST REGULATIONS (HART-SCOTT-RODINO)

The US has a long history of competition legislation. Starting with the Sherman Antitrust Act of 1890, the US government acquired the authority to sue a private company for its business methods. The 1914 Clayton Act broadened Federal powers further. The problem with the Clayton Act was prosecution after the fact. If a merger had to be undone, much consumer harm would already have been done and it cost millions to litigate. The 1976 Hart-Scott-Rodino Act (HSR) was passed to overcome this. It created a screening system at the Federal Trade Commission (FTC) and the Department of Justice (DOJ) so that mergers and acquisitions are reviewed before they happen. The test for lawfulness is similar to the European one: 'Is the merger likely to substantially lessen competition?'.

Although HSR reviews themselves are administrative, US law still requires the government to go to court and be granted an injunction in order for the transaction to be prevented. This is the essential difference between the US and Europe. European antitrust regulations are essentially administrative whereas in the US they are essentially legal. As innocuous as that sounds, it makes for a substantial difference of emphasis between the two systems. For a start, the US system is much more adversarial than the European system. This means that would-be acquirers must be even more careful about the language used in documents concerning US acquisitions.

Under both systems, the last thing a buyer wants is for a document to attract unwelcome attention. At least in Europe there is a chance to explain. In the US, being a legal process, the authorities will only examine documents and if they come across words like 'this deal will allow us to dominate the market' or 'we will put up prices by x per cent by buying this competitor' they will be used, in court, as evidence against you with little regard for the subtleties of the situation. As the US process is assumed to be a precursor to litigation, there is much more mutual suspicion built into the system than there is in Europe where there is a much greater spirit of cooperation.

Basic requirements

Under HSR, all deals under $50 million are exempt from filing. All deals over $200 million must be filed. Transactions in between, that is from $50 million to $200 million, must be notified if the 'size of person' test is met.

The size of person test is usually met if one party has total assets or annual net sales of $100 million or more; and the other party has total assets or annual net sales of $10 million or more. For purposes of HSR, the appropriate entity for measuring size of person is not necessarily the party to the transaction but its 'ultimate parent entity'.

These thresholds apply to mergers, acquisitions of securities, asset acquisitions, and the formation of joint ventures and they are measured *after* the transaction. In other words, even a small transaction could push the acquiring entity over one of the thresholds.

Where the parties and the transaction meet the appropriate tests, US law says that the acquisition cannot take place until:

- both parties have filed pre-merger reports with the Federal Trade Commission and the Department of Justice
- the HSR waiting period(s) expire.

The waiting periods for most transactions are 30 days after both parties file their initial pre-merger reports. If the government requests additional information (a 'Second Request'), there is an additional waiting period of 30 days after completing the response to the Second Request. The main exception is for cash tender offers where the waiting periods are:

- 15 days after filing by the bidder;
- 10 days after response to Second Request.

An Early Termination of the waiting period can be requested and is frequently granted.

Apart from the administrative/legal distinction mentioned above, other differences between the two systems relate to timing, as set out in Table 15.1.

Penalties

The penalty for closing acquisitions in violation of HSR is up to $11 000 per day of non-compliance. This is a provision which is actively enforced, even years after an acquisition has closed.

Table 15.1   Differences between European and US merger regulation

	Europe	USA
Deadline for filing	Within one week of binding agreement or announcement of bid	No deadline but cannot close until the waiting period has expired or the transaction is approved
Pre-filing	Not possible to file prior to a binding agreement	May be possible to submit a formal filing on the basis of non-binding heads of agreement
Ability to control the timetable	Little (timetable imposed by law)	Considerable. It is up to the parties when to: • start the process • comply with the Second Request

Practical issues

1. Confidentiality: information submitted is exempt from public inspection or disclosure.
2. Valuations: transactions are valued at purchase price, unless the fair market value of assets acquired exceeds purchase price. If it does, fair market value is used.
3. Filing fees: there is a three-tiered filing fee structure:

   • For transactions valued in excess of $50 million but less than $100 million, the fee is $45 000.
   • For transactions whose value ranges from $100 million but less than $500 million, the filing fee is $125 000.
   • For transactions whose value equals or exceeds $500 million, the filing fee is $280 000.

A worksheet, with guidelines, is available at the FTC website, www.ftc.gov/bc/hsr.

NATIONAL MERGER CONTROL

If a deal is not trapped by European merger control it could still fall foul of national regulations. The regulations vary by country. UK merger control is covered in the main by the Fair Trading Act 1973 (the FTA). There are three key players:

• The Secretary of State for Trade and Industry
• The Director General of Fair Trading (DGFT) who is head of the Office of Fair Trading (OFT)
• The Competition Commission

The Secretary of State decides, the Director General of Fair Trading advises the Secretary of State whether a merger should be referred, and the Competition Commission investigates mergers that are referred.

The FTA sets out the conditions which must be satisfied for the Competition Commission to investigate. First there must be a merger. This is defined as occurring when two or more enterprises 'cease to be distinct'. This arises either when they are brought under common ownership or control or when there is an arrangement for one of the enterprises to shut down to prevent competition. At least one of the enterprises must either operate in the UK or be controlled by a body incorporated in the UK.

The expression 'control' need not mean holding over 50 per cent of the votes in a company. Material influence is enough to constitute control, that is the ability 'materially to influence the policy or the ability to control the policy of a company or of any person carrying on an enterprise'.

For a merger to qualify for investigation one of two tests must be satisfied:

- Market share test: this is met if, as a result of the merger, the combined enterprise accounts for at least 25 per cent of the supply or acquisition of particular goods or services, either in the UK as a whole or in a substantial part of it. If this was already the case before the merger, the test will be met if, as a result of the merger, the market share is enhanced.
- Assets test: this is satisfied if the gross value of worldwide assets to be acquired exceeds £70 million.

The reality is that a proposed merger will only be referred if it is likely to have a significant effect on competition in the UK. The market share test is therefore much more important than the assets test. Just like the EC regulations, 'substitutability' from the consumers' point of view is central to defining product markets. In the past the OFT has been willing to define markets very narrowly.

A reference is not automatic if the market share test is satisfied. The parties could still avoid a reference if they could show that they could not raise prices or dictate terms, for example because of substantial remaining competition, customer buying power or increased imports.

Time limits

Merger references can be made by the Secretary of State at any time within four months of the merger taking place, or being made public, whichever is the later.

The Secretary of State takes the decision on whether or not to refer a merger in the light of the DGFT's advice. The Secretary of State may accept undertakings in lieu of making a reference. Such undertakings are enforceable.

Implications

Time   An investigation involves a considerable amount of management time. The investigation usually takes three months, although it could take up to six. Management on both sides will be interviewed. Competitors, customers and other interested parties will be invited to make written submissions.

Remedies   If it is concluded that a merger is likely to operate against the public interest, the Competition Commission may recommend remedies. The Secretary of State has wide powers and could:

- Prohibit a merger
- Where the merger has already taken place, insist that the acquirer disposes of the interests in the target

- Prevent the exercise of voting rights
- Control the conduct of the merged company.

What to do

The first thing to decide is whether or not the deal is to be conditional on receiving merger clearance. Thereafter there are a number of courses that can be taken to try and avoid a reference:

- Nothing. There is no obligation to notify a merger to the UK authorities either before or after it occurs. This is clearly a calculated risk which may induce four months plus of uncertainty.
- Seek confidential guidance via the Competition Commission. This involves giving details on a confidential basis and getting an indication on the likelihood of a reference.
- Make an open approach to the OFT. This involves seeking clearance by making a written submission to the Competition Commission. Any decision does not have to be final.
- Make a formal notification to the OFT. This is only an option if the merger has been announced but not yet completed. The major advantage of this option is the certainty of the timetable. The Secretary of State has a maximum of 35 working days to decide whether to refer the merger. If no decision is taken withinin that time limit, no reference can be made.
- Attempt to avoid a reference by making undertakings to sell parts of the business or to conduct the merged business in a particular way in order to make a reference unnecessary.

Antitrust risk

In July 1991, Tetra Pak was fined £52m for a competition law infringement. In the UK the Office of Fair Trading has reported that, 'An "extraordinary" level of illegal price-fixing and market sharing behaviour is leading to one cartel a month being uncovered'.[2] The risks of buying into anti-competitive behaviour are very real and potentially very expensive and if buyers do buy into anti-competitive behaviour, they become liable. Therefore, as well as dealing with merger control filings, there may be other antitrust issues which need investigating prior to completion. For example, the EC Treaty prohibits 'all agreements between undertakings, decisions by associations of undertakings and concerted parties which may affect the prevention, restriction or distortion of competition within the Common Market.'

The possibility of rigged markets is one of the most difficult areas to investigate. Market fixing is a clandestine activity and often top management, let alone in-house lawyers or external advisers, know nothing at all about it. The antitrust violations to watch out for in particular are those which:

1. Directly or indirectly fix purchase or selling prices or any trading conditions through:

   - Abuse of dominant position
   - Market-sharing or price-fixing arrangements with competitors
   - Resale price maintenance – a vertical arrangement under which a supplier requires a purchaser to resell goods at a certain price

2. Limit or control production, marketing, technical development or investment
3. Share sources of supply with competitors
4. Share sensitive information with competitors. This would include sales figures, pricing policy, price lists, discount structures and dates when prices will be increased.
5. Apply dissimilar conditions to equivalent transactions with other trading parties, thereby placing them at a competitive disadvantage
6. Make the conclusion of contracts subject to acceptance by the other parties of supplementary obligations which, by their nature or according to commercial usage, have no connection with the subject of such contracts. This would include, for example, making it a condition that a customer for product A buys product B before it is supplied with product A.

In addition to the above list, because competition law in the EC is supposed to help towards the goal of the single market, the following also need to be added to the list in EC transactions:

- absolute territorial protection of exclusive distributors
- export restrictions within the EC.

Both of these are to prevent national economic frontiers from being recreated by business agreements.

Although the smoke-filled rooms of market rigging folklore are probably a thing of the past, market agreements with competitors certainly are not. Most industries are like extended families, so contact with competitors is usual. The question for due diligence is the nature of those contacts. Trade Association meetings are the most obvious source of potential exposure. Minutes of such meetings and any other Trade Association correspondence should, therefore, be the first port of call.

However, the odds of finding anything written down are slim. Even the law recognizes that most market fixing agreements are verbal.

An agreement exists if the parties reach a consensus on a plan which limits or is likely to limit their commercial freedom by determining the lines of their mutual action or abstention from action in the market. No contractual sanctions or enforcement procedures are required. Nor is it necessary for such an agreement to be made in writing. (*Polypropylene OJ 1972*)

The 'nod and a wink' approach will also fall foul of the rules if it 'substitutes a practical cooperation for the risks of competition' (ICI Ltd Case) or it seeks to

influence the conduct on the market of an actual or potential competitor or to disclose to such a competitor the course of conduct which they themselves have decided to adopt or contemplate adopting (*Cooperative Verenigen Suiker VA* v. *EC Commission 1975*)

Because it is highly unlikely that there will be written records, it is vital for the due diligence team to get out and talk to those people in the target company who have contact with the competition. Sales and marketing and planning personnel would be top of the list. This is because sales and marketing staff are in a position to engage in price fixing, customer allocations, resale price maintenance, export restrictions and distributor or customer terminations, among other sensitive practices. These are also the people who are most likely to generate incriminating internal documents, perhaps describing in exaggerated terms, for example, the actions which the company should take against price-cutting dealers and the like. Employees in the planning department are a high risk group as their market intelligence activities may bring them into contact with competitors and result in exchanges of information that may, in extreme cases, even develop into fully fledged cartels. There really is no substitute for the due diligence team getting in front of these people, seeing the whites of their eyes and watching whether they wince when they ask them their questions.

Any commercial relationships between the target and its competitors (for example, in supply, licensing or joint venture agreements) should also be examined, along with any side deals that go with them.

After carving up the market, trying to fix who can sell what, at what price, comes next on the investigation list. The due diligence investigators should look first at the termination of dealers. Within the EC, terminations, or threats to terminate dealers, because of their pricing or parallel importing, or exporting practices may give rise to substantial antitrust exposure. In many jurisdictions agreements with dealers to maintain their retail prices is a serious antitrust infringement. In the EC, preventing customers from exporting the supplier's products to another EC member country is generally prohibited. A company cannot guarantee absolute territorial protection to a distributor although it can require its exclusive distributor not to *actively* seek customers outside its territory. Many jurisdictions forbid efforts by suppliers to tie in customers, like in the example mentioned earlier, by making them purchase product B as a condition for their being able to purchase product A. In some jurisdictions it may be prohibited for a supplier to discriminate among similarly situated customers; in others, this may be a violation of competition law only where the supplier is in a dominant position. The rules are different in different jurisdictions and whoever is conducting the due diligence needs to be aware of this.

Non-competition restrictions are not always illegal. Where a business is sold, non-competition clauses are allowed for a period not longer than would be needed by a third party to set up a similar business.

If the due diligence review uncovers antitrust law violations, the question is how to limit the buyer's exposure. Under EC competition law, a buyer may be liable under certain circumstances for infringements committed by the target before the acquisition if the target merges with or into the buyer. If the target continues to operate as a separate legal entity in the buyer's group after the acquisition, the target itself will remain liable for its prior infringement, unless the seller was itself a party to the infringement with the target, in which case the seller remains liable. Among the alternatives the buyer can consider are the following:

- Pulling the deal
- Adjusting the purchase price to compensate for the risk
- Obtaining an indemnity from the seller
- Stopping any infringements by the target immediately after the acquisition
- Establishing a clear compliance policy for the future.

ENFORCEABILITY OF CONTRACTS

In the EC, the work does not end with finding and dealing with antitrust exposure. Here there is an additional risk under Article 81 of the EC Treaty which says that clauses of an agreement which restricts competition cannot be enforced. This has given rise to a 'Euro-defence' in private law suits over contractual disputes. What happens is that one party brings a suit against the other seeking damages for breach of contract or for specific performance. The other party will then raise as a defence that the contract, or the clauses at issue, are unenforceable because the contract violates Article 81.

Parties would normally have to go to the Commission and seek formal exemption from the provisions of Article 85 (which deals with restrictive practices) in order for what could otherwise be deemed restrictive agreements not to be illegal and therefore to escape the risk of non-enforceability under Article 81. Article 81 does, however, allow certain types of agreement to stand without the parties having to seek formal exemption. Such block exemptions apply to agreements which improve the production or distribution of goods or promote technical or economic progress and at the same time give a fair share of the benefits to consumers. Block exemptions exist for agreements relating to:

* Exclusive distribution
* Selective distribution, where the supplier appoints dealers on the basis of technical qualifications, the suitability of trading premises and stipulates that such dealers must not sell to unqualified dealers
* Exclusive purchasing
* Patent licensing
* Motor vehicle distribution and servicing
* Research and development
* Specialization
* Know-how licensing
* Franchising
* Subcontracting arrangements
* Joint venture agreements involving R&D, and/or Production.

On top of these, the Commission's Notice on Minor Agreements also allows agreements where the combined market share of the parties is 5 per cent or less if the parties operate at the same level of the market (horizontal competitors). The market share limit is 10 per cent or less if the parties operate at different levels of the market, for example between an upstream supplier of product and a downstream user or reseller of product.

The due diligence exercise should, therefore, be on the look-out for these kinds of agreements and should check whether they meet all of the conditions for coverage by a block exemption regulation. As a further complication, it is not yet clear whether a block exemption at EC level provides protection against prohibition and inability to enforce an agreement at national level. It may be necessary, therefore, to check the status of such agreements under national laws.

If an agreement is not covered by a block exemption, parties can seek an individual exemption from the Commission. Needless to say, obtaining an individual exemption decision is time consuming – it may take several years. As a consequence, most notifications result in the Commission issuing comfort letters. These are not legally binding on national courts but serve as evidence of the Commission's view. In the event of a dispute between the parties to the agreement, or a third party challenge, either or both parties can request the Commission to adopt a formal exemption decision. The persons carrying out the due diligence will, therefore, want to check for any formal exemption decisions or comfort letters.

Conclusion

In most cases the transaction cannot be implemented until clearance is obtained, so it goes without saying that looking at merger control filing is an essential part of the due diligence process on bigger deals. Smaller deals may or may not be caught by national regulations if they cause sufficient concentration to worry the national authorities. Competition filings are territorial, that is they must be considered for each jurisdiction where the buyer and target have operations and/or assets. For this reason, it pays to look at antitrust filings early on in the process. Forgetting to file or filing too late can be expensive and cause delay.

As well as merger control filings, antitrust due diligence should be concerned with the possibility of buying into anti-competitive behaviour. Flouting competition laws can be very expensive, so again it is a fundamental part of due diligence to try to identify as early as possible any specific areas to do with competition law which may be of concern and to determine whether the remedies needed are such that they make the transaction unattractive. Finally, the due diligence process should also seek to identify contracts that may be unenforceable because of antitrust law.

16 *Insurance and risk management due diligence*

The basic, driving philosophy behind risk management is that as losses are funded either directly or through the payment of insurance premiums, they should be seen as a cost which can be reduced.

Insurance due diligence is not usually a top priority in the frantic due diligence timetable. In fact, all too often there is none at all. It is, however, worth saying a few words about the process:

- First, the topic of risk management seems to be one which is gaining momentum.
- Second, risk management due diligence is something which is now being introduced early on in the due diligence process in North America and, where America leads, the rest of the world often follows.
- Third, it is a topic which should not be overlooked during the pre-acquisition investigations. Had Federal Mogul understood the full extent of the asbestos risk it was taking on when it bought T&N in 1998, it might have avoided Chapter 11.
- Finally, taking a positive approach to risk management at the due diligence stage will have a knock-on benefit once the deal is done. An acquisition provides the perfect opportunity to reappraise custom and practice.

Areas to address

At the very least, insurance due diligence should address:

- Present, future and, most importantly, past exposures of the business
- The structure and cost of the existing programme
- Creating a risk management structure.

The starting point, just as in every other due diligence discipline, is a detailed analysis of what the target company actually does. This should establish where the real risks to the business are, whether they can be mitigated by risk management and how insurance, can be best used.

PAST, PRESENT AND FUTURE EXPOSURES

Pre-deal, the purchaser should have access to all the vendor's files dealing with the placing of policies, the notification and handling of claims and risk management measures taken. Risk management uses a qualitative approach to examining potential exposures faced by the business. The risk management audit will examine the manner in which the target addresses the following:

1. The identification of risk
2. The evaluation of risk
3. The reduction of risk
4. The prevention of loss
5. How losses are reviewed:

   - Centrally
   - In the operations

6. Measures being taken to reduce losses:

   - frequency
   - magnitude.

7. The status of any disaster planning
8. The status of any planned health and safety programme

The answers to these questions will, of course, also offer some very revealing insights into the way the business has been managed.

THE STRUCTURE AND COST OF THE EXISTING PROGRAMME

The initial analysis will begin with existing arrangements. For example, if buying a subsidiary of a larger company there will normally be high levels of self-insured risk retention with captives (offshore insurance companies owned by the vendor) often playing a major role. This can pose one or more of the following problems:

- Credit worthiness: captives will not have strong balance sheets.
- The assessment of future claims: a former parent can be expected to take a robust line when assessing claims from an ex-subsidiary.
- The acceptance of future claims: getting a claim from an ex-subsidiary accepted will likewise call for a lot more evidence and persuasion than would be the case if the vendor still owned it.

The form in which insurance has been arranged can also be very significant. There are two different forms of policy:

- Occurrence/Claims Arising. Here the policy covers only incidents which occur during the policy period. So, for example, with asbestos claims, which are reported some years after exposure to the wretched stuff, it would be necessary to look to the policy which was in force during the time of exposure.
- Claims Made. For a claim to be met under a Claims Made policy it must be made while the policy is still in force. Once it has expired no further claims against it can be made.

The type of policy which applies can be very important when assessing the extent to which any claims for the target's accumulated liabilities can be met by insurance. Recent litigation surrounding industrial diseases plus new legislation, such as the EU's Product Liability Directive, have said that liability can be backdated to when a company might reasonably have been expected to know that a process or material was potentially harmful. For this reason, there should be an indemnity in the sale and purchase agreement for any loss of insurance coverage under historic policies due to material non-disclosure or breach of the policy.

CREATING A RISK MANAGEMENT STRUCTURE

Clearly, then, the post-deal risk management programme must offer not just cost-effective protection of the assets and shelter from the current/future liabilities of the target but also cater for any of the target's residual liabilities which may have accumulated as a result of its past actions.

The two points are linked. Dealing with the second point means establishing an accurate insurance history. All too often this is either not possible or investigations reveal that there are gaps in cover. The ability to purchase cost-effective 'retrospective' cover could be of great importance in determining the shape and structure of the future programme.

Finally, the risk management structure must strike a proper balance between risk and cost if it is to give the right coverage at the right cost. Often selecting the right insurance broker can have a significant influence on cost. A broker's track record is important as the insurer is likely to give the most competitive quotes to brokers who can demonstrate that they have carried out the sort of thorough risk analysis described above and, just as important, can communicate the process and results.

Conclusion

Risks are generated by past as well as present and future actions. The aim of insurance and risk management due diligence is to reduce the costs of risk. However, even taking a more focused approach to risk management will not mean the elimination of every risk which due diligence identifies. There will be areas where insurance is not cost-effective or quite simply unavailable. The end result, though, should be a situation that allows risk to be actively managed rather than dealt with in a reactive way. A risk management programme should highlight those areas where insurance is appropriate and provide options based on variable levels of self-insured risk retention combined with practical steps to reduce exposures, whether insured or not.

The following individual due diligence checklists are intended to be as exhaustive as possible. They should provide most of the questions that a prospective buyer could ask. In some situations, some will be unnecessary or inappropriate. They overlap so, for example, the financial due diligence checklists contain questions about employees and tax, two areas for which there are separate checklists. A purchaser will need to edit them to suit its purposes. There is little likely to annoy a target more than being asked for the same information, or asked the same question, three or four times by different advisers or being asked questions that are just not relevant to the target business – especially when it knows that the purchaser knows that they are irrelevant. For this reason, Appendix A2 is an integrated information request list with an indication of which due diligence discipline(s) are interested in which information. Any irrelevant requests should be struck out.

A1 *Purchaser pre-deal due diligence checklists*

Selecting (and working with) advisers

PREPARE

- Discuss the proposed acquisition, and due diligence, with those most likely to be involved in and affected by it.
- Make sure everyone who needs to understand is clear about what due diligence is about and the advantages of bringing in advisers and what they are expected to do.

CONSIDER

- Should you set up a management team?
- Who will prepare and agree the initial brief?
- Who will choose your advisers and on what criteria?
- Who will be the main contact for the advisers?
- How will your firm be kept in touch with the progress of the acquisition/due diligence process?

BRIEF

- Set out the firm's aims/mission.
- Identify all key issues and potential problems that may arise during the course of the due diligence process and during the course of working with your advisers.
- Discuss options with your advisers and set out your initial targets for the advisers.
- Propose an initial budget and timescale and discuss additional expenses.

SELECT

- Compile a criteria checklist for choosing advisers.
- Give likely or interested advisers details of your organization, why you need them and an initial brief.
- Ask advisers to submit an initial proposal and estimate for the work.
- Check references, if given.
- Interview the most promising candidates.

INTERVIEW

1. Make sure you meet the person/persons who will carry out the due diligence and those that will be your principal contacts.
2. Discuss:

   - Who will do the work and how many will be involved
   - Their relevant experience
   - The schedule for the job
   - The fee and how it will be paid
   - Estimated costs
   - Whether payments should be linked to completion of specific stages in the work.

AFTER THE INTERVIEW

- Eliminate those not suitable.
- Compare strengths and weaknesses.
- Compare fees and estimated timescale.
- Check any points that are unclear.
- Assess genuine interest, commitment and professionalism of those interviewed.
- Balance advantages and disadvantages.
- Decide which you like and with whom you get on well.

AGREEING THE FINAL BRIEF

- Discuss your initial brief and the adviser's proposal and refine final brief.
- Agree on the timescale, and how fees and costs will be calculated and paid.

ON APPOINTMENT

- Draw up and sign a contract with your advisers.
- Inform all those that need to know when work will commence and who is to be the main contact for the advisers.
- Make arrangements (allocate a person) to provide the advisers with information, equipment, and the space they require.

MANAGING ADVISERS

- Keep in close contact with your advisers.
- Have regular feedback sessions.
- Make sure arrangements for working with your advisers are running smoothly.

RECEIVING THE RESULTS

- Decide how you want the advisers to report their recommendations and conclusions to you.
- Check its accuracy and conclusions before making it available to others within your organization.

ASSESS THE OUTCOME

- Consider if you have got what you asked for, in the form you wanted it, and its value to your decision-making.
- Discuss the report with your advisers and its implications, and negotiate amendments or additions where the report fails to meet the agreed brief.

AFTER DUE DILIGENCE

- Decide if you want further advice or guidance and on what financial basis that might be given.
- Approve and implement any specific recommendations.

Buyers' pre-deal diligence checklist

1. What is the business strategy?
2. How do acquisitions fit into the business strategy?
3. Does the target fit the strategy?
4. Have we carried out sufficient pre-acquisition planning?
5. Are we sufficiently prepared for the due diligence exercise?

- Which areas are we going to investigate? Why?
- Are we giving enough attention to 'soft' areas like culture and management?
- Do we know what we really need to know in each area of investigation?
- Do we have enough time to complete the process? If not, what are we going to do about it?
- Do we have the information to brief advisers properly?

6. Do we know, do we really really know, where the synergies are going to come from?

   - Have we tried to quantify them in detail?
   - What further information is needed?

7. Have we set a walk-away price?
8. Have we worked out an adequate implementation plan especially for the Human Resources issues? For example:

   - How will individuals be chosen to fill available positions?
   - What are the selection criteria?
   - Who will make the decision?
   - Will incentives be needed to keep talent in place?
   - When will we work out who will be surplus to requirements?
   - Have we worked out the termination packages and the timing of terminations?
   - Who is responsible?
   - Have we a communication plan in place to deal with staff changes?

9. Have we considered any organizational redesign opportunities the acquisition creates, for example outsourcing as an alternative to in-house resources?
10. Have we explored all the consequences of the deal, for example the effects on current operations, existing personnel, the industry and competitors?
11. Have we set material limits for the due diligence investigation?
12. What is our attitude to risk? Is this the same for all types of risk?

A2 *Information to be requested from the target*

Information request list

INFORMATION	DD TOPIC

Accounting policies
Financial
- Copies of last 2 years auditors' management letters
- Copies of accounting manuals
- Are all key accounting policies disclosed in the Annual Financial Statements?
- Have they changed recently?
- Have reported profits been affected by changes in accounting policies?

Accounts
Financial
- Copies of audited accounts for the last three years
- Copy of the latest management accounts
- List of year-end journals and reconciliation between management and statutory accounts

Agreements
Copies of:
Legal

- Agreements with major customers
- Distribution contracts, including all agreements with independent sales representatives, distributors, and franchisees
- Warranty agreements
- Contracts with suppliers
- Subcontractor agreements
- Partnership or joint venture agreements of any partnership in which target or any subsidiary is a member
- Sponsorship agreements

- Property lease and maintenance agreements entered into by the target
- All leases and tenancies granted by the target along with details of tenants and terms and assignment of leases where the target or a subsidiary company was the original lessee

Legal, property

- Standard service agreements, employee terms and conditions, union agreements, management contracts, termination contracts, parachute and profit share agreements, employment agency contracts and consulting agreements

Legal, Human Resources, management

- All contracts relating to the acquisition or disposal of companies or businesses during the last six years

Legal, tax

- Hire purchase, lease and rental agreements
- Loan agreements

Legal, financial

• All agreements dealing with intellectual property rights, including licensing agreements (in both directions, that is both by and to the target)	Intellectual property, legal

Antitrust   Antitrust
- Information required to file with appropriate antitrust authorities
- All covenants not to compete, confidentiality agreements, and other restrictive agreements
- Details of membership of, and representation on, any trade associations or other industry bodies such as standards committees

Capital commitments
- Details of the current capital expenditure budget   Financial
- Has there been significant CAPEX over the past three years? Are any major CAPEX requirements expected in the next three years?
- Details of any capital commitments

- Details of any contingent liabilities   Financial, legal

Cash flow   Financial
- A summary of the month-end bank and cash book position for the current year and previous two years
- Copies of the latest bank reconciliation with supporting bank statement
- An explanation of the major variations in the net cash position over the last three years
- An explanation of intra-month variation in the net cash position. Is the overall pattern of cash flow affected by seasonal factors?
- Are there any exceptional cash inflows or outflows?
- What are the principal uses of cash generated by operations?

Compliance   Legal, financial
- Does the business comply with generally accepted standards of corporate governance (such as Cadbury, Greenbury and Turnbull)?
- Has the target complied with statutory requirements to file documents at Companies House? In particular, have all charges on the company's assets been properly recorded and filed?

Consents   Legal, financial, environmental
- Details of all licences or consents, permits or authorities necessary to carry on business
- Copies of reports or other documents filed with governmental agencies that have regulatory power over the target or a subsidiary.

Contingent liabilities   Financial
- Are there any contingent liabilities (for example guarantees, warranties)?
- Are there material future commitments under rental/operating lease agreements?

Corporate records and structure   Legal, tax, financial
1. Exact corporate name
2. Address
3. Memorandum and Articles of Association, and all amendments of target and each subsidiary of target
4. Location of certificate of incorporation
5. Location of all statutory books of the target and its subsidiaries

6. Is the target UK resident?
7. Is the target a close company? If so, has it made any loans to participants?
8. Legal structure of company and subsidiaries:

   a. A list, with details, of all dormant, joint venture, subsidiary, group and associate companies
   b. A family tree showing the relationship between them and ownership chain to ultimate beneficial owners
   c. Details of any branch, place of business or substantial assets outside the UK
   d. Details during the last [six] years of any:

      • Incorporations
      • Acquisitions
      • Disposals
      • Joint ventures or strategic alliances
      • Windings up

9. Minutes of all Board of Directors, committee and shareholders meetings
10. Material information or documents furnished to shareholders and to directors during the last two years

Customers

Commercial, financial

• Degree of customer concentration
• Evidence of customer satisfaction
• Significant customers lost/won in last 3 years?
• Are special terms given to any customers?
• Management's assessment of customers' key purchase criteria

Debt

Legal, financial

• Details of all borrowing facilities (amount, repayment or conversion terms, interest rates, covenants and copies of trust deeds) including loan agreements, notes, mortgages, and security agreements and all financing arrangements, including sale and leaseback arrangements, capital leases, and hire purchases including security or guarantees given
• Details of charges over assets of the group
• Copies of correspondence with lenders
• Details of any debt arrangements, guarantees or indemnification between officers, directors or the shareholder(s) and the company. Are there any loans from shareholders or connected parties that could be repayable in the short term?
• Schedule of loans made giving details of borrower, authority for loan, amount due, security, interest and repayment terms
• Details of any financial guarantee or indemnities given to secure credit to third parties
• Has the target applied for or received any government grants?
• Are borrowing facilities appropriate to cash requirements?

Dispensations

Legal

Has a resolution been passed by the target or any group company to take advantage of any of the dispensations contained in the 1985 Companies Act, that is to dispense with:

• accounts before an AGM?
• annual appointment of auditors?

- holding AGMs?
- the need to renew the duration of an authority to allot shares and debentures beyond five years?

Disputes   Legal, financial
Details of any disputes, for example with:

- customers
- suppliers
- sub-contractors
- employees
- neighbours

Distribution   Legal,
- A list of licensing or distribution agreements   intellectual
- Names of any selling agents and a summary of goods sold by them   property,
                                                                           commercial,
                                                                           financial,
                                                                           antitrust

Employee information – directors and senior managers
1. Profile of each director and senior manager: Management,
                                                                           legal, Human
    - Previous experience before joining business   Resources,
    - Qualifications and degrees   financial,
    - Duties throughout the period under review   pension,
    - Age   taxation
    - Years of service and date of appointment to Board (if applicable)
    - Current remuneration
    - Service agreements
    - Pension arrangements
    - Other benefits (for example use of company car), share options/incentive arrangements
    - Directorships of companies that carry on business of any kind with the target or its subsidiaries
    - Details of any restrictive covenants, confidentiality provisions and 'golden parachutes'

2. Copy of documented organization chart. If none, why not?   Management,
3. Do the management team meet regularly to review business   Human
    performance? Are these meetings minuted?   Resources
4. Details of management succession plans

5. Are any payments made to senior managers' wives, related parties or   Tax
    related companies?

6. List of former directors and senior executives who have left during the Commercial
    last three years, with brief details

Employee information – staff
1. Details of all staff including date of birth, age, date of commencement Human
    of employment, length of service, salary, benefits, notice period,   Resources
    department and location
2. Copy of any union agreements and list of staff in each trade union
3. Details of employee representatives, who they are and who they represent, terms of office and so on
4. What is the industrial relations record of the business?

5. Details of:

- dismissals, including redundancies in the last six months
- disciplinary and grievance procedures and all recent instances of their use
- sickness records

6. Details of arrangements to be followed in the event of redundancies
7. List of part-time and disabled employees
8. Details of employees on sick leave, maternity leave or secondment
9. Details of employees employed on fixed-term, temporary and casual contracts
10. Details of staff turnover rates. Are they low or high by industry standards? What is the trend?

11. Brief outline of salary/wage payment structure, management levels and staff grading system
12. Copies of personnel policies
13. Copies of staff manuals and employee handbooks
14. Holiday pay arrangements
15. Any promised changes to terms and conditions, including pending pay increases
16. Details of employees' average weekly hours; list of employees who have opted out of the Working Time Regulations
17. Details of training spend
18. Are the growth prospects of the business threatened by skill shortages?

Human Resources, financial, intellectual property

19. Details of any consultants or other people such as agents who provide regular services

Human Resources, intellectual property

20. Details of any correspondence with:

- Commission for Racial Equality
- The Data Protection Commissioner
- Disability Commission
- Equal Opportunities Commission
- any health and safety authority

Human Resources

Environmental
- Details of past environmental assessments
- Copies of any notices of environmental claims, violations, prosecutions, employee claims/complaints or insurance claims
- Copies of correspondence with environmental regulators or third parties

Environmental

History
Brief account of history, location and nature of business

All

Information systems
- Copies of consultancy reports on internal systems and controls
- Are the management information systems fully integrated?
- Is the business dependant on third parties for software/hardware maintenance?
- Have systems weaknesses been noted in auditors' management letters?
- Are the management information systems producing timely and reliable information?

Financial, IT

- What key performance indicators does the business use to monitor its performance?
- Are there systems to ensure effective cash management?

Financial

- Confirmation that the company's systems, software and technology is owned solely by the company and does not infringe any other party's rights

Legal, IT

Insolvency

Legal

- Has any order been made, or resolution passed, for the winding-up of the target or any subsidiary?
- Has any administration order been made, or any petition for such an order presented, in respect of the target or any group company?

Insurance

Risk management, financial, legal, environmental

- Schedule or copies of all material insurance policies covering property, liabilities and operations, including product liabilities
- Schedule of any other insurance policies in force such as 'key man' policies or director indemnification policies
- All other relevant documents pertaining to the company's insurance and liability exposure
- Have the levels of insurance cover been reviewed recently?

Inter-group transactions

- Schedule listing all inter-company balances, both debit and credit. Classify between trading, management charges, rent, interest and so on and financing.

Financial, taxation

- Details of intra-group assets transfers
- Details of group tax matters, for example group income election, VAT grouping
- Copy of transfer pricing policy. Management assessment of practice. Have there been any intra-group transactions not on an arm's length basis?

Taxation

Intellectual property

Intellectual property, legal, Human Resources

1. Details of all patents, trademarks and copyrights granted or applied for, showing countries covered and, for applications outstanding, an estimate of likely date of grant. Details of inventors/authors.
2. Details of other IPRs, for example domain names or unregistered IPRs such as copyright
3. Does management believe it has all necessary patents, trademarks and IPRs?
4. Are there any restrictions or limitations on the use of IPRs or third-party ownership rights?
5. Details of:

   - any trade secrets
   - licences and other agreements to which the target is a party. Revenue streams or royalty obligations associated with each licence
   - any non-disclosure agreements
   - any challenges to intellectual property rights, any infringement claims and all litigation involving IPRs
   - procedures for ensuring that IPRs are protected
   - current R&D projects. Management's assessment of the likelihood of such projects giving rise to a patentable invention
   - maintenance fees for patents and trademarks
   - employment agreements relating to IPRs

Litigation

• Details of any litigation, actual, threatened or pending	Legal
• A summary of any administrative proceedings, governmental investigations, or inquiries against or involving the target or any subsidiary	
• Copies of correspondence with customers or suppliers relating to complaints or disputes	
• Details of any disputes with suppliers, competitors, or customers	
• How frequently has the business been involved in litigation in the past?	
• Are there any outstanding employment claims such as discrimination and wrongful dismissal cases? Please do not limit to Employment Tribunal proceedings	Human Resources, legal

Marketing

Commercial, financial

- What is the marketing strategy?
- Has advertising/sales promotion spend or direction changed recently?

Markets and competitors

Commercial, financial

1. Information on market and competitors, including market shares, competitor profiles:

   - Who are the winners and losers?
   - Why?
   - Do any have a lead technologically or otherwise?

2. Management's assessment of markets:

   - Size?
   - Are markets expanding?
   - Are there new product/geographical markets to attack?
   - How price sensitive are customers?
   - Is this true of all of them?
   - What are the major factors driving the size and growth of the markets?
   - Barriers to entry?
   - What R&D/development would be needed to improve the target's competitive position or take it into new markets?
   - Degree of changes in legislation/regulation?
   - Competitive forces – for example consolidation, restructuring, diversification?
   - How cyclical is the market?
   - Impact of economic variables, for example recession, interest rates, exchange rates?
   - Market positioning v. competitors?
   - Sources of competitive advantage?

Operations/production

Commercial, financial, operational

- Brief description of the production methods and techniques and the relative position of the business in relation to the 'leading edge' in the industry in which it operates
- Summary of recent production problems
- Constraints on production capacity
- Immediate CAPEX requirements

Pensions

- Summary of pension arrangements
- Details of pension or retirement schemes, including a copy of the trust deed and rules (including amendments), members explanatory booklets and any announcements, the latest scheme accounts and accounts for the previous year, list of members, latest and previous actuarial reports, copies of any correspondence on latest actuarial position
- Please confirm that CA approval has been obtained and that there is no OPRA interest
- Are defined benefit schemes fully funded?
- Are equal pay and increases provided for?
- Details of any unfunded pension commitments

Pensions, financial

Product information

- Product catalogues and price lists

All

- Copies of any recent industry or product surveys
- Copies of any recent reports on the target or its products produced by the target or a third party
- Management's description of products' role in the value chain, any complementary products and services and alternative applications for products and services
- Management's assessment of strengths and weaknesses of key products and services

Commercial, financial, technical

- Description of the product improvement process
- How often is each product up-dated?
- What triggers a new product release?
- Access to product complaint letters and recent lost sales reports

Commercial, technical

- Details of product/service warranties and provisions for such warranties

Financial, legal

- Does the product incorporate any third-party intellectual property such as shareware?

Legal, intellectual property, technical

Projections and forecasts

1. Are regular budgets produced, are variances monitored and are budgets updated during the year?
2. A copy of the current year's budget and estimate of trading results for the current year
3. Copies of profit and loss and cash flow projections (1–2 years) together with underlying assumptions
4. Have budgets/forecasts in the last two years been accurate? If not, what reasons do management give for this? Have the projections been prepared especially for the due diligence review or are they normal operating budgets? Were operational as well as financial staff involved in their preparation?
5. Do the projections assume any changes in accounting policies or bases?
6. Are reductions being projected in stock levels or debtor days? Justification?
7. Are increases being projected in creditor days? Justification?
8. Have the projections been approved by the Board?
9. Are there any projected cost savings that depend upon future actions?

Financial

10. Details of any medium term (3–5 years) forecasts. Are projected sales levels higher than recent/current levels? Is projected sales growth consistent with industry growth? To what extent are they reliant on something new, such as: **Financial, commercial**

- market share gains?
- new products?
- new markets/new market segments?
- new major customers?
- new sources of supply?

11. Is projected sales growth volume- or price-based?
12. How sensitive is the target's performance to external factors such as:

- economic cycle?
- fashion?
- proposed legislation?

13. Are projected changes in gross margins supported by known price rises, cost reductions or firmly priced orders/contracts?

Property
- Details of premises used by the target giving complete address, a description of its function, terms of ownership, location, size, description, dilapidation clauses, rent and rates payable and any recent valuations carried out   **Legal, property, financial**
- Do recent valuations differ significantly from book value?
- Sight of any recent independent or internal valuations or insurance reports
- Copies of all appraisals
- Copies of any dilapidation schedules served and presented by landlords
- Details of past payments of rent and rates with a summary of amounts outstanding or prepaid
- Comments on availability of any spare land
- Details of any premises not currently in use
- Management's assessment of future premises requirements

- Are the directors aware of any environmental problems?   **Legal, property, financial, environmental**
- Copies of all studies, site evaluations, and governmental filings and reports prepared by consultants or employees concerning the presence of hazardous materials or toxic substances on, under or about any property owned or leased by target or any subsidiary

Purchasing and supply
- Degree of supplier concentration   **Operational, financial**
- Details of alternative arrangements for important materials which are currently single-sourced
- Have disruptions in supply arisen recently?
- Details of subcontractors
- Are subcontracting arrangements well established, with alternative suppliers in place?
- Have there been any recent changes in subcontractors?

- What factors affect the price of purchases and are prices generally stable?   **Financial**
- Are there alternative sources of supply?

- Are there any unusual payment terms to suppliers?
- Are there any contracted forward purchase commitments?
- Are volume rebate agreements in place?

- Are any purchases made on a non-arm's length basis?   Financial,
                                                                         taxation

- Please supply details of technology and know-how licensed by the   Legal,
  company.   intellectual
                                                                         property,
                                                                         commercial,
                                                                         financial

Regulatory
Is the business subject to any regulatory matters, for example government
quotas or consents, health and safety, consumer credit, licensing or price
controls?

Legal,
operational,
environmental,
Human
Resources

Research & development
- Is the research and development function integrated with production?   Financial, IT,
- If so, how?   technical

- Has the R&D function been successful in the past?   Financial,
                                                                         intellectual
                                                                         property

Sales
- List of major customers with whom there are agreements and a   Legal,
  summary of those agreements   financial,
- Are there agency agreements?   commercial,
                                                                         antitrust

- Details of membership of any trade association or professional body   Legal,
  and of any code of practice or any other rights or obligations imposed by antitrust,
  such membership   financial,
                                                                         commercial

Financial,
commercial

- Has the sales mix changed over the last three years? If so, why?
- Have returns, guarantee or warranty claims increased recently?

- Are there any exceptional/non-recurring revenues?   Financial
- Have unit prices increased or come under severe pressure?
- Degree to which discounting is a regular trading feature
- Has the basis of calculating discounts changed in the last three years?
- Are sales seasonal?
- Impact of exchange rate movements on pricing?

- Extent of sales to related parties.   Financial,
                                                                         taxation

• Are any sales made on a non-arm's length basis?	Taxation
• How is the sales force motivated/rewarded?	Financial, commercial, Human Resources

Shares and shareholders

Legal, taxation, financial

- Authorized and issued shares of target and each subsidiary
- Description of shares
- Rights of each class of share capital
- Details of any shares created or issued in the last [six] years
- Details of any other changes in share capital in the last [six] years
- Details of any issue of, or proposals to issue, share capital since the last year-end
- Are there any unusual reserves or restrictions on distributions to shareholders?
- Have any distributions been made or promised since the last accounts?
- Has the company ever redeemed any shares or debentures from profits or reserves?
- Is any interest treated as a distribution for tax purposes?
- Names of shareholders and holdings.
- Are any shareholders under any legal disability (for example as a result of mental illness)?
- Do any of the major shareholders have any interests in other businesses which could be in competition with the target?
- Are there warrants, options, and other rights to acquire shares?
- Details of stock options, stock purchase and other employee benefit plans and agreements
- Copies of shareholder agreements
- Are there any encumbrances over shares?
- Copies of all correspondence and other communications with shareholders

Strategy

Commercial, financial

- Copy of any business plans in existence
- What is the essence of the company strategy?
- Who is involved in setting the strategy?
- When was the strategy last updated?
- Has the strategy changed recently?
- Have external consultants advised on strategy?

Tangible fixed assets

Financial

- General description, including age, categorized by type of plant and machinery (or copy of fixed asset register)
- Are there any recent independent asset valuation reports?
- Have any new capital commitments been taken on since the last accounts?

• Has any interest, own labour or materials been capitalized? • Details of all investments in other companies	Financial, taxation
• List of all motor vehicles owned, leased or hired and users' names	Financial, management, Human Resources

Taxation

- Summarize tax provisions for the last [3]/[6] years
- Reconcile the tax charge shown in the accounts to the prevailing statutory rates
- Describe deferred tax provisioning policy
- Are recent tax computations agreed by the Inland Revenue?
- If not, what issues are outstanding or being disputed by the Inland Revenue?
- Are there any years still open?
- Has the company been engaged in any schemes for tax avoidance? If so, please give details and copies of any related documentation (for example legal opinion).
- What is the status of overseas tax audits? What have been the previous outcomes of such tax audits?
- Describe relations with the tax authorities: have submissions always been on time?
- Has tax always been paid on time? Has the company ever been subject to penalties? Has the company ever been investigated by the tax authorities?
- Details of any correspondence with the Inland Revenue/local tax authorities
- Copy of the tax computation and correspondence, covering the last 3/6 years
- Are any concessionary tax treatments being followed?
- Copy of any apportionment clearances which have been obtained
- Is there a backlog of tax payable to any authority?
- Has the business entered into any tax planning schemes in recent years?
- Are any agreed tax losses restricted in their availability?
- Summarize any past rollover/holdover claims that impact on tax base cost of significant assets
- Copies of Industrial Buildings Allowance history
- Confirm all relevant elections have been validly made on time
- Copies of all tax clearances sought/received
- Confirm VAT status
- Copy of VAT returns for the current year and previous year
- A copy of the VAT account (including VAT bad debt account), PAYE and NIC account
- If member of a group, confirm that VAT and corporation tax implications of management charges and so on have been considered
- Document any special arrangements and compliance with them
- Confirm VAT payments and returns are up to date with no default surcharge notices
- Details of the latest control visits by PAYE, DSS and VAT authorities and the outcome
- Copies of the latest P11Ds. Copies of any P11D dispensations. Details of any taxation or stamp duty schemes.
- Has the company been party to any transactions where Section 765 Income and Corporation Taxes Act 1988 could apply? (This requires UK companies to obtain consent from the Treasury before certain transactions can be carried out by overseas subsidiaries.)
- Has the company made any claims under double tax relief treaties?
- Does the company have unremittable overseas income or gains?
- Have all relevant documents been duly stamped?
- Does the company have any exposure to Stamp Duty Reserve Tax?

Trading results – historic

- Details of the latest order book (with comparative figures)
- Monthly totals of sales for the current year and previous two years.

- Monthly gross profit percentage for current year and previous two years. Have gross profit percentages changed? If so, why?
- Analysis of purchases from principal suppliers for last three years
- Basis of allocation of costs between different subsidiaries, activities, or divisions?

- Analysis of turnover by main product groups for last three years
- Analysis of turnover by main customers and geographical markets for last three years

Financial, commercial

- Analysis of intra-group trading for the past [three] years – and whether on normal commercial terms

Financial, tax

Trading results – current

Financial

1. Since the last accounts date, details of any:

   - Significant changes in the nature or scale of the business compared with the previous year
   - Transactions or liabilities entered into other than in the normal course of trading
   - Material adverse change in turnover or financial or trading position
   - Actions by the target to prejudice its own goodwill
   - Abnormal factors affecting the business
   - Foreign exchange contracts open at, and opened since, the last accounts date to which the target is a party
   - Letters of credit in issue at, or issued since, the last accounts

2. What is the impact on recent profitability of provisions being created or released?

Working capital – cash

Financial

- Is the level of cash at the balance sheet date representative of the cash held throughout the month/year?
- What are the overdraft facilities?
- How is surplus cash managed?

- What are the terms of bank loans/overdrafts?

Financial, legal

Working capital – stocks

Financial

- Particulars of basis of valuation of stocks and work in progress at each year-end
- Have stock qualities been physically verified recently?
- What levels of stock loss have arisen on recent stock counts?
- How are obsolete and slow moving stock provisions calculated at the year-end and at intermediate dates?
- Have stock levels increased or decreased?
- Why?

Working capital – debtors

Financial

- Most recent aged listing of trade debtors
- Is the ageing of trade debtors improving or deteriorating, and is it acceptable?
- Is the business vulnerable to one or two large debtors defaulting?
- Summary of current bad debt provisions
- What is the past experience of bad debts?
- Are normal credit terms being enforced with all customers?
- Are there any unusual sundry debtors or prepayments?

- Schedule of accruals showing the basis upon which these have been calculated

Working capital – trade creditors   Financial

- Most recent aged list of trade creditors
- Are there any unusual sundry creditors or accruals?
- Is the business under pressure to pay creditors more quickly?
- Do any creditor balances attract interest or offer discounts for early payment?
- How is deferred income calculated?

A3 *Briefing checklist*

The following is intended as an aid to briefing advisers and others working on a transaction.

1. Code words for transaction and parties involved
2. Companies/assets being acquired
3. Type of transaction, that is assets deal, share deal or mixture
4. Companies to be investigated
5. Period to review
6. Description/history of target company
7. Target's:

   - Product and company literature
   - Group structure.

8. Copy of sale memorandum (if there is one)
9. Target's business plan (if there is one)
10. Timetable
11. Copies of confidentiality agreements
12. Outline of which advisers are doing what
13. Contacts list:

    - Target
    - Acquirer + who is responsible for what
    - Advisers

14. Reasons for acquisition:

    - Strategic rationale
    - Other perceived benefits.

15. Is the transaction driven by technology considerations? If using outside experts to evaluate technology, how will the know-how they investigate be protected?
16. Copies of any internal papers justifying the deal
17. Materiality limits

18. Post-acquisition plans:

    - Asset sales
    - Business closures
    - Development plans (when, where and timescales/priorities)
    - To what extent will the target be integrated? Over what timescale?

19. Buyer's existing knowledge
20. Buyer's concerns:

    - Identified
    - Other

21. Audience for due diligence reports (Board, bankers and so on)

22. Written terms of reference for each adviser:

    a. Financial due diligence:

- IT
- Tax
- Pensions.

    b. Legal due diligence:

- Antitrust
- Environment
- Human resources
- Property
- Intellectual property.

    c. Commercial due diligence:

- Operational
- Technical
- Management.

A4 *Financial due diligence checklist*

Executive summary

Provide a short executive summary dealing with the main financial risks and opportunities for the buyer in doing this deal along with an assessment of the likelihood of those risks materializing and the costs if they do. Summarize what warranty/indemnity protection should be negotiated, along with an indication of the priority for each point.

History and commercial activities

Provide a short history and development of the target and the activities undertaken along with a description of the Group's activities and its commercial objectives and policies.

- Outline the target's corporate structure.
- Give a breakdown of turnover by categories for the last [three] years and, where possible, an assessment of the size and development of the principal markets in which the target operates, its main customer type, potential customers and assessment of market share. Commercial due diligence colleagues may be able to help here.
- Outline the target's relationships with suppliers, assess the relative importance of each major source of supply and provide details of any particular commercial relationships.
- Show how the target finances its activities, including any special financial arrangements.
- Summarize any new activities planned, recently commenced or terminated.
- Provide details of trade associations, bonding arrangements, and so on.
- Provide details of the activities of and relationship with any other companies owned by, or in which an interest is held by, the shareholders or directors of the Company, having a trading or other relationship with the target.
- Assess the target's vulnerability to changes in market conditions, interest rate and any other significant factors.
- Liaise with legal due diligence and provide details of the target's properties including location, form and terms of tenure, current usage, date of acquisition, cost and current valuation, planned future expenditure, a schedule of the net book values of the properties (a professional open-market valuation of the properties may be undertaken by a firm of Chartered Surveyors and Valuers) and, in the case of any let properties, details of tenants, terms of lease, rental income and so on.

Organizational structure and employees

1. Provide details of:

   - management structure
   - directors and senior management, terms of employment including service contracts, bonus or commission payable, pensions, benefits, loans and expenses, if applicable.

2. Comment on any changes planned following the proposed acquisition.
3. Assess any management succession plans.

4. Liaise with [employment/legal] due diligence and provide broad details of the workforce including terms of employment, numbers, remuneration policy and staff relations, noting Trades Unions that are recognized, dates of salary/wage reviews and their current status, dates of profit-sharing and bonus schemes.
5. Comment on availability of staff, recruitment policy and training.
6. Liaise with [pensions/legal due diligence] and give details of pension schemes and an indication of their funding position.
7. Summarize any important relationships with outside contractors and professional advisers and the extent of the target's reliance upon them.

Accounting policies and information systems

1. Summarize the accounting policies adopted by the target and details of any recent changes in policy.
2. Describe and assess:

   * The financial records produced by the target and the systems of internal control. Compare with the acquirer's policies.
   * The target's costing systems and the budgetary control and forecasting systems.
   * The management information produced by the target including an assessment of auditors' management letters.

Trading results

* Provide a summary of the consolidated results of the target covering the last [three] years.
* Break down gross profit and analyse by each main activity for the last [three] years together with an explanation of significant variations.
* List adjustments to be made to the profit and loss accounts and balance sheets over the review period to reflect consistent accounting policies or the impact of exceptional items.
* Analyse overhead expenses and comment on significant fluctuations.
* Explain the major fluctuations in turnover and profits during the review period.
* Explain and comment on trends in the results and note any exceptional profits or losses.

Net assets

1. Provide a summary statement of the consolidated balance sheets of the target for the last three (or five) years.
2. Analyse and comment on the main assets and liabilities in the target's balance sheets for the last three (or five) years. In particular, comment on whether stock is valued appropriately, particularly where overheads are included, how long-term WIP is valued and profit recognized, and whether the depreciation rate is appropriate.
3. Compare notes with legal and give summary details of:

   * any material long-term and/or onerous contracts.
   * banking facilities available to the target, including covenants and any onerous conditions, breaches and renewal dates.
   * the target's capital structure.

Cash flows

Show the target's cash flows for the last three (or five) years, reconcile profit and cash and comment on the target's ability to continue to generate cash on the same basis.

Taxation

After discussion with tax and legal give summary details of the current position with regard to the agreement of taxation liabilities, deferred taxation, shortfall clearances and assessments and details of any unusual PAYE or VAT practices and the findings of the last inspection of these areas.

Financial projections

1. Review the target's profit and cash flow projections including:

    *   The method of preparation
    *   Arithmetical accuracy
    *   The commercial assumptions made by the directors. Comment on any assumptions that appear unrealistic
    *   Cash flow projections v borrowing facilities.

2. Provide a sensitivity analysis of the projections in relation to the key assumptions upon which they have been prepared and taking into account the findings of commercial due diligence.

Other matters

Discuss with legal due diligence and give summary details of any current, pending or threatened litigation or legal proceedings against or involving the target, details of any contingent liabilities and a summary of the target's insurance cover.

A5 *Legal due diligence checklist*

Executive summary

Provide a short executive summary dealing with the main legal risks and opportunities in doing this deal, from the buyer's commercial point of view, along with an assessment of the likelihood of those risks materializing and the costs if they do. Summarize what warranty/indemnity protection should be negotiated, along with an indication of the priority for each point.

Corporate records

1. Determine exact corporate name and address.
2. Summarize Memorandum and Articles of Association, and all amendments of target and each subsidiary of target.
3. Verify location of certificate of incorporation and all statutory books of the target and its subsidiaries.
4. Summarize legal structure of company and subsidiaries. Provide:

   a. A list, with details of corporate name, address, activities and so on, of all dormant, joint-venture, subsidiary, group and associate companies.
   b. A family tree showing the relationship between them and the ownership chain to ultimate beneficial owners.
   c. Details of any branch, place of business or substantial assets outside the UK.
   d. Details during the last [six] years of any:

      - incorporations
      - acquisitions
      - disposals
      - windings-up

5. Review:

   - minutes of all Board of Directors, committee and shareholders' meetings.
   - material information or documents furnished to shareholders and to directors during the last two years.

Shares

1. Determine the capitalization and authorized and issued shares of the target and each subsidiary.
2. Provide a description of shares, summarize rights of each class of share capital.
3. Determine names of shareholders and holdings and whether any shareholders are under any legal disability (for example, as a result of mental illness).
4. Do any of the major shareholders have any interests in other businesses which could be in competition with the target?

5. Determine the existence of warrants, options, and other rights to acquire shares.
6. Summarize shareholder agreements and report on their effect, if any, on the proposed transaction (and, if they are to survive) the effect on any future transactions: for example agreements or other arrangements restricting the transfer or ownership of shares or the voting of shares.
7. Investigate whether any shares of stock of the target or any subsidiary have been issued in violation of company law.
8. Report on any encumbrances over shares.
9. Summarize stock option, stock purchase and other employee benefit plans and agreements.
10. Obtain and review copies of all correspondence and other communications with shareholders.
11. Confirm all dividends or distributions declared, made or paid since incorporation have been declared, made or paid in accordance with the Articles and the Companies Acts.
12. Obtain details of any

   - shares created or issued in the last [six] years.
   - other changes in share capital in the last [six] years.
   - issue of, or proposals to issue, share capital since the last year end.

Dispensations

Has the target or any group company passed a resolution to take advantage of any of the dispensations contained in the 1985 Companies Act, that is to dispense with:

- accounts before an AGM?
- annual appointment of auditors?
- holding AGMs?
- the need to renew the duration of an authority to allot shares and debentures beyond five years?

Debt

- Investigate the indebtedness of the target and subsidiaries, including a review of loan agreements, notes, mortgages, and security agreements. This should include a review of all financing arrangements, including sale and leaseback arrangements, capital leases, and hire purchases and terms and assignability of any loan agreements and must include any off-balance sheet financing arrangements and the use of Special Purpose Vehicles where there is recourse to the target.
- Review correspondence with lenders and demonstrate compliance with financial covenants.
- Report on any debt arrangements, guarantees or indemnification between officers, directors or shareholders and the company.

Insolvency

- Has any order been made, or resolution passed, for the winding up of the target or any subsidiary?
- Has any administration order been made, or any petition for such an order presented in respect of the target or any group company?

Property

1. Compile a list of relevant property, including complete addresses of all property owned or leased along with a description of their function and whether owned or leased.

2. Review:

    * title documents to property.
    * leases – term, renewal rights, rent, assignability.

3. Obtain copies of all appraisals.
4. If not covered elsewhere, obtain copies of all studies, site evaluations, and governmental filings and reports prepared by consultants or employees concerning the presence of hazardous materials or toxic substances on, under or about any property owned or leased by target or any subsidiary.

Intellectual property (if not covered elsewhere)

Confirm that the company's systems, software and technology are owned solely by the target and do not infringe on any other party's rights.

Agreements

Review major contracts, including contracts currently under negotiation (for term, appropriateness post-acquisition, assignability and any disputes and their term). Will the acquisition have any adverse effect on the trade of the target or be in breach of any contractual obligation?:

* sales contracts
* distribution contracts, including all agreements with independent sales representatives, distributors, and franchisees
* warranty agreements
* supply agreements
* employment contracts
* union agreements
* management contracts
* profit-share agreements
* consulting agreements
* licence/franchise arrangements granted by the target
* details of all licences or consents, permits or authorities necessary to carry on business
* partnership or joint-venture agreements of any partnership in which the target or any subsidiary is a member. If any partnership is material, additional due diligence will be necessary
* sponsorship agreements
* pension plans
* all insurance agreements in force with respect to target and each subsidiary
* all other material contracts. A material contract is one calling for the payment or receipt by target or a subsidiary of more than a specified amount during any 12-month period.

Employment (unless dealt with separately)

1. Obtain a list of the target's officers, directors, and employees earning more than a specified level.
2. Obtain a schedule showing the total number of employees, their job classifications, average compensation and location of employment.
3. Review:

    * all of the target's and subsidiaries' profit-sharing, pension, retirement, deferred compensation, incentive compensation, stock option, health and welfare, and other benefit plans and all correspondence relating to such plans, including with correspondence the tax authorities and actuaries. Review actuarial reports.

- all personnel policies.
- all employment, consulting, termination, golden parachute, and indemnity agreements.
- all collective bargaining and other labour agreements.

4. Investigate all pending litigation or administrative matters involving employees, including discrimination charges and unfair dismissal claims.

Compliance

1. Obtain and comment on:

   - any licences and permits needed to carry on business.
   - all governmental licenses and permits and all judgments, orders, or decrees to which target or any subsidiary is subject.
   - copies of reports or other documents filed with governmental agencies that have regulatory power over the target or a subsidiary.

2. Verify that the target complied with statutory requirements to file documents at Companies House. In particular, have all charges on the company's assets been properly recorded and filed?

Litigation

- Provide a summary of all pending or threatened material legal actions, administrative proceedings, governmental investigations, or inquiries against or involving the target or any subsidiary.
- Summarize recent or pending changes in the law that might affect the target's business.
- Review correspondence with customers or suppliers relating to complaints or disputes.
- Analyse and comment on any disputes with suppliers, competitors, or customers.
- Review correspondence with auditors or accountants regarding threatened or pending litigation, assessment or claims.
- Summarize and comment on any decrees, orders or judgments of courts or governmental agencies.
- Review settlement documentation.
- Obtain a description of any investigations pending or in progress into the affairs of the target.

Antitrust (unless covered elsewhere)

- Provide a list of where antitrust filing is required and a timetable for filing in each jurisdiction.
- Obtain the information required to file with each antitrust authority.
- Review all covenants not to compete, confidentiality agreements, and other restrictive agreements.
- Report on any anti-competitive behaviour, real and potential.

Insurance (unless covered elsewhere)

- Provide a summary of, and commentary upon, all the target's material insurance policies covering property, liabilities and operations, including product liabilities and any other insurance policies in force such as 'key man' policies or director indemnification policies.
- Review all other relevant documents pertaining to the target's insurance and liability exposure.

A6 *Commercial due diligence checklist*

Executive summary

Summarize the main findings including an assessment of the trends in the target's market, its competitive position and an overall assessment of prospects for sales [and gross margin], both for the target and for the combined entity (if applicable). The target's stand-alone prospects should be summarized in such a way that findings can be fed into the valuation model.

Analysis of the market for each product/service area

- Define the role of the target's [combined entity's] products in the value chain. Identify any complementary products and services and any alternative applications for products and services.
- Quantify market size, import penetration.
- Assess market cyclicality and the impact of economic variables, for example recession, interest rates, exchange rates.
- Describe market structure (market shares, routes to market and so on), how the structure has changed over time and determine the drivers of change, for example technology, legislation/regulation, consolidation, globalization, impact of e-commerce and their likely impact over the next 3–5 years.
- Segment the market and describe the differences in market trends between segments. Where does the target sit?
- Quantify relevant past growth and likely future growth. Give an opinion on the outlook for volume.
- Describe and assess the relevance for the target [combined entity] of each of the competitive forces based on Porter's five forces analysis (barriers to entry, bargaining power of buyers, bargaining power of suppliers, pressure from substitute products and industry rivalry). Give an opinion on the outlook for prices
- Assess industry attractiveness.

Customers (by segment)

Why do customers favour certain suppliers over others? Determine the relative importance of customers' key purchase criteria (KPCs). Rank the criteria and show the target's performance on each of the criteria relative to the competition. Key purchase criteria may include some, or all, of the following:

- quality/performance
- price
- technical support
- service
- delivery
- availability of stock
- availability of spare parts

- purchase decision process
- single-supplier v. multiple-sourcing.

The target company

- Describe and evaluate the target's market positioning v. competitors.
- Rate the target's performance against customers' key purchase criteria.
- Assess the target's [combined entity's] sources of competitive advantage.
- Conduct customer references.
- Assess target's market strategy.
- Comment on the relative strengths and weaknesses of the target's key products and services.

Competitors

Profile competitors:

- ownership
- size
- summary financial information
- main activities
- customers and segments served
- commitment to each market area
- sources of competitive advantage
- performance relative to KPCs
- relative strengths and weaknesses.

External views on management

Capture the market views (for example, those of customers, suppliers and competitors) on the capabilities and effectiveness of the target's top management both as individuals and as a team.

A7 *Human Resources due diligence checklist*

Executive summary

Summarize the main commercial issues arising from the Human Resources investigation. They might include the costs of complying with regulations, rationalization costs, the costs of integrating two workforces (for example in terms of enhanced pay and rations for one), the essentials of post-acquisition rationalization, the costs and dangers of inheriting certain union agreements or trying to merge two opposite cultures. Advise on warranty, indemnity and any other protection required.

Employee information

1. Obtain and analyse a full list of all employees, by process/function:

    - dates of birth
    - dates of commencement of employment
    - notice periods.

2. Obtain and review lists of:

    - part-time employees
    - disabled employees
    - employees on sick leave, maternity leave or secondment
    - employees employed on fixed-term contracts
    - employees employed on temporary and casual contracts
    - people employed as contractors
    - any consultants or other people such as agents who provide regular services.

Payroll information

1. Document, review and summarize remuneration packages, including:

    - pay
    - benefits
    - bonus schemes
    - pension schemes
    - profit-sharing plans.

2. Document and summarize:

    - planned retirements
    - relocations in progress
    - details of anyone receiving less than the minimum wage
    - outstanding leaves of absence
    - status of pension planning.

Staff structure

Summarize management levels and staff grading system.

Terms and conditions

Document, review and summarize:

1. Standard service agreements and terms and conditions

    *   any exceptions to the above
    *   any promised changes to the above (including pending pay increases)

2. Agency contracts
3. Staff manuals
4. Restrictive covenants and confidentiality provisions
5. Details of employees' average weekly hours
6. Employees who have opted out of the Working Time Regulations
7. Any arrangements to be followed in the event of redundancies
8. Holiday pay arrangements
9. Golden parachutes.

Industrial relations

Obtain and review details of:

*   dismissals, including redundancies in the last six months
*   disciplinary and grievance procedures and all recent instances of their use
*   disputes and litigation (past, present, threatened and pending) and not just limited to employment tribunal proceedings
*   sickness records
*   union membership
*   union recognition
*   collective agreements
*   employee representatives, who they are and who they represent, terms of office and so on.

Relations with statutory bodies

Report on any correspondence with:

*   Commission for Racial Equality
*   The Data Protection Commissioner
*   Disability Commission
*   Equal Opportunities Commission
*   any health and safety authority
*   the Inland Revenue.

Legal

Document, review and summarize:

*   consulting agreements
*   employee handbooks
*   internal investigations/corrective actions
*   status of personnel files.

A8 *Management due diligence checklist*

Key individuals and groups

Table A1   Identify action to be taken for key managers and key groups

	Impact of loss	Message to deliver	Date message delivered	Person responsible	Follow-up required
Key individuals					
Name 1					
Name 2					
Name 3					
Name 4					
Key groups					
Group 1					
Group 2					
Group 3					

Organizational design

1. Summarize:

   - Target's organization chart and division of responsibilities
   - Strengths and weaknesses of management team.

2. Give recommendations on:

   - The most appropriate final organizational structure
   - The most appropriate interim organizational structure
   - Which individuals should be in which position.

A9 *Pensions due diligence checklist*

Executive summary

- summary of the funding position
- recommendations on warranties
- recommendations for future pension provision.

Pension schemes

1. A full list of those transferring along with details of age, pay and length of service and contracts of employment, including details of employees earning more than the pensions cap.
2. Commentary on changes planned in the context of the proposed acquisition.
3. Copy of target's accounts.
4. For each scheme from which employees are transferring:

   - the Trust Deed and Rules
   - members' handbook
   - announcements made since both of the above were last updated
   - confirmation that equal pay and increases are provided for
   - the latest scheme accounts
   - latest actuarial report/review
   - information on any unfunded pension commitments, both approved and unapproved.

5. Verification that Revenue Contributions Agency (CA) approval etc. has been obtained.
6. Confirmation that there is no Occupational Pensions Regulatory Authority (OPRA) interest.

A10 *Taxation due diligence checklist*

Executive summary

Provide an overall assessment of the degree and likelihood of the buyer being exposed to any past tax liabilities, the transactional risks and the likelihood of them crystallizing, and advise on any tax planning opportunities. Give recommendations for contract negotiations.

Accounts

- Summarize tax provisions for the last [x] years.
- Obtain/perform reconciliations of the tax charge shown in the accounts to the prevailing statutory rates.
- Investigate reasons for significant differences.
- Describe deferred tax provisioning policy.
- Verify closing balance sheet provision.

Corporation tax

1. Obtain copies of computations, returns, assessments and correspondence with the Inland Revenue for last [x] years.
2. Document status of the above.
3. Review filing of returns and quarterly payment compliance.
4. Describe significant areas of correspondence with the Inland Revenue.
5. Identify any concessionary tax treatments being followed.
6. Detail items still unresolved and under negotiation: quantify amounts and likely risk.
7. Compare above with accounts provisions. Are provisions adequate?
8. Summarize carry-forward tax assets.
9. Confirm extent to which tax assets have been agreed with Inland Revenue.
10. Assess extent to which above tax assets are vulnerable to:

    - Anti-avoidance measures
    - Not being available to the purchaser for any other reason.

11. Confirm and document tax base cost of significant assets.
12. Summarize any past rollover/holdover claims that impact on tax base cost of significant assets.
13. Obtain copies of Industrial Buildings Allowance history.
14. Confirm all relevant elections have been validly made on time.
15. Review intra-group assets transfers.
16. Confirm group matters, for example group income election.
17. Obtain copies of all tax clearances sought/received.
18. Review status and outcome of overseas tax audits.
19. Assess overseas subsidiaries for Controlled Foreign Companies Legislation.
20. Obtain copies of transfer pricing policy. Review and comment on practice.

Payroll taxes

- Review forms P11D.
- Discuss arrangements for expenses, benefits, casual payments and so on and check to P11Ds.
- Review correspondence in respect of most recent PAYE/NIC audits.
- Critically review any 'consultancy' and 'contractor' arrangements for employee status.
- Identify any share options/incentive arrangements and review for compliance/exposure for PAYE and NIC.
- Obtain copies of any P11D dispensations.
- Reconcile balance sheet provision for PAYE/NIC to monthly/year-end returns.
- Review for overseas payroll exposures, for example seconded employees and so on.
- Assess major risk areas.

VAT/Customs

1. Review workings supporting last [x] VAT returns.
2. Confirm VAT status.
3. Document any special arrangements and compliance with them.
4. Review correspondence in respect of most recent audit inspection.
5. Confirm payments and returns are up to date, and there are no default surcharge notices.
6. Discuss and review procedures for:

   - discounts
   - disposals of assets
   - miscellaneous sources of income
   - bad debts
   - non-deductible items.

7. Review and document customs duties arrangements.
8. Assess risk areas.

Previous reorganizations/transactions undertaken by target

- Obtain details of past M&A transactions involving the target.
- Review clearances.
- Review due diligence.
- Review warranties and indemnities.
- Summarize implications for current transaction.

Transaction, structuring and integration issues

1. Identify potential warranty/indemnity issues.
2. Advise on Stamp Duty.
3. Assess the Impact of the transaction on:

   - losses and other reliefs carried forward
   - option schemes. PRP schemes and so on
   - the vendor's tax planning.

4. Report on tax issues to be considered during integration planning.
5. Summarize any tax planning issues to be taken into account when structuring the transaction.

A11 *Environmental due diligence checklist*

Executive summary

Summarize and assess the main environmental risks arising with the transaction and give appropriate recommendations for contact negotiations.

Issues to be covered

1. A summary of:

   - the previous uses of the site(s) and the previous occupiers of the sites during the last 40 years and, where ascertainable, during the last 100 years.
   - the present use or uses of the site(s) including details of any deposit, storage, disposal and treatment of waste or sewage.
   - manufacturing and other processes and operations, abstractions of water, mining operations, discharge of use of chemicals and any other substances.

2. Details of any plant and operating processes.
3. A description of:

   - the geological and hydro-geological features of the site and of land within 1000 metres of the site including the potential migration or pathways of any pollutants or contaminants from the site.
   - the condition or use of any neighbouring land.

4. Details of the location of any asbestos, PCBs or formaldehyde.
5. Details of the drainage system.
6. Details of the measures for containment and prevention of pollution.
7. Details of environmental permits and whether they are in full force and effect.
8. Details of any works or other expenditure required within the next five years to maintain compliance with environmental standards, the presence or former presence of any underground or surface storage tanks.
9. Details of any previous audits, assessments or other reports.
10. Details of any actual or threatened prosecutions or civil proceedings.
11. Provide copies of corporate environmental policies.
12. Provide approximate costings for any remediation works.
13. Give recommendations for stage 2 audit, if any.
14. Highlight any ethical issues:

    - What is the level of understanding and awareness of ethical issues among staff?
    - Are there mandatory training courses designed to raise integrity awareness?
    - Are the target's rules of behaviour accessible and easy to understand?
    - Do they genuinely help staff to know what to do?
    - Are the rules applied consistently?
    - Is the target doing enough or just going through the motions?

A12 *IT due diligence checklist*

Executive summary

Provide a summary of the target's IT and PT equipment and software and report on its security, functionality, ownership and any outstanding commitments. Assess the degree to which IT and technology supports the business on a day-to-day basis and make recommendations for any changes. Assess the sufficiency of the IT resources and production technology for the future and make recommendations for any changes. Give recommendations on the most appropriate and cost-effective IT organization once the transaction is complete, including costings and timetables. Assess the current IT and technical staff both as individuals and as a team.

IT team

Assessment of:

- technical skills
- team spirit
- leadership
- management.

Business processes

Assess effectiveness of:

- departmental structure
- policies and procedures
- project management
- QA process
- documentation
- training.

Users' perceptions of IT department

- Skill base
- Responsiveness

The future

- Are there well-developed plans for future development?
- Do these support the business plan?

A13 *Technical due diligence checklist**

Product

- Conduct a telephone survey of all customers who purchased each product recently. Select the customers randomly from invoices.
- Conduct a telephone poll of random customers that have used the product for over a year.
- Review complaint letters to top management. Call the customers who wrote those letters.
- Review credit memos. Call customers who wanted their money back.
- Get a recent lost sales report. Call customers who selected competitive products.
- How often is each product updated? What triggers a new product release? Elapsed time? New features available? Critical bug fixes available?
- How are new features determined/prioritized? Development Group? Marketing? User Group feedback?
- What is the number and severity of bugs logged against each product?
- Does the bug list adequately reflect the defects reported during the telephone poll?

Software Development Group

- Is the Software Development Group appropriately staffed? Quantity? Quality?
- Is the Software Development Group supplied with adequate development hardware and development software?
- Is the development process appropriately documented?
- Are the products appropriately documented?
- Is the design documentation adequate?
- Has it been updated to reflect design changes and enhancements?
- Is the documentation of the data structures adequate and current?
- Is the documentation of the module structure and control flow adequate?
- Is the documentation of the data structures adequate and current?
- Coding standards and code walk-throughs?
- Structured code?
- Comments in code?
- Design documentation?
- LAN-based source code back-up?
- Frequent off-site source code back-up?
- Virus check all development machines?
- Documented process for release to software QA?

Software QA (Software Design Verification) Group

- Is the SQA Group appropriately staffed?
- Is the SQA Group supplied with adequate test hardware and software?

---

* Copyright © 1997–1998 MasterTeam, Inc and Jonathon L. Huie. The checklist was designed for use when acquiring a software company, but most of the points are valid for other technologies. The original author is Jonathon L. Huie (jhuie@terapacket.com; Voice (303) 517-5617; Fax (303) 664-9842).

- Is the SQA test process adequately documented?
- Does the SQA test process reliably catch regression and other defects?
- Does the SQA test process test all appropriate hardware/software configurations?
- Is testing performed in various LAN environments?
- Does the SQA test process test with appropriate application software?
- Are the Alpha and Beta test processes adequate, and are they well documented?
- Is there an appropriate computerized bug-tracking system with bugs listed for the production release, all test releases, and all prior releases?
- Do the SQA group, the development group, and the technical support group all access the same bug-tracking system?
- Are all releases virus-scanned?

Technical Support Group

- Conduct a telephone poll of customers who called technical support recently.
- Conduct a telephone poll of random customers.
- Is the Technical Support Group appropriately staffed?
- Is the Technical Support Group supplied with adequate test hardware and software?
- Is the Technical Support Group adequately documented?
- Is the technical support response adequate? What hours are available?
- Are in-bound calls immediately directed to a tech support person, or are they logged for call back? What is the average time for callbacks? Worst-case time for callbacks?
- What is the escalation procedure? When is the SQA group or the development group informed of a support issue? When is top management informed of a support issue? When is the salesman on the account informed of a support issue?
- Do the SQA Group, the Development Group, and the Technical Support Group all access the same bug tracking system?
- Is there a computerized log?
- Are reports generated to categorize the reasons for the calls? Call duration? Whether call back needed? How many calls to resolve the issue? Escalation to a second level tech support or to development? Bug fix required to address the issue?
- How are emergency bug fixes handled? How delivered? How tracked? How integrated into next product release? How coordinated with SQA?
- Is there a bulletin board? Does it have troubleshooting tips? Bug list? Bug fixes? New product releases? Beta releases? Can customers and tech support leave messages for each other?

Corporate culture

How do the corporate cultures match?

Hard-driving	v.	Laid back	
Patch it quick	v.	Do it right	
Anything for a sale	v.	Keep the development team focused on the next release at all costs	
Technology-driven	v.	Marketing-driven	v. Sales driven product development strategy
Managers	v.	Leaders	

- How formal are relationships across levels of management?
- Working hours: usual and during deadline crunches?
- Dress code?
- Perks: coffee, snacks, parties, meals during deadline crunches, and so on?
- Compensation? Salaries? Cash bonuses? Stock options?

Personnel: Who is critical to continued success?

- Who has critical undocumented knowledge?
- Historic patterns of attrition?
- Who is currently dissatisfied? Why?
- What happens to stock options in a buyout?
- Who might become dissatisfied by a buyout? Why?
- Who might become too satisfied by a buyout (for example, have all stock options to vest)?

Intellectual property issues

- Has the product documentation, the marketing collateral, or any advertising ever inaccurately represented the capabilities of the product?
- Does an appropriate software licence agreement accompany all products shipped?
- Does the company have full rights to all the source code it uses?
- Did any of the source code originate outside the company? Where? Who has rights? Is the original copyright retained in the source code?
- Has any of the company's source code ever been licensed to another entity? Is there an appropriate signed licence agreement?
- Are there copyright notices in all source code, documentation, and disk labels?
- Does the company own any patents? Are they enforceable?
- Does the company infringe anyone else's patents?
- Are current non-disclosure agreements in place? For employees? Contractors? Customers? Vendors? Partners?
- Is the company or any employee under non-disclosure to any other entity?
- Are all copies of development software and office software paid for and registered?
- Does the company meet all licence agreement terms for all development software used?
- Are royalties payable for any software component bundled with the company's product? Are the royalty payments current?

A14 *Intellectual property checklist*

Executive summary

Provide an executive summary which confirms or shows otherwise the existence and validity of, and title to, the IPRs the buyer thought it was buying. Highlight any 'contractual protection' issues. Assess the importance of IPRs in the creation and maintenance of competitive advantage.

All IPRs

1. Obtain a list of:

   - All intellectual property rights (IPRs) owned by the target which are to be transferred. (Do not forget domain names under this heading or unregistered IPRs such as copyright.)
   - All patent, trade mark and design applications outstanding with an estimate of likely date of grant.
   - Which IPRs cover which products.
   - Any restrictions or limitations on the use of IPRs or third-party ownership rights. Check for security interests, for example, collateral assignments.

2. Obtain copies of all:

   - Licences and other agreements to which the target is a party. (Licences can work both ways so remember the target could be a licensor or a licensee, or indeed both.) Identify revenue streams or royalty obligations associated with each licence.
   - Non-disclosure agreements.

3. Obtain details of:

   - Any challenges to the intellectual property rights owned, claimed, licensed or used by the target company or business.
   - Any claims that the target is infringing another company's IPRs.
   - Inventors/authors. Check that rights have been properly transferred.
   - Arrangements to ensure that the company owns any IPRs created by work done by employees or outside parties.
   - The target's procedures for ensuring that IPRs are protected.
   - How IPRs have been enforced in the past.
   - All litigation involving IPRs.
   - Current R&D projects and an assessment of the likelihood of such projects giving rise to a patentable invention.
   - Payment of maintenance fees for patents and trademarks.
   - Employment agreements relating to IPRs. Do the agreements include non-compete clauses? Does the target remind employees of their confidentiality obligations?
   - Copies of all other agreements dealing with intellectual property rights, for example rights in inventions, secrecy and non-compete agreements with research bodies such as universities and consultancies, and joint-venture partners.

Licences

The principal areas to investigate are:

- Extent of the grant (both geography and the extent to which the licensed technology can be used)
- Exclusive or non-exclusive?
- Royalty and minimum royalty payments
- Compliance with competition law
- Obligations to maintain the rights, for example whether there is a responsibility for paying renewal fees
- The obligations, if any, to disclose improvements and the rights to use those improvements
- Restrictions on developing alternative technology
- Duration
- Termination conditions
- Assignability
- Change of control
- Outstanding breaches of the licence.

Trademarks and copyrights

- Has there been any non-use of trademarks? For what period of time?
- Has there been any prior assignment of trademarks?

Trade secrets

- To the extent possible, identify all trade secrets and know-how used in or associated with the acquired business. Particularly identify confidential information that the target has acquired from third parties.
- Identify the target's procedures for protecting confidential information.
- Identify the target's procedures for releasing information, for example in marketing materials or technical symposia.

B

The following appendices are to give further illustration to some of the points mentioned in the main text and as such they cover a wide variety of issues.

B1 *Financial due diligence – an example of breaking down the numbers*

A summary profit and loss account for a company making a specialized type of plastic which is used in the truck industry might be as shown in Table B1. On the figures presented, there is a good progression of sales and profits. Sales have rebounded strongly from the 1999 low and are forecast to continue their upward progression. Profits growth is even more impressive, with the operating margin forecast to go from 3 per cent to 11 per cent. Financial due diligence seeks to get behind these numbers and understand them a little more.

Table B1 Summary profit and loss account

	1999 Actual £000	2000 Actual £000	2001 Actual £000	2002 Forecast £000	2003 Forecast £000	2004 Forecast £000
Sales	10500	13000	12800	14000	15000	15750
Cost of sales	(8617)	(10303)	(10039)	(10400)	(10850	(11200)
Gross profits	1883	2697	2761	3600	4150	4550
Overheads	(2008)	(2349)	(2346)	(2076)	(2127)	(2158)
Operating profits	(125)	348	415	1524	2023	2392

Table B2 Summary profit and loss account

Year ending 31 December	1999 Actual £000	2000 Actual £000	2001 Actual £000
Turnover	10500	13000	12800
Direct costs	(5317)	(6571)	(6447)
Contribution	5183	6429	6353
Overheads:			
Production	(3300)	(3782)	(3492)
Administrative	(710)	(975)	(890)
Distribution	(151)	(154)	(161)
Marketing	(1147)	(1170)	(1395)
Operating profit	(125)	348	415

Notes:
Direct costs are material, subcontract costs and direct labour.
Production overheads are mainly indirect labour costs, building maintenance, utilities and depreciation.
Administrative overheads are occupation costs, employee costs and professional services.
Distribution overheads are employee costs and carriage charges.
Marketing overheads are employee costs, advertising, promotions and PR.

Each of the figures in Table B1 will be analysed and explained in detail. The very skimpy highlights given might be expanded as shown in Table B2. The investigating accountants go to work and soon their analysis of the marketing overheads shows a need for adjustments. The breakdown of the reported marketing figures is shown in Table B3. Table B4 further analyses special promotions. Product X was launched at the end of 1999 and discontinued in April 2001. The figures included for Product X will not therefore recur.

Table B3   Analysis of marketing overheads

Year ending 31 December	1999 £000	2000 £000	2001 £000
Advertising	90	85	95
PR	20	25	25
Wages & salaries	50	55	60
Special promotions	982	1000	1210
Other	5	5	5
Total	1147	1170	1395

Table B4   Analysis of special promotions

Year ending 31 December	1999 £000	2000 £000	2001 £000
Product X	2	760	250
Other	230	240	260
Overriding discounts	750	—	700
Total	982	1000	1210

Overriding discounts are given to customers who achieve very high levels of purchases. Discounts are based on sales to 31 December. They are calculated and paid early in the calendar year after the year in which they are earned. Because of competitor activity in 1999 no overriders were earned and therefore no overrider discounts were paid in 2000. Several big accounts were won in 2000. Sales overriders were an important factor in winning their business. Their sales to December were enough to qualify them for overriding discounts. These were recognized in the special promotions account for 2001.

Table B5   Overrider analysis

Year ending 31 December	1998 £000	1999 £000	2000 £000	2001 £000
Overriders recognized	—	750	—	700
Overriders actually payable	750	—	700	650

Recording and paying overriders in the year after they are earned is an incorrect accounting treatment. Overriders should have been accrued through the year and accounted for as a deduction from sales. As a result, profit in 1998 has been overstated by £750 000, understated by £750 000 in 1999, overstated by £700 000 in 2001, and understated by £50 000 in 2001, as shown in Table B5. The Product X and overriding adjustments lead to adjustments of the marketing figures (see Table B6) and the sales figures (see Table B7).

The accountants continue their work, and find a host of similar non-recurring items and adjustments to the figures provided by the target. The non-recurring items, like Product X,

Table B6   Recurring marketing costs

Year ending 31 December	1999 £000	2000 £000	2001 £000
Advertising	90	85	95
PR	20	25	25
Wages & salaries	50	55	60
Special promotions	982	1000	1210
Less Product X promotion	(2)	(760)	(250)
Overriding discounts	(750)	—	(700)
Other	5	5	5
Recurring special promotions	230	240	260
Total	395	410	445

Table B7   Sales adjustment

Year ending 31 December	1999 £000	2000 £000	2001 £000
Sales	10500	13000	12800
Overriding discount adjustment	—	(700)	(650)
Adjusted sales figure	10500	12300	12150

Table B8   Non-recurring and exceptional items

Year ending 31 December	1999 £000	2000 £000	2001 £000
Product X promotion	2	760	250
Overriding discounts	750	—	700
Group charges	175	190	215
Rent	(300)	(300)	(300)
Stock provision	50	(50)	—
Computer spend	—	200	100
Building provision	—	100	—
Provision reversal	25	—	(25)
Insurance	(80)	(80)	(80)
Customer B price adjustment	—	—	(50)
Total non-recurring items	622	820	(910)

Notes:
- Group charges: Charges appear to be a levy and not related to specific services.
- Rent: Property is held centrally. This is actual rent net of depreciation for buildings used.
- Stock provision: The reversal of an over-provision made in 1999.
- Computer spend: Non-recurring costs of installing the new ERP system in 2000.
- Building provision: An over-accrual for building maintenance in 2000.
- Provision reversal: Legal charges were provided for in 1999 but case subsequently dropped.
- Insurance: Group hold insurance centrally. This is the stand-alone charge.
- Customer B price adjustment: Customer B had a one-off price adjustment for 2001 only.

Table B9   Summary of profit adjustments

Year ending 31 December	1999 £000	2000 £000	2001 £000
Profit adjustments (above)	622	820	910
Adjustment to sales (overriding discounts)	—	(700)	(650)
Overhead adjustment	622	120	260
Operating profit as reported	(125)	348	415
Adjusted operating profit	497	468	675

and other exceptional items the accountants found are shown in Table B8 and summarized in Table B9.

This all leads to the profit and loss account being restated as it is in Table B10. Table B11 applies the same process to forecasts provided by target management.

Table B10   Summary profit and loss account

Year ending 31 December	1999 £000	2000 £000	2001 £000
Turnover	10500	13000	12800
Less overriding discounts	—	(700)	(650)
Adjusted sales figure	10500	12300	12150
Recurring costs:			
Direct costs	(5317)	(6571)	(6447)
Recurring contribution	5183	5729	5703
Recurring overheads:			
Production	(3300)	(3782)	(3492)
Administration	(840)	(915)	(930)
Distribution	(151)	(154)	(161)
Marketing	(395)	(410)	(445)
Recurring operating profit	497	468	675
Non-recurring items	(622)	(120)	(260)
Operating profit as reported	(125)	348	415

So now we have quite a different picture, certainly for the target's history. What was a loss in the first year actually turns out to be a healthy profit, and historical profits look altogether better than they did. This should give the buyer much more comfort. Now scepticism should be turning to the reduced, but still huge, 'hockey stick' in the three forecast years.

Having cleaned up the numbers, the FDD team will now produce tables which explain the numeric basis to the differences between the years. These will go something like Table B12 for historic numbers and Table B13 for forecast numbers.

Table B11   Summary P&L forecasts

Year ending 31 December	2002 Estimate £000	2003 Forecast £000	2004 Forecast £000
Turnover	14000	15000	15750
Less overriding discounts	(700)	(700)	(700)
Adjusted sales figure	13300	14300	15050
Recurring costs:			
Direct costs	(6900)	(7350)	(7700)
Recurring contribution	6400	6950	7350
Recurring overheads:			
Production	(3500)	(3500)	(3500)
Administration	(920)	(950)	(960)
Distribution	(165)	(170)	(175)
Marketing	(450)	(460)	(470)
Recurring operating profit	1365	1870	2245
Non-recurring items	159	153	147
Operating profit as reported	1524	2023	2392

Note:
Overheads have been forecast on a line-by-line basis.

Table B12   Operating profit bridge – historic

	£000
1999 recurring operating profit	497
Volume/price	889
Increase in margin	(343)
Increase in overheads:	
Production	(482)
Administrative	(75)
Distribution	(3)
Marketing	(15)
2000 recurring operating profit	468
Volume/price	(70)
Decrease in margin	(44)
Increase in overheads:	
Production	290
Administrative	(15)
Distribution	(7)
Marketing	(35)
2001 recurring operating profit	675

Table B13   Operating profit bridge – forecast

	£000
2001 recurring operating profit	675
Volume/price	(535)
Increase in margin	162
Increase in overheads:	
Production	(8)
Administrative	(10)
Distribution	(4)
Marketing	(5)
2002 recurring operating profit	1365
Volume/price	481
Decrease in margin	(69)
Increase in overheads:	
Production	—
Administrative	(30)
Distribution	(5)
Marketing	(10)
2003 recurring operating profit	1870
Volume/price	348
Decrease in margin	53
Increase in overheads:	
Production	—
Administrative	(10)
Distribution	(5)
Marketing	(10)
2004 recurring operating profit	2245

B2 *Human Resources legislation*

There is a large amount of Human Resources legislation which is relevant to due diligence, including:

- Minimum wage legislation
- Working time provisions
- Data protection legislation
- Maternity leave and parental leave regulations
- Protection for part time workers
- Protection for whistleblowers
- Unfair dismissal legislation
- Discrimination legislation
- IR35.

B3 *Commonly sought management competencies*

The five main subject headings below form a framework of competencies against which to assess management in either interviews or tests (or both).

Individual competencies

- *Flexibility:* the ability to change direction or modify the way in which the individual does things. Flexibility would include a willingness to try, adaptability and a positive outlook.
- *Decisiveness:* this is the readiness to take decisions and to act, that is coming to conclusions and taking appropriate action.
- *Tenacity:* the ability to stick with a problem until it is solved (and to recognize when there is no solution).
- *Independence:* the willingness to question the accepted way of doing things.
- *Risk taking:* the extent to which a manager is prepared to take calculated risks.
- *Integrity:* the recognition and maintenance of high personal standards and the implementation of appropriate moral and ethical norms.

Interpersonal competencies

- *Communication:* the ability to convey information clearly, both orally and in writing. The ability to listen.
- *Impact:* the ability to create a favourable first impression.
- *Persuasiveness:* the ability to persuade and influence others.
- *Personal awareness:* the awareness of other people and the need to take into account their thoughts and feelings before acting.
- *Teamwork:* contributing in an active and cooperative way with the rest of the team; supporting others; making decisions by consensus.
- *Openness:* the ability to take constructive criticism. The ability to build on the contributions of other people.

Analytical competencies

- *Innovation:* the ability to come up with imaginative and practical solutions to problems.
- *Analytical skills:* the ability to break problems down and work on them sequentially.
- *Numerical problem solving:* the ability to understand and analyse numerical information.
- *Problem solving:* the ability to evaluate a situation and come up with solutions which meet customers' needs.
- *Practical learning:* being able to absorb, learn and apply new methods.
- *Detail consciousness:* the ability to process large amounts of complex information.

Managerial competencies

- *Leadership:* the ability to guide the actions of, and achieve results through, other people.

- *Empowerment:* the concern for developing other people and allowing them freedom of manoeuvre.
- *Strategic planning:* the ability to hover above the day-to-day detail and see the bigger picture.
- *Corporate sensitivity:* an understanding of where the business is going.
- *Project management:* the ability to define the requirements of a project and lead a group towards its satisfactory completion.
- *Management control:* the appreciation of how a business needs to be controlled and subordinates organized.

Motivational competencies

- *Resilience:* the ability to 'bounce back' when things are not going to plan.
- *Energy:* otherwise known as stamina and drive.
- *Motivation:* the ability to motivate self and others.
- *Achievement orientation:* the drive to set challenging targets and the drive to meet them.
- *Initiative:* the ability to spot and solve problems before they arise and to act on opportunities when they present themselves.
- *Quality focus:* the commitment to getting a job done well.

B4 *Myers-Briggs Type Indicators®*

The *Myers-Briggs Type Indicator®* (*MBTI®*) is designed to give information about Jungian psychological type preferences. *MBTI®*, results indicate the respondent's likely preferences on four dimensions with each dimension made up of a pair of preferences. All eight preferences are valuable, and everyone uses each of them at least some of the time. However, each individual tends towards one preference of each pair and generally uses it more than its opposite. The four dimensions and eight preferences are as follows:

- Ways of gaining energy: Extraversion (E) or Introversion (I)
- Ways of taking in information: Sensing (S) or Intuition (N)
- Ways of making decisions: Thinking (T) or Feeling (F)
- Ways of living in the world: Judging (J) or Perceiving (P)

Basically, these are interpreted as shown in Table B14.

Table B14   *MBTI®* indicators

Ways of gaining energy	Extraversion (E)	Introversion (I)
	A focus on the outside world Energy through interacting with people and doing things	A focus on the inner world Energy through reflecting on information, ideas and concepts
Ways of taking in information	Sensing (S)	Intuition (N)
	Trust and notice facts, details and present realities	Attend to and trust inter-relationships, theories and future possibilities
Ways of making decisions	Thinking (T)	Feeling (F)
	Make decisions using logical, objective analysis	Make decisions to create harmony by applying person-centred values
Ways of living in the world	Judging (J)	Perceiving (P)
	A preference to be organized and to make decisions quickly	Prefers to be flexible and adaptive and to keep options open

Results on the indicator are generally reported with letters representing each of the preferences, of which there are 16 possibilities. The following is a very brief overview of the summary profiles for each of the 16 types:

- ENFJ. 'Pedagogue'. Outstanding leader of groups. Can be aggressive at helping others to do their best.
- ENFP. 'Journalist'. Uncanny sense of the motivations of others. Life is an exciting drama; emotionally warm; empathic.

- ENTJ. 'Field Marshall'. The basic driving force and need is to lead. Tends to seek a position of responsibility and enjoys being an executive.
- ENTP. 'Inventor'. Enthusiastic interest in everything and always sensitive to possibilities. Non-conformist and innovative.
- ESFJ. 'Seller'. Most sociable of all types. Nurturer of harmony. Outstanding host or hostess.
- ESFP. 'Entertainer'. Radiates attractive warmth and optimism. Smooth, witty, charming, and clever. Fun to be with. Very generous.
- ESTJ. 'Administrator'. In touch with the external environment. Very responsible. Pillar of strength.
- ESTP. 'Promoter'. Fiercely competitive. Action man. Often uses shock effect to get attention. Excellent negotiator.
- INFJ. 'Author'. Motivated and fulfilled by helping others. Complex personality.
- INFP. 'Questor'. High capacity for caring. Calm and pleasant face to the world. High sense of honour derived from internal values.
- INTJ. 'Scientist'. Most self-confident and pragmatic of all the types. Decisions come very easily. A builder of systems and the applier of theoretical models.
- INTP. 'Architect'. Great precision of thought and language. Can readily discern contradictions and inconsistencies. Motivated by the need to understand.
- ISFJ. 'Conservator'. Desires to be of service and to minister to individual needs – very loyal.
- ISFP. 'Artist'. Interested in the fine arts. Expression primarily through action or artform. Keen senses.
- ISTJ. 'Trustee'. Decisiveness in practical affairs. Guardian of time-honoured institutions. Dependable.
- ISTP. 'Artisan'. Impulsive action. Action is an end to itself. Fearless, craves excitement.

B5 *UK sources for environmental due diligence*

The following is based on a Department of Environment (DoE, now Department of the Environment, Transport and Regions) Consultation Paper dated May 1991, 'Public Registers of Land which may be contaminated'.

Historical maps and plans

- Ordnance Survey (OS) county series 6 inch and 1:10,000
- OS county series 25 inch and 1:2,500
- OS 50 inch (1:1250)
- British geological survey geological maps at a scale of 1:50,000 or 1:63,360

Secondary map sources where applicable

- Tithe survey maps 1836–60
- Enclosure plans
- Settlement plans
- Early county maps
- Parish and ward maps
- Jowett's atlas (details and plans of public and statutory undertakings)
- Goad fire insurance plans 1885–1940 and latest available town centre plans

Local authority records

- The statutory planning registers maintained by the local planning department
- Hazardous substance consents granted by the local planning department
- Environmental assessment reports lodged with the local planning department
- Waste disposal site licences, and licence applications where available, held with the local Environmental Health Department
- Applications. Authorisations, compliance and enforcement actions under environmental legislation and all other available registers held by the local Environmental Health Department

The Environment Agency

- Public registers of integrated pollution control processes and radioactive substances
- Records of groundwater pollution and public register of boreholes. Environment Agency plans indicating groundwater vulnerability
- Waste disposal licences held by the Environment Agency

Statutory authorities and public registers

- Radon atlas of England, published by the National Radiological Protection Board in 1996
- English Nature lists of sites of special scientific interest and other sites designated by statute
- The local water company as statutory sewage undertaker
- The DoE 1973/74 survey of landfill sites
- The Aspinwall's Sitefile Digest 1989–1997

Historical and archive records

- Local street directories published from 1850
- Kelly's street and other trade directories
- Post Office street directories
- Local commercial directories
- Local archives, company records, newspaper articles and historical society records

B6 *Intellectual property rights*

Patents

A patent gives the right to exploit an invention for a stated period of time. A patent will therefore prevent others from making, using or selling the invention. The holder of the patent can, of course, license others to do these things if he so wishes. Patents can be extremely difficult to get. Basically, the patentee has to prove that the invention is unique, and this can be very difficult (and expensive). In the UK, the rights are set out in the Patents Act 1977. Under its terms they last for 20 years from the date of application to the Patent Office provided renewal fees are paid every year from the fifth year onwards.

International law is roughly the same. The 1994 Agreement on Trade-Related Aspects of Intellectual Property (TRIPS) says that patents are issued for a non-renewable period of 20 years from the date of application. Fees and when they need to be paid are significantly different throughout the world so watch out for this if buying a company with patents registered in lots of places.

A patent will lapse if renewal fees are not paid – never to be restored – so watch out for that too!

If buying a company with patents pending, the other thing to remember is the time typically taken between patent application and when it is granted. The process takes about 2 years, but do not be surprised if it takes longer. The application must be accompanied by a detailed description of the invention and a set of claims which define the requested patent's scope. The patenting authority will then carry out a search to see if anybody else has had the idea. This is called 'prior art' and for it to exist only the same idea needs to have been published before. It does not need to have been patented or even tested, let alone commercialized. To be successful, a patent must show novelty and 'inventive step' (that is be new and different from what has gone before).

An application made at the British Patent Office will give you a British patent only. Applicants who want to register their inventions in more than one country can use two international systems:

- The Patents Cooperation Treaty
- The European Patent Convention

The Patents Cooperation Treaty (PCT) is operated by the World Intellectual Property Organization. Applicants apply to their national office, specifying the countries where they are seeking protection. The application is sent to each of the countries and they each carry out a search as if the application had been a national application under their own laws.

The European Patent Convention means that an application can be made at the European Patent Office in Munich specifying the member states in which protection is sought. The application is searched and examined centrally by Munich and if it is satisfied, grants separate national patents. This of course means that renewal fees must be paid in each state according to their usual terms.

If a patent is infringed, the patent holder is entitled to an injunction, to have any infringing articles handed over and to damages or the infringer's profits.

Copyright

Copyright exists in every original work and is automatic in Europe. It arises when the work is created and does not have to be registered. (It must, however, be registered in the US.) Works covered by UK copyright law include:

- Literary, dramatic, musical and artistic works
- Their typographical arrangements
- Sound recordings, films and TV programmes

The above includes original works such as computer programs, even where they are supplied in electronic form.

Copyright protects the holder against somebody else:

- Copying the work
- First circulating it
- Performing it or showing it in public (which would include broadcasting)
- Renting it out
- Adapting it.

'Fair use' of the work is allowed. Fair use is not defined but will depend on factors such as how much is copied and why. Copying does not have to be exact, just similar.

The author will be the first person to have the copyright. There can be more than one author, and if there is, joint owners can only exercise their rights jointly. They cannot grant licences individually.

Protection can last for the life of the author plus 70 years in the UK and US. The time period for photographs, films and sound recordings is shorter – just 50 years from publication. Typography is protected for 25 years.

There are a number of organizations which license copyrighted works. The Performing Rights Society in the UK is the most obvious. This is the body which licenses music to be broadcast, not just on the radio but also in other public places such as shops.

Design

There are two systems in the UK for protecting designs. Registered designs are covered by:

- The Registered Designs Act 1949 (as amended)
- The Design Right (Semiconductor Topographies) Regulations 1989

Unregistered designs are covered by the Copyright Designs and Patents Act 1988.

REGISTERED DESIGNS

Registered design right is available for shape, configuration, pattern or ornament applied to an article by an industrial process. The test is whether the feature gives 'eye appeal' to the article. The design cannot be purely functional as the Act specifically excludes aspects of design which allow it to fit with something else so that it or the other article can perform its function. It relates to three-dimensional products.

In the UK, registration is with the originally named Designs Registry. Registered design right is initially for five years, renewable up to a maximum of 25 years.

Semiconductor chip designs have their own system of protection. The regulations protect the topography (but not the functions) of the chip. The owner of the chip topography has the same exclusive rights as the owner of design rights.

UNREGISTERED DESIGNS

Unregistered design rights do not require 'eye appeal'. An unregistered design right is granted to 'the design of any aspect of the shape or configuration (whether internal or external) of the whole or part of an article'. It is not available for surface decoration, for example, wallpaper designs.

Unregistered design right is automatic, like copyright. It lasts for 15 years or ten years from the end of the first sale of articles with that design.

The owner of the design has the right to reproduce the design for commercial purposes. Design rights enable the owner to prevent anyone else copying that design, except with unregistered rights where the owner cannot stop copying in the last five years of the design's protection but can only charge reasonable royalties for that copying.

The first owner of the design right is the designer unless the design is commissioned or produced in the course of the designer's employment, in which case it is the designer's employer – unless, of course, someone had commissioned the design. There is primary infringement (for making registered items) and secondary infringement (for importing and or dealing).

Design rights are territorial.

Trademarks and brand names

The law defines a trademark as 'any sign capable of being represented graphically which is capable of distinguishing goods or services of one undertaking from those of other undertakings'. Unregistered trademarks are protected by the common law tort of passing off. Registered trademarks are protected by statute. In the UK, The Trade Marks Act 1994 was passed to implement EC Council Directive 89/104/EEC which sought to harmonize laws on trademarks and make provision for a Community trademark.

The owner of a registered trademark has its exclusive use. Anybody using it without his consent is infringing it. Unauthorized use in relation to goods is a criminal offence. When a trademark is granted to two or more persons, each is entitled to an equal share in the mark. Transactions in registered trademarks, for example if they are assigned, have to be registered.

Registered marks are valid for ten years and renewable for further periods of ten years. If registration is not renewed it will removed from the register.

The mark can also be revoked, in the following circumstances:

- It has not been used in the five years after registration, and there is no good reason for this.
- It has not been used in any continuous five-year period, and there is no good reason for this.
- It ceases to distinguish the goods or services of its owner, for example, when it has become a 'generic' name.
- It is likely to mislead the public about the product or service for which it is registered.

Objects marketed under a registered trademark should have 'Reg Trade Mark' on the product or the packaging. Common law marks are identified by words like 'ABC is a Trade Mark'. The advantage of registration over reliance on the tort of passing off is the ease of enforcement. With a registered mark there is no need to prove that the infringer is confusing customers and thereby reaping the rewards of the goodwill generated by the rightful owner of the mark.

Trade secrets

Trade secrets are slightly harder to define. They are the know-how and confidential information that contributes to the success of the business. Their exclusivity relies on their being kept secret. Usually they are protected through non-disclosure contracts with employees and contractors but legal action is possible if confidential information is handed over on the understanding that it will be kept confidential but is used to the detriment of the original communicator. It is usually transferred in an acquisition by disclosure subject to confidentiality obligations. These must not be so restrictive that the buyer cannot use the trade secrets. Also the buyer should do a very thorough and careful preliminary review to make sure that trade secrets or variant of trade secrets are not already in use.

Notes

Chapter 1

1. Searby, F. (1969), 'Control of post-merger change', *HBR* September–October 1969.
2. Hunt, J.W., Lees, S., Grumbar, J.J. and Vivian, P.D. (1987), 'Acquisitions: The Human Factor', London: London Business School and Egon Zehnder International.
3. KPMG (1999), 'Unlocking Shareholder Value: Keys To Success', London: KPMG.
4. KPMG, op. cit p.13.
5. KPMG (1998), 'Merger and Acquisition Integration', London: KPMG.
6. Hubbard, N. (1999), *Acquisition Strategy and Implementation*, Basingstoke: Palgrave.
7. See for example Hubbard, op. cit.
8. *Glassman* v. *Computervision* (1996), quoted in Alexandra Reed Lajoux and Charles Elson (2000), *The Art of M&A Due Diligence*, New York: McGraw-Hill.
9. Lajoux and Elson, op. cit., summarizing the US case *Escott* v. *BarChris Construction Corp.* (1968).

Chapter 2

1. Alexandra Reed Lajoux and Charles Elson (2000), *The Art of M&A Due Diligence*, New York: McGraw-Hill.
2. Joseph L. Bowyer (2001), 'Not all M&As Are Alike and That Matters', *Harvard Business Review* March 2001.
3. Quoted in Lajoux and Elson.

Chapter 3

1. David Montagu-Smith, *Financial Times*, 21 February 2002.
2. Department of Trade and Industry (2001), *Mirror Group Newspapers*, London: Stationery Office.
3. *Weekend Financial Times*, 31 March/1 April 2001 p.6.
4. Department of Trade and Industry, *Mirror Group Newspapers*, op. cit.
5. *Weekend Financial Times*, 31 March/1 April 2001 p.6.
6. Jon Moulton, managing partner of private equity firm Alchemy and Partners quoted by Reena SenGupta in *Financial Times*, 10 October 2001.
7. Quoted by Reena SenGupta, *Financial Times*, 10 October 2001.

Chapter 4

1. Stephen Bourne (2000), *Financial Due Diligence*, London: Pearson Education Limited.
2. The term 'accounting policy' refers to the overall policy adopted by the company. For example, stock may be valued at 'the lower of cost or net realizable value'. The 'accounting treatment' refers to the bases and assumptions used by management to apply that policy. For example a company may write down a particular line of stock if it is not sold within six months of purchase. Clearly any change of accounting policy or treatment from one year to another can result in the profit trend being distorted.
3. A negative assurance is where the view expressed is in the form of 'nothing has come to light which would cause us to believe that the assumptions do not provide a reasonable basis for the projections'.

Chapter 5

1. James Dyson (2001), *Against The Odds: An Autobiography*, London: Texere.

Chapter 6

1. *Financial Times*, 6 May 2002.
2. Haarmann Hemmelrath Management Consultants, *Stahl und Reisen*, 119(8), quoted in *The McKinsey Quarterly*, 2001 (4).
3. Booz Allen & Hamilton (1996), 'Lessons From Failed Corporate Marriages', *Strategy & Business*, Fourth Quarter 1996.

Chapter 7

1. Davey, J.A., Kinicki, A., Kilroy J. and Schenk, C. (1988), 'After the Merger: Dealing with People's Uncertainty', *Training and Development Journal*, November.
2. EEA countries are all EC countries plus Iceland, Liechtenstein and Norway.
3. The IR35 legislation in the UK seeks to make sure that people who are working as 'disguised employees' pay the same tax and national insurance contributions as regular employees. It was enacted in response to the growing numbers supplying their services through own limited company.
4. In recent years the courts have reined in the employer's discretion, for example on whether or not to pay a bonus or give an annual pay increase. Their approach has been to imply a term in written contracts which controls the exercise of an employer's discretion. The net result is that discretionary bonuses are not necessarily totally discretionary and much will depend on the wording of individual contracts. For example, in *Clark* v. *Nomura International Plc*, Mr Clark's contract stated quite clearly that Nomura's bonus scheme is discretionary and not guaranteed. It also said that any bonus was dependent on individual performance and was only paid to people employed on the date of payment. Mr Clark was about to leave Nomura and the company exercised its

discretion not to give a bonus. The High Court found that the only criteria that should apply were Mr Clark's performance (which had been impressive) and that he was still employed on the date of payment (which he was). He was awarded £1.35 million in compensation.

5. Richard Koch, London, 1995, speech given to *Acquisitions Monthly* 'Acquiring in Europe' Conference.
6. *Business Week*, 11 October 1999, in a review of *Sony: The Private Life*, Houghton Mifflin, 1999.
7. Quoted in Gerry Johnson and Kevan Scholes (2002), *Exploring Corporate Strategy*, London: Financial Times/Prentice Hall and adapted from R.E. Miles and C.C. Snow (1978), *Organizational Strategy: Structure and Process*, New York: McGraw-Hill. Johnson and Scholes make the point that 'although this is now an old reference, it is still a useful way of characterising culture.'
8. Quoted in Johnson and Scholes, *Exploring Corporate Strategy*, and adapted from C. Handy (1997), *Understanding Organisations*, 4th edition, Harmondsworth: Penguin.
9. Johnson and Scholes, *Exploring Corporate Strategy*.
10. Ibid.
11. Charles Hampden-Turner & Fons Trompenaars (1994), *The Seven Cultures of Capitalism*, London: Piatkus.

Chapter 8

1. *Daily Telegraph*, 22 February 2002, referring to Energis's share price collapse.
2. Sue Cartwright and Cary L. Cooper (2000), *HR Know-How In Mergers and Acquisitions*, London: Institute of Personnel and Development.
3. Department of Trade and Industry (2001), *Mirror Group Newspapers*, op. cit.
4. *Weekend Financial Times*, 31 March/1 April 2001 p.6.
5. KPMG (1998), op. cit.
6. Geoffrey H. Smart (1999), 'Management Assessment Methods in Venture Capital', *Venture Capital*.
7. Daphne M. Keats (2000), *Interviewing. A Practical Guide for Students and Professionals*, London: OUP.
8. Ira T. Kay and Mike Shelton (2000), 'The people problem in mergers', *McKinsey Quarterly*.

Chapter 9

1. A scheme must be approved by the Pension Scheme Office if all tax reliefs are to be obtained and inheritance and capital gains tax are to be avoided. CA approval is about contracting out.
2. *Barber* v. *Guardian Royal Exchange*. The ruling of the European Court of Justice on 17 May 1990 effectively ruled that females were entitled to pension benefits on an equal basis with males. Since most part-timers are female it effectively ruled that part-time workers were also entitled to pensions.

Chapter 10

1. A capital loss is the opposite of a capital gain, that is it arises on disposal of a chargeable asset. Any such loss may be set against capital gains made now or in the future. A chargeable asset is one defined by the revenue as subject to capital gains tax. In practice in the UK just about every asset sold for more than £6000 is chargeable.

2. In the UK, a controlled foreign company (CFC) is a company which is:

   • resident outside the UK
   • controlled by persons resident in the UK
   • subject to a lower level of tax in the country of residence than it would suffer in the UK.

   Unless the CFC falls within one of five exemptions, the Revenue may direct that its profits (except chargeable gains) are apportioned among UK corporate shareholders with at least 10 per cent holdings and subjected to UK corporation tax.

3. If you are in business making taxable supplies, you are liable to register for VAT if:

   • at the end of any month the value of your taxable supplies in the previous 12 months has exceeded the annual sales threshold, or
   • there are grounds at any time for believing that the value of taxable supplies in the next 30 days will exceed the annual sales threshold.

   Taxable supplies are goods that are either:

   • standard-rated (within the scope of VAT and taxable at 17.5 per cent); or
   • zero-rated (within the scope of VAT and taxable at 0 per cent).

4. A group of companies may register each company separately for VAT, but there is an option for group registration in which only one representative company registers. With group registration, no VAT is charged on intra-group transactions and only one VAT return is necessary each quarter to cover the whole group.

Chapter 11

1. Environmental Law is not something which is relatively new, driven by new legislation which reflects the worries of a society increasingly concerned with protecting the environment. The common law tort of nuisance has been around for many hundreds of years. Contamination on a site may well give rise to liability under the common law for nuisance. As far back as 1868 the English courts established in the case of *Rylands* v. *Fletcher* that anyone making a 'non-natural' use of land, who brings something on to it which is likely to do mischief if it escapes, is responsible for all the damage it causes if it does escape. Finally, in the UK at any rate, Local Authorities have long had the right to take action to stop statutory nuisance.

2. Barrie Pearson (1989), *Successful Acquisition of Unquoted Companies*, Aldershot: Gower.

3. Because its business involved animal experiments, the employees, customers and shareholders of Huntingdon Life Sciences were targeted by the Stop Huntingdon Animal Cruelty group (SHAC) in a campaign aimed at forcing the business to close.
4. In the UK, environmental liability falls first on the 'causer' or 'knowing permitter'. Buying assets rather than the shares of a company in which environmental liabilities may reside will end any connection with that company's historical liabilities.
5. Contaminated land provisions only apply under UK law:

   - where it is necessary to deal with unacceptable risks to health or to the environment which arise from the current use of the contaminated land in question.
   - where there is a breach of an environmental licence.

   Unacceptable risks will only arise where contamination is such that significant harm is, or is likely, to be caused. Examples of significant harm will include:

   - death or serious injury in humans
   - death or disease to livestock and/or crops leading to a substantial fall in value
   - wholesale changes in habitats
   - serious damage to buildings

6. Draft Statutory Guidance on the Environment Act 1995 (September 1996).
7. William Butterworth (2001), 'Environmental Due Diligence', in *Venture Capital and Private Equity: A Practitioner's Manual*, London: City & Financial Publishing.
8. Contamination may produce third-party claims or demands from regulatory authorities for the performance of clean-up work and the financial burden of revocation/revision of licences/consents. Remember, clean-up can be required even where there is no breach of any laws.

Chapter 12

1. See for example Cathy Hayward, 'Plug & Pray', *Financial Management*, February 2002.
2. Giga Information Group.
3. Michael E. Porter (1998), *On Competition*, Harvard: Harvard Business School Publishing Corporation.
4. According to Porter, these are:

   - Bargaining power of suppliers
   - Threat of new entrants
   - Bargaining power of buyers
   - Threat of substitutes
   - Rivalry amongst existing competitors.

5. Ibid.
6. Ibid.
7. ibid.

Chapter 13

1. Saikat Chaudhuri and Benham Tabrizi (1999), 'Capturing the Real Value in High-Tech Acquisitions', *HBR* September–October.
2. Booz Allen & Hamilton (1997), 'Growth By Acquisition: The Case of Cisco Systems', *Strategy & Business*, Second Quarter.
3. Nigel Verdon, Evolution Consulting Group Plc.

Chapter 14

1. Lajoux and Elson, *The Art of M&A Due Diligence*, op. cit., p.286.

Chapter 15

1. *Financial Times*, 21 November 2001.
2. *Financial Times*, 11 April 2002.

Index